THE ECONOMICS
OF DEFENCE POLICY

Also available from Brassey's

BLUNDEN & GREENE
Science and Mythology in the Making of Defence Policy

DANDO & ROGERS
What if Nuclear Disarmament were Attempted?

DROWN
A Single European Arms Industry?

GOLDBERG
Avoiding the Brink

HIGGINS
Plotting Peace

POOLE
Independence and Interdependence

THE ECONOMICS
OF DEFENCE POLICY

Keith Hartley

BRASSEY'S (UK)

Member of Maxwell Macmillan Pergamon Publishing Corporation

LONDON · OXFORD · WASHINGTON · NEW YORK · BEIJING
FRANKFURT · SÃO PAULO · SYDNEY · TOKYO · TORONTO

UK (Editorial)	Brassey's (UK) Ltd., 50 Fetter Lane, London EC4A 1AA, England
(Orders, all except North America)	Brassey's (UK) Ltd., Headington Hill Hall, Oxford OX3 0BW, England
USA (Editorial)	Brassey's (US) Inc., 8000 Westpark Drive, Fourth Floor, McLean, Virginia 22102, USA
(Orders, North America)	Brassey's (US) Inc., Front and Brown Streets, Riverside, New Jersey 08075, USA Tel (toll free): 800 257 5755
PEOPLE'S REPUBLIC OF CHINA	Pergamon Press, Room 4037, Qianmen Hotel, Beijing People's Republic of China
FEDERAL REPUBLIC OF GERMANY	Pergamon Press GmbH, Hammerweg 6, D-6242 Kronberg, Federal Republic of Germany
BRAZIL	Pergamon Editora Ltda, Rua Eça de Queiros, 346, CEP 04011, Paraiso, São Paulo, Brazil
AUSTRALIA	Brassey's Australia Pty Ltd., PO Box 544, Potts Point, NSW 2011, Australia
JAPAN	Pergamon Press, 5th Floor, Matsuoka Central Building, 1-7-1 Nishishinjuku, Shinjuku-ku, Tokyo 160, Japan
CANADA	Pergamon Press Canada Ltd., Suite No. 271, 253 College Street, Toronto, Ontario, Canada M5T 1R5

Copyright © 1991 Brassey's (UK)

First edition 1991

Library of Congress Cataloging-in-Publication Data
Hartley, Keith.
The economics of defence policy/Keith Hartley. – 1st ed.
p. cm.
Includes index.
1. Great Britain – Defenses – Costs. 2. Great Britain – Military policy – Economic aspects. 3. Budget – Great Britain. I. Title.
HC260.D4H37 1990 338.4'76234'0941 – dc20 90-21951

British Library Cataloguing in Publication Data
Hartley, Keith 1940–
The economics of defence policy.
1. Defence. Expenditure by governments
1. Title
355.622

ISBN 0-08-033625-6

Printed in England by B.P.C.C. Wheatons Ltd, Exeter

To

WINIFRED
ADAM, LUCY AND CECILIA

Contents

Preface

DEFENCE POLICY in the UK and elsewhere is of continuing interest and concern. The events in Eastern Europe in 1989, the prospects of successful arms control agreements between the USA and the USSR, and question marks over the future of NATO and the Warsaw Pact have made the subject even more topical. Will NATO continue to exist in its current form in the year 2000 and beyond? Possible arms control agreements offer the prospect of greater security and international stability at lower levels of armaments. In such circumstances, critics will question the value of maintaining both 'strong' defences and the NATO alliance. They will anticipate all manner of wonderful things which will follow from major reductions in defence spending. Resources will become available for spending elsewhere in the economy. In the UK, some commentators are expecting that defence cuts will produce a miraculous improvement in the economy's performance: a topic which is of major interest to economists. Nonetheless, even with defence cuts, the UK and other nations will continue to maintain military forces and the problems which have always confronted defence decision makers will not disappear. The challenge remains of maintaining the security and protection required by society when only limited resources are available for the task: a problem which is also central to the discipline of economics.

This book has three aims. First, to identify the types of questions raised by economists when studying defence policy. Second to show how simple economic analysis can be used to answer these questions and to contribute to our understanding of defence issues. Third, to provide a critique and evaluation of defence policy. The emphasis is on general economic principles, their applications and implications.

Choices and efficiency are central to economics. The range of choices facing any government are outlined and the principles of substitution, competition and self-interest are applied to defence issues, often showing new and controversial insights. Consideration is also given to such issues as programme budgeting, the arms race, alliances, the military-industrial complex, value for money policies, the benefits and costs of collaborative programmes, and the likely barriers to arms control agreements. Throughout, the aim is to subject the myths, emotion and special pleading which dominate defence debates to economic analysis, critical scrutiny and empirical testing.

Despite the importance of defence policy and the size of military budgets, the field has attracted relatively few economists willing to apply their 'tool kit' to the defence sector. This is unfortunate and a sad reflection on the economics profession which has allocated liberal quantities of scarce resources to exploring many other fields, some of which are of dubious value in contributing to the sum total of human welfare and its survival! Indeed, the author believes that defence economics has now developed to the point where it merits recognition as a distinctive and academically reputable specialism alongside such other specialisms as the economics of education, health, industry and labour.

The book is designed for students, practitioners, industrialists, policy makers and general readers. It should be of interest to first, second and third year undergraduates as well as graduates studying applied economics, including industry and public finance specialists. It can also be used for policy study courses as well as by students of politics and international relations, by military staff and civil servants. The aim is to show how, in non-technical terms, simple economic analysis can be applied to defence issues. The principles are sufficiently general to be applicable to all nations with a defence budget.

Many people have contributed to this book, some knowingly, others unwittingly through their advocacy of alternative views and policy solutions. Much of the material was developed and tested on generations of students at the University of York where I have taught a second-year course on the economics of defence. Nick Hooper was a joint author of part of Chapter 8 dealing with the options of imports or domestic equipment. Others who have helped, sometimes unknowingly, include David Greenwood, Michael Intriligator, Gavin Kennedy, Ed Kolodziej, Todd Sandler, Ron Smith and Christian Schmidt. Thanks are also due to Ministry of Defence staff; to participants at various seminars organised by RAF Cranwell, Shrivenham, the University of Aberdeen and Brassey's; and to Dr F. Welter, NATO. Financial support for various research projects in defence economics was generously provided by ESRC and a NATO Research Fellowship (1987–88). The usual disclaimers apply. Margaret Johnson had the unenviable task of typing the end-product and completed the job admirably. Jenny Shaw offered support and extreme patience in awaiting the final product. And the greatest burden was borne by my wife, Winifred, whose contribution was invaluable.

January 1990

CHAPTER 1

Economics and Defence Policy: An Overview

Introduction: continuing controversy

Defence is controversial. Much depends on people's views of the threat and whether 'strong defences' are a pre-condition for successful arms control or a cause of a 'dangerous arms race'. Moreover, defence is a field where many different disciplines are relevant, represented by engineers, scientists, statisticians, experts on international relations and professional soldiers. Natural and applied sciences are reflected in the technical requirements of modern defence equipment such as nuclear weapons, guided missiles and space satellites. Moral issues involving life and death cannot be avoided. Examples from the Second World War included submarine warfare against merchant shipping; the treatment of prisoners-of-war; the large-scale bombing of cities such as Dresden, Hamburg and London; and the use of nuclear weapons at Hiroshima and Nagasaki. Current examples include the use of chemical and nuclear weapons, with the latter posing major moral dilemmas possibly involving the future of civilisation and the continued existence of our planet. Questions also arise about whether there is such a thing as a 'just war'; and the morality of producing weapons and exporting arms when large numbers of people in the world are poor, ill, starving and lack housing. These are all important issues which cannot be the sole preserve of the philosopher. They place this book into context. At the same time, it has to be recognised that ethics and morality are not costless and have an economic dimension.

Economists have a contribution to make to debates about defence policy since defence is a major user of limited and scarce resources which have alternative uses. The aim is to show how economic principles can be applied to defence issues, using the UK as a case study. Nonetheless, the principles are sufficiently general to be applicable to other nations.

In the UK, defence policy has been a continuing focus of public debate. Since 1945 a variety of questions have been raised about UK defence policy, all of which have an economic dimension. Questions continue to be raised about the following issues:

i. The appropriate size of the defence budget and whether Britain spends too much or too little on defence. Here, comparisons are often made with the defence budgets of other European NATO nations and there are continuing debates about the threat;

ii. Whether defence is a burden or benefit and whether membership of NATO is worthwhile;

iii. The UK's defence commitments, particularly whether it can afford an independent nuclear deterrent, a complete range of modern balanced forces, a continuing role outside NATO and a sizeable all-volunteer force;

iv. Whether the UK can continue to support a defence industrial base with the capability of developing and producing a complete range of modern high technology equipment. Instead, should more defence equipment be imported or be produced jointly with other nations, particularly with the Europeans?

v. The efficiency of the armed forces, the Ministry of Defence and domestic defence contractors, and whether they provide good value for money. Project management is a major source of controversy, reflected in increasingly expensive equipment, cost overruns, delays, gold-plating and cancellations (*eg* TSR-2; Nimrod AEW);

vi. Whether arms races lead to war or contribute to peace, and the implications for policy towards arms control.

The following Chapters show the contribution of economics to these and other debates about UK defence policy. Initially, it is necessary to outline some of the broad stylised facts about British defence policy, with budgets as an obvious starting point.

UK defence spending and policy

A substantial amount of economic and statistical information on UK defence spending is published regularly in the Ministry of Defence (MoD) annual *Statement on the Defence Estimates* and by the House of Commons Defence Committee. Total UK defence expenditure, its percentage growth and numbers of personnel for the period 1975–92 are shown in *Table 1.1*. This period involved both Labour and Conservative governments, the NATO commitment to raise annual real defence spending by 3 per cent between 1979–80 and 1985–86, and the Falklands conflict of 1982. Also, during the 1980s, there were a number of costly equipment purchases including the Tornado aircraft, the decision to acquire the Trident nuclear deterrent, together with the cancellation of the Nimrod AEW aircraft and its replacement with the Boeing AWACS (*HCP 383, Statement on Defence Estimates 1989*). In 1986, the debate about the Westland helicopter company and the cancellation of Nimrod

AEW raised important questions about the future of the UK's defence industrial base (see Chapter 8). The defence industrial base was also affected by MoD's competitive procurement policy introduced in 1983 and by a substantial programme of privatisation (see Chapters 6 and 8). Indeed, the 1980s were increasingly dominated by a concern with improving efficiency through competition, contracting-out, Responsibility Budgets, reorganisation of the MoD and a more effective use of Service and civilian manpower. Between 1979 and 1990, the numbers of UK-based civilians employed by MoD fell by over 40 per cent (*Table 1.1* and *Cmnd 675-I, 1989*). In fact, in 1988, total UK-based Service and civilian personnel employed by MoD and in UK defence industries exceeded one million people. However, by the late 1980s, there was increasing concern about difficulties of recruiting and retaining sufficient Service personnel to maintain the current size of all-volunteer force (*Table 1.1* and Chapter 4).

Real defence spending rose from over £15 billion per annum between

TABLE 1.1 *UK Defence Spending*

Year	Defence expenditure (£ms)		Percentages (%):		Personnel (000s)	
	Current prices	Constant 1987–88 prices	Annual real growth	RPE	Service	Civilians
1975–76	5,394	15,733	2.1	−2.2	346.4	295.6
76–77	6,216	16,016	1.7	3.6	340.4	289.4
77–78	6,857	15,534	−3.0	−0.8	337.1	278.8
78–79	7,545	15,413	−0.8	−0.3	332.5	266.8
79–80	9,273	16,242	5.4	2.5	330.0	263.3
80–81	11,231	16,593	2.2	−0.6	330.2	255.3
81–82	12,670	17,056	2.8	1.3	340.6	242.3
82–83	14,481	18,205	6.7	0.7	334.7	230.2
83–84	15,686	18,847	3.5	1.3	333.1	219.1
84–85	16,949	19,407	3.0	1.4	335.8	213.6
85–86	18,029	19,570	0.8	−0.5	334.2	208.8
86–87	18,526	19,456	−0.6	1.4	331.5	200.7
87–88	18,790	18,790	−3.4	0.6	327.6	180.3
88–89	19,228	17,929	−4.6	−1.5	327.5	177.2
89–90	20,143	17,803	−0.7		324.2	173.4
90–91	21,190	18,004	1.1		312.7	173.1
91–92	22,100	18,233	1.3			

Notes: (i) Figures are for out-turns to 1988–89 and planned spending 1989–92.
    (ii) Figures include Falklands costs and 1987–88 prices were derived using GDP (market prices) deflators.
    (iii) Annual real growth is percentage growth over previous year.
    (iv) RPE is the Relative Price Effect for the total defence budget and is an index of defence prices divided by the GDP deflator.
    (v) Service personnel include locally entered personnel. Civilians comprise industrial and non-industrial staff plus locally-engaged staff employed by MoD.
Sources: HCP 495, 1988; HCP 383, 1989.

1975 and 1979 to a peak in 1985–86, followed by a substantial decline to 1989–90. Nonetheless, planned real spending in the early 1990s will be some 16 per cent greater than in the mid-1970s: a result which has occurred during a period of relative peace! Such outcomes reflect the fact that equipping armed forces with modern equipment is a costly business (see Chapters 2 and 4). Some estimates suggest that on current cost trends, in 25 years time, the UK will only be able to afford to buy one-third as many aircraft as it buys today (Coxhead, 1987).

Further indicators of defence burdens both within the UK and in relation to NATO nations are shown in *Table 1.2*. Between 1975 and 1979, UK defence as a share of gross domestic product declined from 4.9 per cent to 4.5 per cent, after which it rose to a peak of 5.3 per cent in 1984, followed by a further decline to some 4 per cent in the late 1980s. Interestingly, throughout much of the period 1979–90, defence and health absorbed similar shares of national output and each raises questions of whether society obtains good value for money from such expenditures (see Chapters 2, 3 and 6). International comparisons are also used to assess the UK's defence burden, particularly in relation to its major European allies. *Table 1.2* shows the performance of a group of NATO nations against the NATO 3 per cent target and the average for the period 1979–88. The UK, France and Italy each achieved the NATO target or thereabouts in three years, West Germany in one year and the

TABLE 1.2 *UK Defence Burdens*

	UK percentage of GDP (%)		Annual real growth in NATO defence expenditure (%)				
	Defence	Health	UK	France	West Germany	Italy	USA
1979	4.5	4.5	2.1	2.9	1.5	2.6	3.3
1980	4.9	5.0	2.9	3.8	1.9	4.9	4.3
1981	5.0	5.3	1.8	4.3	3.4	−0.5	4.6
1982	5.2	5.1	4.9	2.1	−0.4	3.1	7.0
1983	5.2	5.2	3.0	1.7	0.9	2.5	7.9
1984	5.3	5.2	1.8	−0.3	−0.7	2.8	4.7
1985	5.2	5.1	1.3	−0.4	0.2	3.0	7.3
1986	5.1	5.1	−1.1	0.3	−0.5	1.0	6.7
1987	4.6	5.2	−3.7	3.1	−0.1	5.8	0.1
1988	4.3	4.6	−3.4	−0.4	−0.3	−1.1	−4.9
1989	4.1	4.6					
1990	4.0	4.6	(0.9)	(1.7)	(0.6)	(2.4)	(4.0)

Notes: (i) GDP is Gross Domestic Product for the UK at market prices.
(ii) Figures for 1988–90 are estimates based on planned spending.
(iii) Real growth figures are for annual year on year growth using GDP deflators for Germany and defence specific price deflators for all other nations. The UK data in *Table 1.1* are based on GDP deflators.
(iv) Figures in brackets are averages for 1979–88.
Sources: Cmnd 621, 1989; Cmnd 675–II, 1989; HCP 383, 1989.

United States, as the alliance leader, exceeded the target in every year of the commitment: hence the continuing debate about burden-sharing in NATO and whether the Europeans are free-riding at the expense of the USA (HCP 37, 1985; see also Chapters 4 and 7).

Defence budgets are often expressed in real terms, eliminating the effects of inflation, so that meaningful comparisons can be made over a number of years. Frequently, however, real terms are defined with respect to the GDP deflator which measures general inflation in the economy rather than with respect to defence-specific price deflators (*Cmnd 621, 1989*, p. 6; and *Tables 1.1* and *1.2*). This is where the Relative Price Effect (RPE) is important. The buying power of the defence budget is affected by the RPE for equipment, pay and other items. The RPE shows the difference between the rate of inflation for defence items compared with the general inflation rate for the economy as a whole. For the period 1975–89, the median RPE for all items in the defence budget was some +0.7 per cent per annum, varying within a range from −2.2 per cent to +3.6 per cent. For equipment, the corresponding figures were a median of +1.3 per cent per annum within a range from −3.5 per cent in 1988–89 to +7.2 per cent in 1976–77 (*HCP 383, 1989*, p. 46). A positive RPE means that defence prices rise faster than the general rate of inflation so that a defence budget based on the GDP deflator will be inadequate to keep pace with inflation in military markets.

A simple example is shown in *Table 1.3*. In this case, assume the government commits itself to maintaining the defence budget in real terms (*ie* level funding). Initially, the budget is £100 (say units of millions or tens of millions of pounds). To maintain this in real terms, the goverment applies the GDP deflator at, say, 3 per cent and allocates £103 for defence in the next year. If, however, defence prices rise at 10 per cent, then level funding in real terms requires a budget of £110. Alternatively, if defence prices fall by 5 per cent and the government allocates £103 for military expenditure, there is a net benefit to the defence budget. Indeed, the negative RPE in 1988–89, especially for equipment, probably reflected greater competition leading to increased industrial efficiency as well as better management of the defence programme. Moreover, it has to be

TABLE 1.3 *Real Defence Budgets*

Defence budgets in:			
Year one	Required in year two for level funding in real terms		
	GDP deflator at 3%	Defence price inflation at:	
		+10%	−5%
100	103	110	95

stressed that the RPE is based on input prices so that it takes no account of productivity improvements for defence goods and services (reflecting the difficulties of measuring output). Finally, variations in the RPE can also reflect exchange rate changes (*HCP 383, 1989*, p. xi).

The UK defence budget is used to buy manpower, equipment and supporting inputs required to provide protection and security. Some of the results in terms of front line units over the period 1979–90 are shown in *Table 1.4*. Over a period when real defence spending rose (*Table 1.1*), a substantial number of front–line units either declined or remained unchanged. In the Navy, there were expansions in the numbers of submarines and patrol ships at the expense of the destroyer and frigate fleet.

TABLE 1.4 *UK Front-Line Units*

	Unit	1979	1990
Royal Navy			
Submarines	Vessels	22	24
Carriers and assault ships	Vessels	3	4
Destroyers and frigates	Vessels	53	44
Mine counter-measures	Vessels	35	37
Patrol ships	Vessels	19	32
Royal Marines	Commandos	4	3
Regular Army			
Royal Armoured Corps	Regiments	19	19
Royal Artillery	Regiments	22	22
Royal Engineers	Regiments	9	13
Infantry	Battalions	56	55
Special Air Service	Regiments	1	1
Army Air Corps	Regiments	6	4
Royal Air Force			
Strike attack	Squadrons	14	11
Ground-offensive support	Squadrons	5	5
Air defence	Squadrons	9	9
Maritime patrol	Squadrons	4	4
Reconnaissance	Squadrons	5	2
Airborne early warning	Squadrons	1	1
Transport	Squadrons	10	12
Tankers	Squadrons	2	3
Search and rescue	Squadrons	3	2
Surface-to-air missiles	Squadrons	7	7
Regular Forces	Numbers (000s)	315.0	304.6
of which: Navy	Numbers (000s)	72.5	63.9
Army	Numbers (000s)	156.2	151.3
Air Force	Numbers (000s)	86.3	89.4
Reserve Forces	Numbers (000s)	259.7	340.1
of which: Navy	Numbers (000s)	37.1	35.4
Army	Numbers (000s)	193.9	264.0
Air Force	Numbers (000s)	28.7	40.7

Notes: (i) 1979 figure for destroyers and frigates includes cruisers.
     (ii) Service personnel figures exclude locally-engaged personnel.
Sources: Cmnd 8212-II, 1981; Cmnd 1022-II, 1990.

In the Army, there was an increase in the number of regiments of Royal Engineers, and reductions in the Air Corps and infantry. For the Air Force, there were reductions in the number of strike and reconnaissance squadrons and an expansion in the tanker and transport fleet. During the same period, the size of the Regular forces has declined slightly. The Air Force share of total manpower has increased at the expense of the Navy, whilst the Army as the manpower-intensive service continued to account for almost half of the total number of Regular personnel. Finally, between 1979 and 1990, there was a substantial increase in the size of the Reserve forces, particularly in the Army. Against this defence background, what is the contribution of economics?

The contribution of economics

Economics is about the study of scarcity and choice. It focuses on the behaviour of individuals and groups as represented by households, firms, governments and their bureaucracies (see Chapter 5). To explain the behaviour of these agents, it is necessary to know what motivates them: what are they trying to achieve and what are the restrictions or constraints on their behaviour? For example, natural resources, income, information, knowledge and the law all act as constraints on the behaviour of individuals and groups. Since the various agents make independent and separate decisions, some mechanism is required to bring them together. Private markets and prices are one possible co-ordinating and allocative arrangement; others include voting systems, bargaining and barter, central planning and dictatorship, inheritance, force, fraud, deceit and bribery.

Regardless of the method, the need for some allocative mechanism reflects scarcity. Resources have many alternative uses and users. By choosing one thing individuals, groups and society are sacrificing something else. Allocating resources to national defence involves a sacrifice of civil goods and services. This is what is meant by opportunity cost, namely, the sacrifices incurred by using scarce resources for, say, defence rather than for hospitals, schools, roads, cars and videos. And in considering alternatives, choices cannot be avoided. This is a simple proposition but it is amazing how often governments, the Ministry of Defence and the armed forces ignore opportunity costs and believe that their plans will not involve any sacrifices. Examples include the sacrifice of conventional equipment by purchasing the Trident nuclear deterrent, the sacrifice of equipment by buying from a costlier UK defence industrial base, and the sacrifice of numbers involved in choosing more expensive high quality weapons.

Starting from the study of choice, economics provides a body of knowledge (theories) designed to explain how parts of the economy work, known as micro-economics, and how the whole operates, known as macro-economics. Micro-economics studies the behaviour of consumers, firms, industries and markets such as those for cars, clothes, food, foreign exchange, houses, and workers. Macro-economics studies broad aggregates for the whole economy, such as total consumption, aggregate demand, inflation, unemployment, the balance of payments and growth. In applying economic theory in a policy context, economists use an established methodology.

Methodology

The methodology of economic policy involves a three-stage approach to policy issues whether they be in the field of defence or elsewhere:

(i) Policy objectives have to be specified. What is the Government, the Ministry of Defence and the armed forces trying to achieve?

(ii) The relevant economic theory has to be identified. Which economic theories 'best' explain the problems facing policy makers in defence?

(iii) A policy solution has to be chosen from a range of alternatives. For example, air defence can be provided by ground-based missiles or manned aircraft; whilst military personnel can be provided by men or women, by younger or older age groups, and by UK nationals or foreigners.

Throughout, choices cannot be avoided: governments and the Ministry of Defence have to choose between different objectives, competing economic theories and alternative policy solutions. What does all this mean for defence economics?

Defence economics

Defence economics is not solely about budgets and money. Broadly defined it embraces all aspects of the economics of defence, disarmament and peace. Examples include peace and war economics, arms races and arms control agreements; the economic impact of defence spending in both developed and developing countries; weapons procurement policies, defence industries and the arms trade; military alliances and burden-sharing; economic warfare and terrorism; disarmament and conversion. Further topics can be grouped around the general concern with managing defence resources efficiently involving budgeting, the military production function, incentive systems and performance indicators; military manpower, namely, recruitment, training, retention and the choice between a conscript and an all-volunteer force; the opportunities for substitution; together with studies of internal markets in the armed forces, different forms of organisation and their performance. A reading of the Ministry of Defence *Annual Statement on the Defence Estimates* shows the breadth of the subject area of defence economics. Typically, there are chapters on arms control, on the armed forces, their roles and equipment, on procurement, on resources and management, and on the balance of forces between NATO and the Warsaw Pact (*Cmnd 675, 1989*).

Defence economics applies economic theory to the defence sector broadly defined. This embraces the Ministry of Defence, the armed forces, the defence industries and their direct and indirect effects in both a domestic and international context. Often the greatest insights are obtained by applying simple economic ideas to complex problems. One simple but invaluable contribution is for defence economists to analyse defence issues and policy as choices involving the sacrifice of something else. The economic problem is to choose the strategy, technology and force structure which achieves the aims of defence policy at least cost in a world where resources are limited. The task is to make the armed forces decide on these issues whilst subjecting them to budget constraints and output targets. In this way, decision makers bear the costs of their choices; but they also need to be offered rewards for good performance and penalties for failure. On this basis, the Army, for example, might only be able to buy a new tank at the expense of some of its infantry battalions or at the expense of its attack helicopter force.

Compared with other parts of the discipline, defence economics has attracted relatively few economists. Pioneering work was undertaken in the USA, particularly at the Rand Corporation, and reflected in a classic contribution on *The Economics of Defense in the Nuclear Age* (Hitch and McKean, 1960). Hitch and McKean's book inspired generations of academic researchers. There have been economic studies of the arms race, military alliances, weapons markets and procurement policies, the costs and benefits of defence spending, and the effects of disarmament, together with case studies of projects and countries (Hartley and Hooper, 1990(a); Hartley and Sandler 1990(b); Kennedy, 1983; Schmidt, 1987; Schmidt and Blackaby, 1987). By 1990, there was sufficient academic interest and support to launch a specialist journal in the field (Hartley and Sandler, 1990(a)). Nonetheless, there remains a massive research agenda for defence economists, lots of questions to be asked and answered and numerous myths to be exposed. As always there is a lack of resources available to study the issues!

Conclusion

This Chapter has outlined some of the issues, stylised facts and general concepts which form the material for this book. Many of the points will be developed in subsequent chapters which deal with how economists analyse defence; budgets; the determinants of defence expenditure; public choice; procurement policy; NATO standardisation; the UK defence industrial base; collaboration; and arms control. A final section presents some questions for discussion.

References

Cmnd 8212-II, 1981, *Statement on the Defence Estimates 1981*, HMSO, London.

Cmnd 621, 1989, *The Government's Expenditure Plans 1989–90 to 1991–92*, HM Treasury, HMSO, London.

Cmnd 675, 1989, *Statement on the Defence Estimates 1989*, HMSO, London, Volumes I and II.

Cmnd 1022, 1990, *Statement on the Defence Estimates 1990*, HMSO, London, Volumes I and II.

Coxhead, C. D., 1987, Pressure for change in military aviation, *Air Clues*, vol. 41, 4, April, pp. 123–127.

Hartley, K. and Hooper, N., 1990(a), *The Economics of Defence, Disarmament and Peace, An Annotated Bibliography*, Elgar, Cheltenham.

Hartley, K. and Sandler, T., (eds.), 1990(a), *Defence Economics: The Political Economy of Defence, Disarmament and Peace*, Harwood, London.

Hartley, K. and Sandler, T., (eds.), 1990(b), *The Economics of Defence Spending: An International Survey*, Routledge, London.

Hitch, C. and McKean, R. N., 1960, *The Economics of Defense in the Nuclear Age*, Harvard University Press, Cambridge, USA.

HCP 37, 1985, *Defence Commitments and Resources and the Defence Estimates 1985–86*, Defence Committee, HMSO, London.

HCP 495, 1988, *Statement on the Defence Estimates 1988*, Defence Committee, HMSO, London.

HCP 383, 1989, *Statement on the Defence Estimates 1989*, Defence Committee, HMSO, London.

Kennedy, G., 1983, *Defence Economics*, Duckworth, London.

Schmidt, C., 1987, *The Economics of Military Expenditures*, International Economic Association, Macmillan, London.

Schmidt, C. and Blackaby, F., 1987, *Peace, Defence and Economic Analysis*, Macmillan, London.

CHAPTER 2

How Do Economists Analyse Defence?

Introduction: choices and the defence budget

In UK defence policy, choices are being made continually and cannot be avoided. Decisions are required on the appropriate size of the defence budget (guns v. butter or Trident v. NHS), and its allocation between manpower and equipment, between nuclear and conventional forces, between air, land and sea forces, and between the UK, Europe and the rest of the world. The result of this complex set of choices is reflected in the defence budget which shows the costs of the UK's major commitments (*Table 2.1*). These consist of the nuclear deterrent, the defence of the UK, a major land and air contribution to the defence of Europe, a major maritime capability in the eastern Atlantic and a commitment beyond the NATO area. Some of these commitments are costly. For 1990–1991, the annual direct costs of BAOR were £3.1 billion; maritime commitments cost £2.7 billion; while nuclear strategic forces cost £1.5 billion and RAF Germany cost almost £1 billion. Expenditure on military R & D was also substantial at £2.5 billion *pa*, which effectively represents a commitment to support a domestic defence industrial base. Other commitments are relatively cheap, such as expenditure on Polaris, reserve forces and future Falklands costs (estimated at £55–60 million *pa* in 1990).

Not only are defence choices complex, but they have to be made in a world of uncertainty. Consider the assumptions required in formulating UK defence policy to the year 2000 and beyond. Assumptions have to be made about the state of international terrorism, arms control agreements and the likely threat; about technical progress in new equipment; about the behaviour of our allies (*eg* the possibility of US troop withdrawals from Europe); about the growth and competitiveness of the UK economy; and about the political composition of the UK governments in the 1990s and their preferences for defence and social welfare spending. No one can predict accurately the future: today's modern air bases might be tomorrow's ancient castles! In such circumstances, policy makers are

TABLE 2.1 *Costs of UK's Defence Commitments 1990–91*

Commitments	Costs (£m, 1990–91 prices)
1. Strategic nuclear deterrent	1,480
2. Defence of UK home base	2,557
3. Defence of Central Front:	4,135
of which BAOR (including reinforcements)	(3,125)
RAF Germany	(947)
Berlin	(63)
4. Maritime operations:	2,672
of which Eastern Atlantic	(2,086)
Channel	(586)
5. Others:	858
of which UK Mobile Force	(256)
Amphibious capability	(130)
Cyprus	(94)
Gibraltar	(82)
Falklands Islands	(73)
Hong Kong	(47)
Belize	(29)
Total of 1–5 above	11,702
Total defence budget	21,223

Note: Costs are directly attributable expenditures on major commitments, excluding R & D, training, equipment support, stocks and other support.
Source: HCP 383, 1989, p. 47; Cmnd 1022, 1990.

likely to choose a diversified force structure with a mix of specialised and general forces capable of meeting a variety of likely threats.

Economics as the study of choices

A central focus of economics is the study of scarcity and choice. Where resources are scarce, choices cannot be avoided. Economists can represent defence choices in a series of diagrams. *Figure 2.1* shows the classic guns-versus-butter 'trade-off'. If the economy is operating on its production frontier where its resources are fully and efficiently employed, then more defence is purchased at the expense of fewer civil goods and services (*quadrant I, Figure 2.1*). The diagram also provides a simple model for the belief that defence is a burden on the economy. This model links defence spending to investment and growth. If investment depends on the level of civil spending, then more defence expenditure means reduced investment, with adverse effects on the economy's growth rate (*quadrants II and III of Figure 2.1*). However, increased defence spending is likely to produce benefits to society in the form of greater protection and security for its citizens, as shown in *quadrant IV of Figure 2.1*.

The production frontier approach can also be used to illustrate a simple model of the arms race and alliances. Consider two nations in an arms

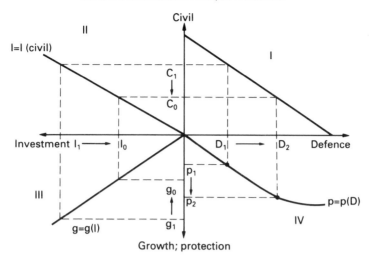

FIG. 2.1. As defence spending rises from D_1 to D_2, civil expenditure falls from C_1 to C_0, hence investment declines from I_1 to I_0 and the growth rate falls from g_1 to g_0. At the same time, at D_2, there is more protection: for simplicity, growth and protection are shown on the same axis.

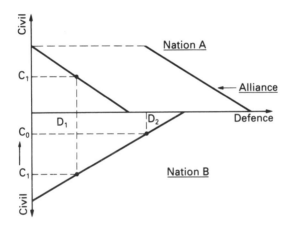

FIG. 2.2. Initially, nations A and B each spend D_1 on defence. Next, if B increases defence spending to D_2, nation A might still be able to compete by joining a military alliance, as represented by a new production frontier.

race, each trying to match the other's defence spending, as shown in *Figure 2.2.* If nation B increases its defence spending sufficiently (to D_2), nation A will no longer be able to compete. Such behaviour by nation B could result from a new strategic defence initiative or reflect 'economic warfare'. However, nation A can adopt a variety of responses: it might resort to a pre-emptive strike on B before it loses the arms race; or it

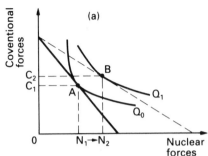
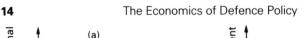
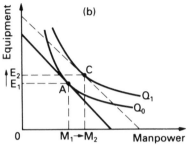

FIG. 2.3. In both a and b, the initial position is shown at A where the defence budget buys C_1, N_1 of conventional and nuclear forces, and E_1 and M_1 of equipment and manpower. If nuclear forces become cheaper more can be bought from a given defence budget as shown by the broken line in (a), and N_2 will be purchased. If the defence budget increases as in (b), more of both equipment and manpower will be bought, as at position C.

might seek a peace treaty; or it could join a military alliance and enjoy the benefits of collective defence.

Once the size of the defence budget has been determined, further choices are required about its allocation between nuclear and conventional forces and between manpower and equipment. These choices are illustrated in *Figure 2.3*. In each case, for a given defence budget and given input prices, there will be a cost-minimising combination of forces to achieve a level of defence output or protection. A larger budget or a lower price for, say, nuclear forces, enables more defence to be bought, as shown in *Figures 2.3 (a) and (b)*.

Pressures on the defence budget

The UK's limited defence budget has to buy manpower and equipment to continue meeting effectively all its defence commitments. Following the end of the NATO 3 per cent commitment in 1986, Britain's defence budget has been squeezed in terms both of its size and its buying power. There are four major pressures on the defence budget. First, the Government's declared commitment to continue with all the UK's major defence roles. Second, manpower for all-volunteer force is expensive. Demographic trends in the 1990s mean that it will become more difficult and costlier to recruit and maintain the current size of an all-volunteer force. A shift in the proportion of expenditure on manpower means less available for equipment and hence for spending on UK defence industries. Third, the 1981 Defence Review was required because the Government believed that even with 3 per cent growth in spending it would not be possible to fund adequately forces of the current size and the plans for their improvement. The underlying budgetary pressures which led to the

1981 Defence Review have not disappeared. At the same time, the House of Commons Defence Committee has repeatedly referred to the substantial pressures on the defence budget, the need for some hard decisions and the possibility of a defence review by stealth (*HCP 37, 1985; HCP 383, 1989*). Fourth, to continue to meet effectively the UK's defence commitments requires modern costly equipment, where the trend is towards rising costs in real terms (*Table 2.2*). The increasing real costs of successive generations of new equipment reflects the higher performance and hence the greater technical complexity required for each new system.

During the 1990s, the UK armed forces have a massive shopping list for new equipment. In addition to Trident, the Navy wants some three new frigates per year, a new helicopter, more submarines, torpedoes and missiles as well as a replacement for its amphibious forces. The Army wants a new main battle tank, anti-tank weapons, and the Multiple-Launch Rocket System (MLRS), and the RAF is awaiting delivery of its Boeing AWACS', and a new European fighter aircraft (*Table 2.2*).

TABLE 2.2

Equipment	Programme costs (£m, 1989–90 prices)	Years of peak expenditure
Tornado GR1 and ADV (435 units)	11,700	Past years
Trident (4 submarines)	9,380	Late 1980s – early 1990s
European Fighter Aircraft (250 units)	2,335 (D)	Early–mid 1990s
Harrier GR5 (96 units)	1,600	1987–90
Boeing AWACS (7 units)	950	1988–92
EH101 helicopter (50 units)	1,110 (D)	Mid 1990s
Trigat Long-Range anti-tank missile	1,900	Late 1990s
Trigat Medium-Range anti-tank missile	800	Late 1990s
Alarm air launched anti-radar missile	680	Late 1980s
Multiple Launch Rocket System Phase I	550	Late 1980s – early 1990s
Warrior Mechanised Infantry Combat Vehicle	1,126	1987–94
Upholder submarines (4 units)	670	1988–91
Type 23 Frigates (7 ships)	1,700	1988–93
Single role minehunter (5 units)	210	1990–92
Tucano trainer aircraft (130 units)	130 (P)	1989–92
Spearfish torpedo	1,357	1988–90
Challenger main battle tank (7 regiments)	725	1984–89
Chieftain replacement demonstration phase	90 (D)	1989–91

Cost trends in real terms: relative production costs of successive generations of equipment:

Trident programme	= 4 × cost of Polaris programme
Type 22 frigate	= 4 × cost of Leander frigate
Harrier GR1	= 3.75 × cost of Hunter
Sea Wolf missile	= 3.25 × cost of Sea Cat
Tornado F2	= 2.75 × cost of Lightning
Challenger tank	= 2.25 × cost of a Chieftain
Sea King helicopter	= 1.75 × cost of a Wessex

Note: D = development costs only; P = production costs only.
Source: HCP 383, 1989; HCP 37-II, 1985; Cmnd 1022-II, 1990.

Choices: what are the policy options?

A limited budget and rising costs of both manpower and equipment suggests that it will be increasingly difficult for the UK to continue meeting effectively all its defence commitments. A larger defence budget would ease the military choice problems, but only at the expense of the civil sector (*Figure 2.1*). Indeed, the 1990 public expenditure plans forecast a 3.0 per cent increase in real defence spending to 1993 (*Cmnd 1021, 1990*). For the longer term beyond 1993, guesses abound, but the trends are unlikely to be upwards and most likely to be towards level funding or cuts in real defence spending. Pressures for cuts will come from possible arms control agreements, competing social welfare expenditure (*eg* the National Health Service and care for the elderly), the desire for lower personal taxation and comparisons with the burdens borne by our European allies and major competitors in world markets (*eg* in 1988, France and West Germany allocated 3.8 per cent and 3.0 per cent, respectively, of their GDP to defence). Indeed, since the 1989 events in Eastern Europe and the possibility of arms control agreements, critics have focused on the prospects of substantial cuts in defence spending (the peace dividend) and the need for a radical re-appraisal of UK defence policy. The prospects of a funding gap and/or substantial cuts in defence budgets means that UK defence policy is faced with some difficult choices in the 1990s.

With only limited resources, the armed forces cannot have everything they ideally need and something will have to be sacrificed. Questions arise about the range of available options and the criteria to be used in choosing. Assuming no increase in real defence spending, the UK has three broad policy options:

(i) Reduce or eliminate a major commitment (the defence review or drastic surgery option).

(ii) Improve efficiency within the armed forces, the Ministry of Defence and the defence industries (better value for money): an option which will need to be pursued whatever the size of the defence budget.

(iii) Accept a gradual reduction in the operational effectiveness of UK forces and in their ability to continue meeting all their current commitments (fudge it).

Although these options are presented as alternatives, it is likely that any goverment will select a mix of these policies.

Drastic surgery

The possibility of a serious funding gap, as suggested by some critics, or an outbreak of peace in Europe will create pressure for drastic surgery such as a re-consideration of the size of BAOR, the RAF and the Navy's surface fleet or ending the commitment to maintain a domestic defence-industrial base (Greenwood, 1985; Small and Kennedy, 1985). Or, the UK could cancel the Trident programme and so eliminate its future strategic nuclear deterrent. Here, a distinction is needed between acquisition and operating or running costs. While cancellation of Trident appears to offer major savings on equipment acquisition costs (capital costs), it should be remembered that spread over the 20-year programme period, this represents an average *annual* saving of some £470 million (1990 prices). On this basis, the true defence costs of acquiring Trident are represented by the annual 'sacrifice', of some three frigates, or two nuclear-powered submarines or 30 Harrier GR5 aircraft. These are only illustrative orders of magnitude since no allowance has been made for the operating costs of each weapon. Nor does it follow that the savings from cancelling Trident would necessarily be re-allocated to the defence budget. Moreover, by the early 1990s, substantial sums will have been incurred or committed so that the cancellation of Trident will no longer offer the major savings which were available at the time of the 1987 General Election. However, if Trident were cancelled in the early 1990s, there would be savings on future operating costs, probably equivalent to under 2 per cent of the defence budget in the mid-1990s.

In considering the options for drastic surgery, the crucial question concerns their effects on defence output in the form of peace and the protection of UK citizens. Which, for example, contributes most to protection: Trident, BAOR, the RAF or the Navy's surface fleet? To some people, even to ask such questions about the costs of these commitments is sufficient to condemn the analyst. Supporters of Trident, or BAOR, or the RAF or of the Navy's surface fleet will assert that these commitments are 'vital' to the defence of the UK, failing to recognise that these options are not costless. However, in the 1980s the Government rejected the 'drastic surgery' option, claiming that the UK would continue to meet all its major defence commitments. The efficiency programme was offered as part of the solution.

Improving efficiency or better value for money

The efficiency programme introduced in 1983–84 has embraced more competition, contracting-out, privatisation, international collaboration, rationalisation, cuts in civilian manpower and the transfer of Service personnel from support activities to front-line units. The Ministry of

Defence was reorganised; a Management Information System for Ministers and top managers (MINIS) together with Responsibility Budgets were adopted; a new Chief of Defence Procurement was appointed with the aim of introducing a more commercial and competitive style of defence procurement; and in 1989 a New Management Strategy with Top Level Budgets and performance indicators was introduced (*HCP 399, 1986; HCP 383, 1989*). The general emphasis of the policy has been on managing defence resources efficiently.

The efficiency programme was originally introduced because it was believed that there were substantial inefficiencies in MoD, in the armed forces and in defence industries and markets. MoD was criticised for employing 'too many' civilians, and for being bureaucratic with 'too many' Whitehall civil servants, 'too little' delegation and with managers lacking budget constraints. Inefficiency in the armed forces was reflected in over-elaboration in equipment requirements, a lack of competition for 'in-house' services, 'wasteful duplication' of training and support activities and too high a proportion of Service personnel in support areas at the expense of front-line units. Finally, UK weapons programmes were criticised for excessive technical sophistication (gold-plating), the high level of costs together with cost overruns and delays (*eg* Nimrod AEW aircraft; Tigerfish torpedo). Cost escalation and delays are often associated with non-competitive markets and cost-plus contracts. In this context, a number of UK high technology industries are characterised by domestic monopolies (aircraft, helicopters, missiles, nuclear-powered submarines, tanks, torpedoes). The absence of rivalry or competition has often been reinforced where production contracts have been awarded automatically to the original development contractor. In other words, UK weapons markets were characterised by a lack of competition and an absence of incentive and fixed-price contracts which imposed financial constraints on contractors.

The efficiency programme has achieved some impressive results. Service manpower has been re-allocated from support to front-line units. For example, the Army's Lean Look programme aimed to save 4,000 uniformed support posts by 1990. Between 1979 and 1990, the number of UK-based MoD civilians was reduced by over 40 per cent from 248,000 to 142,000. In 1989, MoD announced an internal three-year target for efficiency savings of 2.5 per cent per annum. Similarly, contracting-out of support services has led to cost savings of 20–30 per cent, an annual equivalent of £50 million (1989 prices: *HCP 383, 1989*, p. xv). Furthermore, in 1985, the Chief of Defence Procurement declared a target for savings over five years of 10 per cent on the procurement budget (*HCP 399, 1986*, p. xiv). Examples have been reported where competitive procurement has resulted in cost savings ranging from 10–70 per cent, all of which might be taken as indicators of monopoly-pricing and/or inefficiency in UK defence industries.

While the examples of efficiency improvements appear impressive, major doubts remain. The successes claimed for competitive procurement often fail to show the *total amount* of savings which are expected; how quickly the savings will be achieved and their effect on the *annual* defence budget. Examples have been given of substantial percentage savings from competition with no indication of their aggregate value; or, where aggregate figures are reported, no indication is given of the time-period over which the savings will be achieved. In some cases, such as contracting-out, substantial percentage cost savings of 20–30 per cent result in annual savings of a mere £50 million which, while useful, is small in relation to the cost of major equipment projects. Elsewhere, the claimed benefits from competition might reflect bad estimating! Questions also arise as to the effects on the operational capability of UK forces. There is, then, a real danger that presentation in the form of impressive and numerous examples will divert attention from the central issue of whether the efficiency programme will result in sufficiently large savings to enable the UK to continue meeting its defence commitments without a substantial reduction in operational effectiveness. This brings us to the third policy option.

The 'fudge it' option (salami-slicing)

This option involves the UK accepting a gradual reduction in the operational effectiveness of its armed forces and hence in their ability to meet all their current commitments. It can take the form of reduced training, cancellations or delays in ordering new projects and in attrition buys of replacement equipment, and delays in reaching required stocks of ammunition and supplies (none of which are glamorous to users in the Services). Politically, this is an attractive policy option. The government can avoid a major defence review while claiming to meet all its commitments. This does not necessarily mean that the policy should be condemned as inefficient. It might be a socially desirable option, involving only a marginal reduction in output which society might willingly accept. However, unless this option is presented as an element in the public debate about UK defence policy, society will be unable to make an informed choice. Here, economic theory can contribute by providing an analytical framework for evaluating alternative policies.

Does economic theory offer any guidelines for UK defence policy?

Choices and efficiency are central to economics. Five general and related economic principles can be used in evaluating choices and efficiency in UK defence policy:

(i) *The principle of outputs.* Admittedly, the output of defence is difficult to measure. Reference can be made to peace, protection, security and the valuation of human lives. It is, in fact, possible to place a more meaningful interpretation on these vague concepts. For example, the current defence budget might allow the UK to participate in a conventional war in Europe for up to, say, four to five days before using nuclear weapons; or the budget might give the UK the capability to mount a Falklands-type operation. Despite the difficulties, the emphasis on defence outputs shows the limitations of focusing on inputs and intermediate outputs such as a 50-squadron Air Force or a 50-ship Navy or a commitment to maintaining 55,000 troops in Germany, or to raise military spending by 3 per cent per annum. The crucial question is what contribution do these inputs of expenditure, aircraft, ships and troops make to protection and security in the UK?

(ii) *The principle of substitution.* There are alternative methods of achieving protection and security. For example, manned aircraft and cruise missiles could replace Trident submarines; in turn, Trident could replace some conventional forces; Tornado aircraft in Germany could replace soldiers in BAOR; RAF maritime patrol aircraft can replace Navy frigates and aircraft carriers. Equipment can replace manpower. Within equipment, there is a wide range of alternatives such as quality versus quantity; new equipment versus the continued use of existing equipment through longer in-service lifetimes and mid-life up-dating; equipment versus stocks; and British versus foreign equipment. Within manpower, there is a further range of alternatives involving men and women, military and civil personnel, younger versus older personnel, Gurkhas versus UK soldiers and regulars versus reserves. For example, in 1986 the average annual cost of a Regular Army soldier was £12,800 compared with £2,800 for a TA soldier and £770 for a member of the Home Service Force (*HCP 399, 1986,* p. 147).

Economists would expect MoD and the armed forces to substitute relatively cheaper for more expensive forms of protection, regardless of the traditional property rights of each of the Services. This is what happens in the private sector of the economy where there is a continual search for cheaper production techniques, new products and new markets all of which leads to continual change in the profitability and size of firms and industries (*eg* UK cotton, shipbuilding and steel industries). But in the private sector, the incentive to substitute cheaper production methods is provided by competition and the profit-motive.

(iii) *The principle of contestability and rivalry.* Actual and potential rivalry promotes efficiency. Defence offers massive opportunities for introducing and extending rivalry and for creating contestable markets. There are possibilities for more competition involving:

(a) Rivalry between the armed forces. The aim would be to allocate defence budgets on the basis of each Service's comparative advantage (*ie* specialising in what it is good at). Why not allow the Army with land-based guided missiles to compete with the RAF and manned fighter aircraft for the air defence of the UK? Similarly, RAF Germany could compete with BAOR for the defence of central Europe; and RAF land-based aircraft could replace RN frigates and aircraft carriers. For example, the expenditure on a Harrier with six BL 755s could be used to purchase 20 Multiple-Launch Rocket System (MLRS) launchers, each with a supply vehicle and 36 rockets (Davies, 1985). In other words, there are opportunities for reducing the entry barriers associated with the traditional monopoly property rights for each of the Services, thereby creating contestable markets.

(b) Rivalry between the armed forces and private contractors. Firms could be allowed more opportunities to bid for a whole range of activities traditionally undertaken 'in-house' by the armed forces. Competition has occurred for some defence support functions but the moves have been relatively limited and there remain considerable opportunities for further experimentation with the policy (*cf* NHS and local government: Hartley, 1987).

(c) Rivalry between firms seeking defence business, ranging from standard items and services to the supply of high technology equipment. A competitive procurement policy would be characterised by MoD's willingness to shop around; by the removal of barriers to entry into, and exit from, the UK defence market; by rivalry for different specifications and at the design, prototype and production stages of a project's life cycle; and by competitively-determined fixed price contracts with no state regulation of profits.

(iv) *The principle of self-interest.* The search for cheaper substitutes and better value for money depends upon the motivation and behaviour of individuals who have to implement policies. Individuals have no incentive to co-operate in policies aimed at improving efficiency if they bear all the costs and receive none of the benefits (*ie* are made worse-off). Currently, individuals and groups in the armed forces and MoD have every incentive to spend since there are no inducements and rewards for economising. The

Navy is unlikely to economise if all the savings are used to buy more tanks for the Army or more aircraft for the RAF, or if the savings accrue to the Treasury.

(v) *The principle of incrementalism* (or equalising returns at the margin). Economic efficiency focuses on the costs and benefits of small changes (incrementalism or marginalism). Questions have to be asked about the effects on UK security and protection (benefits) if the defence budget were changed by plus or minus 5 per cent (costs); or what would be the costs and benefits of changing the size of the Navy's surface fleet, or BAOR, or RAF Germany by plus or minus 10 per cent. Ultimately, an efficient solution requires the equality of costs and benefits at the margin. On this basis, society, in searching for the most preferred pattern of defence spending, might be willing to change its 'consumption' of, say, nuclear and conventional forces by sacrificing some of one for more of the other; and the value to the community of a force structure will diminish the more of that force structure which is already in existence and being 'consumed'. Applying this principle to UK defence policy suggests that when changes are needed they should be on the basis of a variety of small adjustments across a range of defence activities: a solution which resembles the 'fudge-it' option or which involves small changes in commitments. In contrast, 'drastic surgery' which eliminates a capability might be too drastic. As always, though, simple generalisations have to be qualified. Drastic surgery could be a preferred and efficient solution where there is a major change in technology rendering some forces obsolescent; or where a change of government leads to completely different views and valuations of defence forces (*eg* valuations of a strategic nuclear deterrent).

Barriers to improving efficiency

Clearly some of the above economic principles have been reflected in UK defence policy, particularly in MoD's efficiency programme where efforts have been made to improve the efficiency of meeting existing defence commitments. The emphasis on competitive procurement and contracting-out are obvious examples. There have also been examples of substitutions such as between nuclear and conventional forces, equipment and manpower, military and civil personnel and between men and women. Similarly, the 1985 reorganisation of MoD and the creation of a unified defence staff might be viewed as an effort to reduce the traditional monopoly property rights of each of the armed forces. However, there is a worry that the three Services will collude rather than compete, so continuing the principle of Buggins's turn. Indeed, there are major barriers to securing substantial efficiency improvements in defence markets. These result from employment contracts, a concern with operational capability and a traditional commitment to support UK defence industries.

Organisational changes in MoD, MINIS and Responsibility Budgets are unlikely to be successful in providing efficiency incentives unless they are associated with employment contracts which reward efficient behaviour and penalise inefficiency. Currently, the employment contracts of military personnel provide no inducements to economise and save by searching for lower-cost solutions; individuals and groups (*cf* worker co-operatives) are not rewarded for improving efficiency. There is, then, scope for experimenting with efficiency-promoting employment contracts for military staff and civil servants in MoD. Examples include fixed budgets, output targets, bonuses, sharing in cost savings, promotion, firing and forming the equivalent of worker co-operatives where workers bear the risks of an enterprise.

Recently, some limited moves have occurred in this direction with the introduction of performance-related awards for civilian staff. Also, in 1989, as part of the government's Financial Management Initiative, MoD announced its New Management Strategy (NMS) which is planned to be fully operational in 1991. The NMS is designed 'to allocate budgets and delegate authority to managers and to develop better systems and techniques for performance measurement, applying as appropriate the best private and public sector management techniques' (*Cmnd 675-I, 1989*, p. 43). Under NMS, there will be 22 top level budgets held by commanders–in-chief and senior staff which will be broken down into lower level budgets allocated to individual budget-holders. Budgets will cover all operating costs except spending on the Procurement Executive's equipment programme. Budget-holders will be given 'as much flexibility as possible in using their cash in order to achieve agreed tasks and objectives with maximum efficiency' (*Cmnd 675-I, 1989*, p. 44). However, in practice what actual flexibility will managers really have, bearing in mind that Service pay is determined nationally and that top level budgets will not include defence equipment? Moreover, will managers be compelled to buy central services and will they be allowed to sell surplus land and buildings and retain the proceeds? Furthermore, a range of performance indicators will be required to specify fully a budget-holder's objectives and targets, so ensuring that financial savings are not achieved by unacceptable sacrifices of output (*ie* savings can always be achieved if there are no output targets, assuming that output can be measured). There are also questions about what incentives managers and staff will have to achieve maximum efficiency. Will there be performance-related pay and will it be possible to carry forward savings to future years, or will subsequent annual budgets be revised downwards to reflect savings; and will there be penalties where budget-holders exceed their budgets? Finally, appeals to apply the best private sector management techniques to MoD and the armed forces ignore the fact that private sector efficiency is the result of the profit motive, the threat of take-over and the threat from rival producers. Nonetheless, having stated these reservations about the NMS, it should be stressed that defence is not unique and other parts of the public sector such as health and education are subject to similar problems.

Many of the economic problems in defence are similar to those in the National Health Service (NHS). There are difficulties of measuring output: the defence equivalent of health output expressed as quality adjusted life years (QALYS) might be protection adjusted life years (PALYS). Nor is a great deal known about the relationship between specific inputs and outputs: for example, what contribution do highly-trained nurses make to health output, and what is the contribution of tanks or warships to the protection of Britain? There are also problems of providing staff with incentives to be efficient and to substitute relatively cheaper for more expensive inputs. For instance, in the NHS, there have been managerial changes (Griffiths), budgets for clinicians, proposals for General Practice budgets and internal markets, and debates about possible substitutions between doctors and nurses, drugs and surgery and between different types of nurses; while in the armed forces, the equivalents are the NMS, Responsibility Budgets and possible substitutions between regulars and reserves, and between RAF maritime aircraft and RN frigates.

Despite the substantial progress which MoD has made in introducing and extending competition through the contracting-out of services and through equipment procurement policy, major barriers exist to further efficiency improvements in these areas. Competition for, and the contracting-out of, defence support functions has produced savings of 20–30 per cent, equivalent to a useful £50 million per year in 1989. Examples of services which have been subject to competition from private contractors include catering, cleaning, grounds maintenance, security guarding, managing and manning facilities (*eg* Royal Dockyards), and equipment maintenance (*Cmnd 675-I, 1989*, p. 35). Opportunities exist for a major extension of the policy in repair and maintenance work, air, land and sea transport, air traffic control, search and rescue and training functions.

Critics claim that private contractors offer a poor quality and unreliable service; that they are subject to bankruptcy; they are unable to respond to emergencies (*eg* wars); that they use low bids to buy into an attractive contract and so establish a monopoly position; and that awarding a contract to a private firm can cause industrial relations problems and strikes. These arguments need to be critically assessed and tested empirically. Some of the arguments represent special pleading by those interest groups likely to lose from the policy. In defence, 'operational factors' are the usual objection to contracting-out. Apparently, there are operational difficulties in employing a combination of Servicemen and civilians, especially in servicing at front-line combat units; and there are possibly security problems if contractor's staff have access to secret equipment. However, contracts can specify a contractor's obligation during mobilisation and war, and the security argument is rather strange in view of the extensive use of civilians in the development and production of weapons by private industry. Once again, the objections might reflect the power, influence and knowledge of vested interest groups opposed to contracting-out because they will be the losers. It must also be recognised that 'operational considerations' are not without cost. The armed forces need to be subject to output targets and budget constraints and their staff need employment contracts which provide them with inducements to economise. In this way, the forces would be required to choose between the operational advantages of using, say, a high proportion of Servicemen for maintenance work, and other things such as less training or buying less equipment. Similar choices are needed when considering the purchase of British equipment.

The defence industrial base and the efficiency with which it provides equipment is a major input into the protection of the UK. In buying equipment, 90 per cent of MoD orders go to British companies and 10 per cent to foreign firms (*Cmnd 1022-I, 1990*). Traditionally, the UK has supported its domestic defence industrial base. If buying British means paying more for some defence equipment and waiting longer for delivery, the result is smaller defence forces and less protection for our citizens. Questions then arise as to what the defence budget is buying: is it buying protection for our society or protection for UK defence industries?

The traditional desire to maintain a strong UK defence industrial base reflected a concern with defence and other policy objectives particularly jobs, technology and the balance of payments (*Cmnd 9227-I, 1984*, p. 17). As a result, there were major barriers to achieving substantial cost savings through a competitive procurement policy. Government-created barriers to entry and exit meant that existing firms were protected from rivalry, especially foreign rivals. The opportunities for inefficiency are increased where there are domestic monopolies as in aerospace, tanks, torpedoes and submarines, and where state regulation of defence profits provides contractors with incentives to pursue non-profit objectives (*eg* a quiet life; luxury offices). However, in 1988, MoD announced as part of its competition policy 'a greater readiness to consider non-UK sources where they are likely to offer greater value for money' (*Cmnd 288-II, 1988*, p. 7). Of course, MoD equipment choices need government approval, at which point, politicians will be concerned with the vote-consequences of decisions. Moreover, large defence contractors with domestic monopolies form a major pressure group with an obvious interest in persuading governments to buy British. Inevitably, proposals to buy from abroad, especially from the USA (*eg* AWACS, tanks), will encounter massive opposition from established interest groups likely to lose from a competitive procurement policy. UK defence contractors, unions, scientists and professional associations will scream about the dangers of depending on foreigners, and about the adverse effects on jobs, technology and the balance of payments, all of which will be expressed in terms of the national interest. Economists can contribute by critically evaluating these arguments, by seeking evidence on their validity and by estimating the costs of buying British. Typically, economists will point to alternative uses of resources by asking whether some of the resources used in UK defence industries would make a greater contribution to protection, jobs, technology and, ultimately, to human satisfaction if they were used elsewhere in the economy (see Chapter 8).

Conclusion

Increasing cost pressures on limited UK defence budgets will require difficult choices about its military commitments. These same pressures will require equally difficult choices about the minimum size and composition of the UK's defence industrial base. Decisions are required in a world of uncertainty. Today's threat might be tomorrow's ally; today's high technology equipment might be tomorrow's Dreadnoughts.

Increasingly, economic pressures will require the armed forces to think more radically about the current constraints on their range of choices. Here, the possibilities of substitution need to be explored further, such as equipment for manpower, reserves for regulars, civilians for Service personnel, aircraft replacing surface ships, missiles for aircraft, helicopters replacing tanks and foreign equipment replacing UK equipment. In making such choices, there is a more fundamental problem involving society's preferences for the size and various combinations of defence forces.

A voting system based on General Elections is a limited mechanism for allowing voters to express their preferences on defence issues. For example, in the 1980s, was a vote for the Conservatives expressing a preference for Trident and strong defences, or for lower taxation or for privatisation? Questions also arise about the quantity and quality of information on UK defence policy which is presented to voters and to Parliament on the basis of which choices are made. Here, the obvious starting point for economists is the information provided on the budget in the annual *Statement on the Defence Estimates*. Further information is available from the reports of the House of Commons Defence Committee, from higher education institutions and from independent think-tanks (*eg* International Institute for Strategic Studies, the Royal United Services Institute, the Royal Institute of International Affairs).

References

Cmnd 9227-I, 1984, *Statement on the Defence Estimates 1984*, (HMSO, London).

Cmnd 288-II, 1988, *The Government's Expenditure Plans 1988–89 to 1990–91*, (HMSO, London).

Cmnd 1021, 1990, *The Government's Expenditure Plans 1990–91 to 1992–93*, (HMSO, London).

Cmnd 675, 1989, *Statement on the Defence Estimates 1989*, (HMSO, London).

Cmnd 1022, 1990, *Statement on the Defence Estimates 1990*, (HMSO, London).

Davies, J., 1985, 'The guided missile and its role in the air-land battle', *Air Clues*, MoD, London, November.

Greenwood, D., 1985, Memorandum in *Defence Commitments and Resources and the Defence Estimates 1985–86*, pp. 288–297A. Defence Committee, HCP 37-II, (HMSO, London).

Hartley, K., 1987, Competitive tendering in Jackson, P. and Terry, F. (eds.), *Public Domain 1987*, (Public Finance Foundation, London).

HCP 37, 1985, *Defence Commitments and Resources and the Defence Estimates 1985–1986*, Defence Committee, May (HMSO, London).

HCP 399, 1986, *Statement on the Defence Estimates 1986*, Defence Committee, (HMSO London).

HCP 383, 1989, *Statement on the Defence Estimates 1989*, Defence Committee, June (HMSO, London).

Small, J. R. and Kennedy, G., 1985, Memorandum in *Defence Commitments and Resources and the Defence Estimates 1985–86*, pp. 284–288. Defence Committee, HCP 37-II, (HMSO, London).

CHAPTER 3

Defence Budgets

Introduction

Since the 1960s, there have been major changes in British defence policy and in the organisational, budgetary and financial arrangements for planning and controlling defence expenditure. In 1964 a unified Ministry of Defence was established, the aim being to create '. . . an organisation in which defence, rather than single Service, considerations will be paramount' and which will '. . . help the achievement of a unified defence policy and the efficient and economical provision of our military forces'. (*Cmnd 2270, 1964*, p. 5). These organisational arrangements were reinforced in 1965 when two new techniques, namely, functional costing and cost-effectiveness, were incorporated into Britain's defence decision making process.

Functional costing or programme budgeting is a means of identifying the functions of the defence forces and the costs of these functions. The Ministry's functional costing system was designed to '. . . assist in planning and co-ordinating the Defence Budget', so that those who plan the Budget and have to decide on new projects for the defence programme '. . . will have much more information than in the past about the relative costs of planned forces and weapons systems' (*Cmnd 2592, 1965*, pp. 11–12). Functional costing provides the framework for undertaking cost-effectiveness studies. Such studies estimate the costs and defence effectiveness of alternative force arrangements and various weapons systems in relation to some specified objective such as the destruction of an industrial complex, an airfield or a ship. No attempt is made to place a monetary value on the measure of defence effectiveness, the aim being to select the 'least-cost' method of destroying a target or protecting a city or a military installation.

The various defence choices and reviews which have occurred since the mid-1960s have provided many opportunities for using these new aids to decision making. There have been major differences in the defence policies of the two political parties. They have differed on the appropriate size

28

of the defence budget, on force structures and on the geographical distribution of the UK's forces. The Labour governments of 1964–70 and 1974–79 withdrew from the Far East and the Mediterranean and concentrated Britain's forces in Europe. In addition the Labour government in the mid-1960s cancelled a number of major UK aircraft projects (*eg* TSR-2) and replaced them with the large-scale purchase of US military aircraft. There have also been continued debates between the political parties on the Navy's carrier force and its surface fleet, and on the UK's defence commitments outside the NATO area (*eg* Falklands, Gibraltar).

In 1990–91, Britain's defence budget exceeded £21 billion. A budget of this size with its sacrifices of hospitals, schools and roads as well as of private sector goods and services (*eg* cars, videos, holidays) is obviously a source of public concern. Questions have to be asked about the 'appropriate' size of the defence budget. Is the current budget too large or too small? What is the defence budget buying and does it provide good value for money? Does information on the budget enable Parliament and the electorate to make informed choices about the efficient allocation of military expenditure between nuclear and conventional forces, between air, land and sea forces and between the UK, Europe and the rest of the world? Society is interested in the efficiency with which defence resources are used and whether it is possible for Parliament and the taxpayer to assess such efficiency. In relation to efficiency questions, it is necessary to examine whether the information presented in the defence budgetary statements can be related to any of the economic principles in Chapter 2.

This chapter shows how programme budgeting provides a framework for answering some of the major choice and efficiency questions of UK defence policy. It starts by considering the problems of traditional input budgets, after which it examines and evaluates the functional costing or programme budgeting system as presented to Parliament by the Ministry of Defence. Economists are interested in the impact of programme budgeting on the allocation of resources within defence and on the efficiency with which resources are used.

The production of defence: how does it differ from private markets?

Scarcity and the problem of efficiency in the allocation and use of resources is central to economics. In this sense, defence is not unique and similar problems arise throughout the public sector. Defence can be regarded as an industry which uses resources of land, manpower, capital (*eg* bases, equipment) and entrepreneurship in the form of military commanders. This industry consists of a large number of military units (firms) of different sizes, each producing a variety of different products (air, land and sea forces in different locations) and all concerned with maximising defence output or protection and security. For example, as entrepreneurs, military commanders have the task of combining Hawk, Phantom and Tornado fighter aircraft, surface-to-air missiles, pilots, ground staff and airfields to produce an air defence force which will maximise the number of enemy bombers and missiles destroyed at minimum cost. In principle, this is the same problem that is faced by, say, brewers or car firms which have to assemble and combine various quantities of skilled labour, plant and machinery, to earn maximum profits. In both defence and manufacturing industry, decision makers have the task of using limited resources in the best possible way to achieve their objectives.

Defence, however, differs from other British industries in one resource-relevant way. For products such as beer, cars and television sets, private markets indicate a set of prices for the industry's output. Also, in private markets, competition between rival suppliers can provide a benchmark for assessing a firm's performance, with profitability as the criterion of efficiency in resource use. Within defence, there are no private markets to establish the price of the industry's output or to give society's valuation of the activity; there are no rival suppliers of defence in the UK market, nor can profitability be used to assess the efficiency with which the Ministry of Defence and its military commanders use scarce resources. Indeed, for economists, defence has some distinctive characteristics which classify it as a public good.

Defence as a public good

Defence provided nationally or internationally through a military alliance is usually presented as a classic example of what economists call a pure public good. These are goods where, once produced, one person's consumption does not reduce anyone else's consumption. Other examples are ideas, theories, information, music, flood control, street lighting and traditional types of lighthouses (Hartley and Tisdell, 1981, Chapter 2; Kennedy 1983, Chapter 2).

The central characteristics of a pure public good is its non-excludability: if it is provided to one person, then it is provided to everyone. For example, the UK provides defence for all its citizens and its provision for me implies its provision for everyone else in the community: protection for one is protection for many and my protection does not exclude others from protection (non-rivalry). Similarly, with the US strategic nuclear umbrella which provides deterrence for all members of NATO. Compare this with a private good where the exclusion principle operates and there is rivalry in the consumption of goods and services. For example, if I buy a loaf of bread, it becomes my property; I have the right to exclude you from its consumption and the more I consume the less is available to you.

The public good nature of defence means that, if left to themselves, private competitive markets will fail to provide the socially desirable amount of protection for a community, so that some form of state intervention is required. Once defence is provided, its benefits extend to everyone in the community and individuals cannot be excluded by charging a price. So, if direct prices cannot be charged, some other method is needed to finance the supply of defence. Here, the usual solutions are state finance in the form of taxation (*eg* taxes on income and expenditure) or payments in kind through conscription. But the search for appropriate methods of financing defence raises two problems. First, there are free-rider problems which arise when someone obtains the benefits of defence without contributing to its costs. For example, I have every incentive to conceal my true willingness to pay for defence if the costs will be borne by others in the group (*eg* NATO). How, then, does a group or community obtain an accurate indication of each individual's valuation of defence? Second, if it is difficult to identify each individual's valuation of defence, how does a society or government determine the appropriate or optimum size of the defence budget?

Efficiency and budgets

While recognising its distinctive economic characteristics, the fact remains that defence is a major user of society's limited resources so that it is important to examine the means available for promoting and improving efficiency in this area of decision making. Questions arise as to whether the traditional methods of budgeting provide a framework for assessing the efficiency of resource allocation decisions in defence. Does the budget provide information on outputs and on the objectives of defence decision makers? Does it show the relationship between inputs and specific outputs and are all the inputs shown and correctly valued? In other words, do traditional budgets convey the sort of information about performance that is automatically generated by private firms operating in competitive markets? An example of the traditional form of defence budget is shown in *Table 3.1*.

Table 3.1 is a typical example of an input budget which was used in the UK until the mid-1960s. Admittedly, some of the information can be used for assessing efficiency in resource use. Examples include expenditure on the pay of Service personnel, reserves and civilians, together with outlays on research and production by each of the Services. The remaining budget headings are less helpful, unless decision makers are worried about the relative size of the Army's food bill and its consumption of fuel and light! In general, the traditional budget provides only limited information for debating the difficult choices and questions raised by UK defence policy since the mid-1960s. How much should the

TABLE 3.1 *Traditional form of the UK defence budget, 1965–66*

Item	Ministry of Defence (£m)				Totals £m
	Central	Navy	Army	Air	
1. Pay of Service Personnel	9.90	91.55	166.40	140.21	410.01
2. Pay of Reserve Forces		1.38	21.42	0.77	23.57
3. Pay of Civilians	4.40	62.83	125.68	50.60	275.27
4. Movements	0.50	10.73	23.32	19.60	57.12
5. Supplies: (a) Petrol, oil lubricants	0.01	14.20	6.96	26.35	48.70
(b) Food & ration allowance		116.06	25.76	15.90	52.72
(c) Fuel and light		5.15	10.46	6.73	23.70
(d) Miscellaneous	0.21	0.64	2.78	1.77	5.40
6. Production and Research: (a) Production		297.06	112.46	281.00	739.31
(b) Research and Development	0.10	20.10	6.46		200.65
7. (a) Works, Buildings, Land	7.34	3.63	7.97		161.63
(b) Associated Expenditure					25.24
8. Miscellaneous Services	6.00	3.54	10.09	1.23	21.41
9. Non-effective charges		22.32	35.84	17.61	75.77
TOTALS	28.46	544.19	555.60	561.77	2,120.50

Note: Total figure includes expenditures by Ministry of Aviation, Ministry of Public Building and Works and Atomic Energy Authority.
Source: Cmnd 2592, 1965, Annex B.

UK spend on defence? What are the costs of the nuclear deterrent, or BAOR, of UK air defence and of maintaining the Navy's carrier force and its surface fleet?

The input budget in *Table 3.1* creates at least three problems for any assessment of efficiency in the use of defence resources. First, it does not show any output other than the generally vague heading of 'defence'. Second, it is not possible to relate inputs to outputs. Third, on the inputs side, difficulties arise because it is implied that current defence decisions only involve the use of resources for a one-year budgetary period. In view of their importance for the development of programme budgeting, these problems need further elaboration (Greenwood, 1972; Hartley, 1974).

The input budget shown in *Table 3.1* does not provide any means of relating expenditure to outputs in the defence sector. For example, pay, research and production are all inputs into a variety of defence activities, none of which are apparent from the information given in *Table 3.1*. As a result, decision makers in MoD and in Parliament were unable to relate expenditures on inputs to the objectives of UK defence policy reflected in Britain's commitments. Input budgets did not provide information on the resource implications of changing the composition of defence output through, say, varying the 'mix' of nuclear and conventional forces, or changing the geographical distribution of forces between the UK, Europe and the rest of the world. Nor did traditional budgets show the opportunities for substitution and the implications for various defence outputs. For example, they did not provide any relevant information for assessing the resource and output implications of substituting RAF maritime patrol aircraft for RN frigates or Trident submarines for BAOR or submarines for surface ships. Instead, input budgets focused on the possibilities of substitution between such items as pay, petrol, movements, food and buildings, with no information on the output effects of such substitution.

The defence budget in *Table 3.1* is confined to a one-year period. However, modern weapons systems such as combat aircraft and the Trident nuclear deterrent project can involve a 30–40-year planning period (*eg* 10–20 years for development and production and a 20-year operational life: *HCP 479, 1985*). In these circumstances, traditional budgets did not show the total systems or life-cycle costs of current defence decisions. For example, the decision to order the Tornado aircraft involved relatively small-scale expenditures in the early years of the project but outlays rose as development proceeded and production started with a peak of expenditure occurring around the tenth year of the programme; and these capital expenditures were followed by outlays on the Service operation of the aircraft (*eg* modified bases, training, support, mid-life modifications). In this situation, input budgets which only showed expenditures for a one-year period failed to reveal the total resource costs of current defence decisions. Up to the 1960s, such a limited planning horizon, in which new weapons projects appeared to be relatively cheap in their early stages, might have led the UK to start the development of a number of projects which might never have been undertaken if their total resource costs had been considered. It is possible that a relatively short planning horizon in which projects initially appear to be relatively cheap might have contributed to such controversial defence issues as cost escalation and the cancellation of projects.

Input budgets also fail to show that each Service, as well as a number of government departments, might be pursuing the same objective with obvious implications for inefficiency in the provision of defence output. For example, within nuclear forces, the RAF's V-bombers and the Navy's Polaris submarines could, at one time, have been regarded as substitutes; similarly with the Air Force's land-based strike aircraft and the Navy's carrier force. Further problems with the traditional defence budgets arise because they do not show the defence activities of other government departments. Examples include civil defence and fire fighting within the Home Office, transport services (British Rail), overseas aid and Government policy towards self-sufficiency in food supplies and weapons (Ministry of Agriculture and the Department of Trade and Industry). Nor does the defence budget show military expenditure by our allies, including expenditure by US forces in Britain.

Finally, traditional budgets only show cash expenditure figures. To assess economic efficiency, it is necessary to know whether the cash outlays are an accurate reflection of the scarcity value of resources. Since the UK relies upon voluntary forces rather than conscription, the price of labour in periods of full employment will reflect the scarcity or alternative-use value of resources. However, when there is unemployment in the economy or if weapons such as ships are purchased from areas of high unemployment (Development Areas), the financial outlays shown in traditional budgets will not reflect the fact that in the limit the alternative-use value of labour is zero. And to assess efficiency it is resource costs rather than money outlays that are relevant.

Thus, for a variety of reasons, traditional budgets, while useful for controlling expenditures, are not really suitable for assessing the performance of the Ministry of Defence in using scarce resources: they provide no basis for analysis, planning and informed decision making. How can efficiency in resource use be assessed and improved when traditional budgets do not show the products of the defence industry nor their costs of production? Programme or output budgeting provides a framework for addressing some of these questions. It presents a framework for systematically assessing information and questioning the aims of a Government Department and its use of resources. With its emphasis on objectives, outputs and total resource costs, it is in complete contrast to traditional input budgets: hence the alternative title of output budgeting (Williams, 1967).

What is programme budgeting?

Programme budgeting or a planning, programming budgeting system (PPBS) provides information for answering questions about the efficiency with which the Ministry of Defence uses resources. It seeks answers to four questions. First, what are the objectives of the Ministry of Defence and is it possible to formulate a set of programmes which can be related to these objectives? Second, what are the current and expected life-cycle resource costs of each programme? Third, what are the results or outputs of each programme? Finally, are there alternative methods of achieving each programme and what are the costs and outputs of each alternative (*ie* cost-effectiveness studies)?

The programme budget or functional costing system introduced by the

Ministry of Defence in 1965 originally consisted of 14 major programmes further sub-divided into some 700 programme or functional elements (*eg* an aircraft squadron, a single ship), each of which was costed. In principle, expenditures are allocated to programmes, so leaving miscellaneous categories as small as possible. A 10-year planning period is used for the Ministry's functional costing system. However, the programme budget information presented to Parliament in the annual Defence Statement is restricted to a one-year period with the major programmes subdivided into over 50 elements. Examples of the published form of the functional analysis of defence expenditure for 1983–84 and 1989–90 are shown in *Table 3.2*.

Compared with traditional input budgets, *Table 3.2* shows some of the outputs of the defence industry (*eg* air, land, sea and nuclear forces), their costs of production and the possibilities for substitution. It provides a basis for debating the objectives of UK defence policy and the questions raised by the various defence reviews and policy changes that have occurred since the mid-1960s. For example, in 1990–91, the cost of BAOR was similar to the total budget for research and development and for the Navy's combat forces. Spending on destroyers and frigates was similar to the cost of the RAF's strike and reconnaissance squadrons. Furthermore, if the UK decided that it was spending too much on defence, the information in *Table 3.2* shows some of the options available to policy makers. A 10 per cent cut in the 1990–91 budget, equivalent to annual savings of £2 billion, would require the abolition of most of either BAOR or the Navy, or cancelling most of the R & D programme. Thus, the functional costing system in *Table 3.2* provides information on the costs of maintaining a nuclear deterrent, the 'mix' of nuclear and conventional forces, the geographical distribution of land forces and the weapons composition of sea and air forces.

A critique

The choice of major programmes by the Ministry of Defence is a strange mixture of outputs and inputs arranged partly by individual Service, partly by geography and partly by weapons. Only the first six major programmes in *Table 3.2* are related to the combat activities of the defence forces; the rest simply show the various support activities which are not allocated to the front-line units. Alternative programme arrangements can be devised (Hitch and McKean, 1960). One possibility would be a structure based on four major programmes, say nuclear strategic forces, nuclear tactical forces, conventional forces and special forces. The inputs for each of these programmes would include reserve forces, training, research, production facilities and stocks; inputs which in the present functional costing system form separate programmes. Another

TABLE 3.2. *Functional analysis of the UK defence budget*

	£ million	
	1983–84	1990–91
Nuclear strategic forces	382	1,480
Navy general purpose combat forces	2,149	2,503
Submarines	468	446
Aircraft and ASW carriers	140	99
Amphibious forces	60	102
Destroyers and frigates	722	669
Mine counter-measures vessels	159	72
Other vessels	285	404
Aircraft	242	282
Fleet headquarters	24	127
Overseas shore establishments	49	59
Naval bases and operational support	–	243
European theatre ground forces	2,445	3,387
British Army of the Rhine	1,700	2,319
Berlin	42	63
Home forces	703	1,005
Other Army combat forces	191	206
Mediterranean	62	92
Hong Kong and other Far East	1	45
South Atlantic	105	35
Other areas	23	34
Air Force general purposes forces	3,207	3,668
Air defence	579	753
Offensive support	118	372
Strike/attack/reconnaissance	922	691
Maritime aircraft	139	132
Transport aircraft	231	232
Tanker aircraft	128	101
Civil charter	17	27
Other aircraft	122	133
Operational stations	418	519
Headquarters	68	98
General support	465	610
Reserve and Auxiliary formations	312	458
Navy	15	27
Army	279	397
Air Force	18	34
Research and development	1,896	2,454
Ship construction and underwater warfare	328	368
Ordnance and other Army	177	191
Military aircraft	556	720
Guided weapons	245	384
Other electronics	282	365
Other research and development	308	426
Training	1,230	1,407
Service colleges	85	122
Navy	443	355
Army	428	609
Air Force	274	321

TABLE 3.2. (*Continued*)

	£ million	
	1983–84	1990–91
Equipment support and associated		
facilities in UK	1,040	1,093
Royal Dockyards	128	118
Other repair and maintenance/	401	445
Storage and supply	403	416
Quality assurance	108	114
War and contingency stocks	410	476
Navy	161	153
Army	165	171
Air Force	84	152
Other support functions	2,631	4,031
Whitehall organisations	222	344
Local administration communications		
etc. in UK	1,080	1,654
Meteorological services	34	50
Family and personnel services in UK	241	282
Service pensions	754	1,408
Other support services	300	293
Miscellaneous expenditure and receipts	80	60
Total Defence Budget	15,973	21,223

Source: Cmnd 1022, 1990.

possibility would be a programme structure showing the geographical distribution of all land, sea and air forces. With its emphasis on the UK, Europe, and commitments outside the NATO area (*eg* Belize, Falklands), such a programme structure would provide more complete information than at present for debating the geographical aspects of UK defence policy (see Chapter 2, *Table 2.1*). In other words, alternative programme arrangements are possible, each appropriate for a specific set of policy questions.

There is a further limitation of the published information shown in *Table 3.2*. Expenditure figures are only inputs and any appraisal of efficiency in the defence sector cannot ignore outputs or the combat effectiveness of the armed forces. The annual *Statement on the Defence Estimates* publishes statistics on Service personnel, aircraft squadrons, regiments and ships. To illustrate the potential of the programme budgeting approach both expenditure and output have been combined in *Table 3.3*. However, the published data are usually measures of intermediate, rather than final, output. The number of Service personnel is misleading if their training and productivity are ignored. Similarly, the numbers of aircraft squadrons and ships are misleading in the absence of data on the average age of weapons and equipment and their operational availability both currently and in the future. In other words, the published data presented to Parliament and to the electorate fail to provide any reliable

TABLE 3.3. *Defence expenditure and output, 1990–91*

Programme	Cost (£m)	Output
1. Nuclear strategic forces	1,480	4 Polaris submarines to be replaced by 4 Trident submarines
2. Navy combat forces	2,503	176 vessels of all types
eg aircraft and ASW carriers	(99)	(3 ASW carriers)
destroyers and frigates	(669)	(44 vessels)
submarines	(446)	(24 vessels)
3. European theatre ground forces	3,387	96,800 regular troops
eg BAOR	(2,319)	(53,400 regular troops)
Home Forces	(1,005)	(40,500 regular troops)
4. Other army combat forces	206	15,900 regular troops (*eg* Mediterranean, Hong Kong)
5. Air Force general purpose forces	3,668	50 squadrons of aircraft and helicopters
eg Air defence	(753)	(9 aircraft squadrons plus missile squadrons)
Strike-attack-reconnaissance	(691)	(13 aircraft squadrons)
6. Reserve formations	458	340,100 reserves
7. Research and development	2,454	*eg* EFA, EH101, Trigat, Alarm
8. Training	1,407	*eg* Service Colleges, training units
9. Repair facilities in UK	1,093	*eg* Royal Dockyards
10. War and contingency stocks	476	74 depots for stockholdings
11. Other support functions	4,031	*eg* Whitehall organisations; meteorological services
TOTALS	21,223	Total Service manpower: 304,600 of which Army manpower: 151,300 Air Force manpower: 89,400 Navy manpower: 63,900

Source: Cmnd 1022, 1990.

indications of final outputs as reflected in deterrence, protection, security and, ultimately, the chances of survival in different conflict situations.

At this point, reference must be made to a major qualification. It is not being claimed that programme budgeting will make decisions. The scheme simply encourages decision makers to seek answers to a set of logical questions about the purposes or objectives of defence and the costs of achieving these aims: these are questions which any well-run organisation needs to ask and answer. By encouraging decision makers to seek answers to such questions, it is hoped that programme budgeting will improve the quality of decisions and the efficient use of resources. But programme budgeting does not remove the need for individuals to make decisions. Moreover, in assessing programme budgeting it is useful to distinguish two sets of decision makers, namely MoD and Parliament.

The published programme budget which is submitted to Parliament (*eg*

Table 3.2) presents information which reflects the results of decision making, so by-passing the central issue of just how the expenditure decisions were made in the first place. This makes it much more difficult for Parliament to debate the objectives of UK defence policy. Also, Parliament is never given the 10-year forecasts used in the MoD's functional costing system. Nor does it have access to data on the marginal or extra costs of making small changes in the size of forces, such as the costs of an additional squadron of Tornado aircraft or the cost savings due to reducing the size of BAOR by, say, 5 per cent, or the number of Navy frigates by 10 per cent. Such information on the marginal costs of different forces which is so basic for assessing efficiency is not revealed to Parliament (see Chapter 2). However, this information is available to MoD, which also has access to professional judgements on the final output resulting from UK defence expenditure. There is, though, a further problem with the expenditure figures presented in MoD's functional costing budget.

The difficulties of estimating the total systems costs of a new complex, high technology equipment project (*eg* a new missile or combat aircraft) have been widely reported (*HCP 431, 1988*). The problem of assessing the internal efficiency in defence establishments has received much less attention. In the private sector of the economy, the search for profits and competition between rival firms tends to promote internal efficiency or the search for the lowest cost methods of production. Defence differs in that, while it consists of a large number of different units (firms), there are no market prices for the products of Navy, Army and Air Force bases, nor are military commanders (or civil servants) motivated by the desire for profits. In this type of institutional environment, individuals are most unlikely to minimise costs unless there are strong pressures on them to do so: such behaviour leads to what economists call X-inefficiency (Leibenstein, 1966). As a result, it is likely that the expenditure figures used in the Ministry's functional costing system will be based on X-inefficient solutions, (*ie* they will not be least-cost solutions).

Various solutions have been suggested for improving efficiency within military establishments. They include proposals to create internal markets within the Services, experiments with work study teams, the use of outside consultants and inter-unit comparisons, including prizes for the most efficient units. Recently, internal efficiency has been pursued through Executive Responsibility Budgets, the New Management Strategy and an increased reliance on the private sector through privatisation and contracting-out (see Chapter 2). However, many of the proposals for improving internal efficiency are subject to at least four problems. First, station commanders frequently face constraints on the extent to which they can vary the mix of manpower and equipment. For example, a station commander at an RAF air defence base has to deploy Tornado aircraft and this forms a major element in his annual budget. Second, the incentives to increased efficiency are considerably reduced if some of the benefits do not accrue to either individuals or their unit, but instead are transferred to MoD or even to the Treasury. Third, efficiency incentives need to be related to clearly-specified output targets. Fourth, for the armed forces there are likely to be conflicts or trade-offs between commercial efficiency requirements necessitating a life-time's training and specialisation in one task compared with the traditional policy aimed at giving officers a broad-based training with no more than, say, three years in one unit.

Conclusion

Programme budgeting is a valuable technique for requiring policy makers to think more clearly about the aims, costs and performance of the armed forces. Individuals are still required to make choices and decisions, but programme budgeting provides an information framework which, in principle, can help to improve the quality of decisions affecting efficiency in the use of resources. However, programme budgeting is applied by bureaucracies which are likely to be pursuing their own self-interest rather than the welfare of the community.

Economic models have been formulated in which bureaucracies are viewed as budget-maximising agencies. In such models, efforts to raise their budgets will lead departments to exaggerate the demand for their preferred policies and to under-estimate the costs of policies and projects. As a result, budget-maximising bureaucracies are likely to be too large and inefficient (Hartley, 1985). Applying this approach, MoD is viewed as a monopoly supplier of defence services which are offered to the government in return for a budget. Governments lack information on the minimum budget required for any defence output. In this situation, there is a distinct possibility that programme budgeting will be used to support and reinforce the budget-maximising aims of the Ministry. Critics of programme budgeting claim that:

> . . . better analysis and information are not a general solution to the problems of bureaucracy. The superior performance of market institutions is not due to their use of better or more analysis. The primary differences in the performance of different organisations are due . . . to differences in their structure and in the incentives of their managers (Niskanen, 1971, p. 212).

In the private sector of the economy, the profit-motive, the threat of take-over and competition between rival firms results in efficiency.

References

Cmnd 2270, 1964, *Defence Statement*, (HMSO, London).

Cmnd 2592, 1965, *Statement on the Defence Estimates*, (HMSO, London).

Cmnd 675, 1989, *Statement on the Defence Estimates, 1989*, (HMSO, London).

Cmnd 1022, 1990, *Statement on the Defence Estimates, 1990*, (HMSO, London).

Greenwood, D. 1972, *Budgeting for Defence*, (Royal United Services Institute, London).

Hartley, K., 1974, 'Programme budgeting and the economics of defence', *Public Administration*, vol. 52, pp. 55–72.

Hartley, K., 1985, 'Exogenous factors in economic theory: neo-classical economics, *Social Science Information*, vol. 24, 3, September, pp. 457–483.

Hartley, K. and Tisdell, C., 1981, *Micro-Economic Policy*, (Wiley, London).

Hitch, C. J. and McKean, R. N., 1960, *The Economics of Defense in the Nuclear Age*, (Harvard University Press, Cambridge, USA).

HCP 479, 1985, *The Trident Programme*, Defence Committee, House of Commons, (HMSO, London).

HCP 431, 1988, *The Procurement of Major Defence Equipment*, Defence Committee, House of Commons, (HMSO, London).

Kennedy, G., 1983, *Defence Economics*, (Duckworth, London).

Leibenstein, H., 1966, 'Allocative efficiency vs X-efficiency', *American Economic Review*, 56, June, 394.

Niskanen, W. A., 1971, *Bureaucracy & Representative Government*, (Aldine Atherton, Chicago).

Williams, A., 1967, *Output budgeting & the contribution of micro-economics to efficiency in government*, CAS Occasional Paper 4, HM Treasury, (HMSO, London).

CHAPTER 4

The Determinants of Defence Expenditure

Introduction

Until recently, defence was one of the major components of government expenditure which was frequently ignored by economists and simply assumed to be autonomous (Hitch and McKean, 1960). This chapter outlines a taxonomy and elements of a model which explains the facts of post-1945 UK defence expenditure and which is derived from Ministerial pronouncements and successive *Statements on the Defence Estimates*. Broadly, these suggest that UK defence expenditure has been determined by political, strategic and economic factors. These factors will be related to the conventional economic approach and to models of the arms race and alliances and to the possible economic burdens of defence spending.

The stylised facts

What have been the major determinants of UK defence spending? In answering this question, economists start by formulating a model designed to explain the facts. Some of the major stylised facts are summarised in *Table 4.1* which shows levels and shares of defence spending, military manpower and, for comparison, the share of education expenditure.

Table 4.1 shows that over the last 40 years, the general trend in the level of real UK defence spending has been upwards. Variations around this upward trend have resulted from cuts in military spending associated with Defence Reviews in 1957 (Conservatives), 1965–68 and 1975 (Labour). In contrast, the NATO commitment to raise annual real defence spending by 3 per cent between 1979–80 and 1985–86 resulted in a substantial rise in expenditure reaching a peak in the mid-1980s. At the same time, the long-term trend in the share of defence in national output has been downwards from a peak of some 10 per cent in the early 1950s to about 4 per cent in 1990.

In examining long-run trends in military expenditure, it is noticeable

TABLE 4.1. *UK Defence Expenditure*

Year	Defence spending (£ millions 1984–5 prices)	Defence share of GDP (%)	Service personnel (000's)	Education share of GDP (%)
1950	8,558	5.8	690	2.7
1951	11,234	7.0	827	2.8
1952	13,329	10.0	848	2.8
1953	12,571	9.7	841	2.7
1955	12,195	8.0	784	2.8
1960	11,841	6.3	504	3.6
1965	12,779	5.8	423	4.4
1970	12,128	4.8	372	5.1
1975	13,649	4.9	332	6.5
1980	14,474	5.0	323	5.5
1985	17,324	5.2	326	4.9
1990	15,993	3.9	314	3.8

Notes: (i) Years are financial for levels of defence spending; calendar years elsewhere; 1990 figures are estimates.
(ii) Defence and education shares are shares of GDP at market prices.
Sources: Chalmers, 1985; Cmnd 621, 1989.

that following the end of the Korean war, real defence spending consistently exceeded its pre-Korean levels: a fact which provides some tentative support for a type of 'displacement effect'. During periods of crisis, such as a war, public expenditure rises. This crisis-induced upward shift in public expenditure is called the displacement effect. Once the crisis has ended, public expenditure and taxation do not fall to their original levels. However, other factors have not remained constant and unchanged since 1950. Governments and defence commitments have changed, conscription has been abolished and technical progress has raised both the productivity and the cost of weapons.

Many of these changes in, and influences on, defence policy and the budget have been described in the annual *Statements on the Defence Estimates*. From such official statements, it is possible to deduce a policy model which suggests that since 1945, UK defence policy and military spending have been determined by a combination of political, strategic and economic factors. Efforts to explain defence spending cannot ignore potential enemies, the arms race, wars, alliances, new technology and the economy's ability to pay. Obviously, some of the political, strategic and economic determinants of defence spending are inter-related. For example, there are economic models of alliances, while the strategic choice between nuclear and conventional forces can also be determined by political or economic factors. For example, in the early 1980s, Conservative and Labour parties held completely different views on the future of the UK's strategic nuclear deterrent (Trident). At the same time, economic factors are not irrelevant since estimates suggest that nuclear weapons are relatively cheaper than conventional forces. US studies show that for each dollar spent on nuclear weapons, five dollars would be needed for the same level of effectiveness using conventional forces (Gansler, 1989, p. 26). Consideration now needs to be given to these various determinants of defence spending.

Political factors: the role of governments

Perceptions of the threat to the UK's national interests are an obvious starting point in any explanation of military spending. For much of the period since 1945, the Soviet Union, the Warsaw Pact, the cold war and the arms race have dominated the perceived threat and the UK's response has been reflected in its defence commitments, including its membership of the NATO military alliance. In addition, since 1945, there were occasions when the UK was involved in local conflicts associated with its United Nations, Commonwealth and national commitments. These included Malaysia, Korea (1950–53), Africa, the Middle East and, more recently, the Falklands and Northern Ireland. Two of these conflicts particularly – the Korean war and the rearmament programme of the early 1950s and the Falklands conflict (1982) – had a clearly identifiable impact on UK defence spending. In addition, between 1979 and 1986, Britain accepted a NATO commitment to raise its defence spending by 3 per cent annually in real terms (*Table 4.1*). Of course, the perceived threat is characterised by uncertainty. Which nations are likely to be the UK's potential adversaries in the year 2020? Will the threat come from, say, chemical weapons in Third World nations or from international terrorism?

Clearly, the interpretation of the threat, the choice of allies, the range of defence commitments, the acceptance of NATO spending targets and, ultimately, society's willingness to pay for security and protection will be reflected in the political determinants of defence spending. Throughout the period since 1945, the major political parties have taken different views about the desirable levels of defence spending, and about the size, roles and geographical distribution of the armed forces (*eg* nuclear weapons; US bases). Some of these differences were reflected in major Defence Reviews. For example, Labour governments were associated with Defence Reviews which reduced planned military spending (1965–68; 1975), cancelled new UK aircraft and carrier projects (*eg* TSR-2 in 1965; new aircraft carrier in 1966) and withdrew British forces from East of Suez (1968). In contrast, the Conservative government between 1979 and 1986 implemented the NATO commitment to raise annual real defence spending by 3 per cent. Similarly, Labour and Conservative administrations have often differed in their preferences for state expenditure on military and civil goods, such as education and health. On this basis, it might be hypothesised that periods of rising real defence expenditure are associated with Conservative administrations and falling real defence spending with Labour governments. Such an hypothesis might be related to the voting system.

The voting system provides a crude and limited mechanism whereby individuals in society can express their preferences for different defence policies. For example, if they anticipate a period of international tension, they might prefer a government committed to strong defences. Or, expectations of a more peaceful world might lead voters to favour a government committed to arms control, disarmament and greater social welfare spending. Of course, the UK voting system has its limitations as a mechanism for expressing individual preferences. Elections occur infrequently, they take a general form and the majority party captures the entire market. For example, in the 1980s, was a vote for the Conservative Party a reflection of its policies on defence, income taxes, privatisation, the welfare state or the EEC?

Simple generalisations relating political parties and defence expenditure are complicated by other influences. The economy might be subject to external shocks such as the oil crisis of the 1970s or UK involvement in a local conflict. Similarly, while Labour administrations are likely to prefer civil government expenditure, the reductions in defence outlays under Labour between 1964 and 1970 coincided with a series of economic crises, especially in the balance of payments. Defence cuts were part of the deflationary policy aimed at 'correcting' the balance of payments. However, in formulating economic policy, governments can choose between different policy instruments (*eg* exchange rates, import controls, deflation) and between different components of aggregate demand when deflating (*ie* defence cuts are sufficient, but not necessary, for deflation). Also, the data show a long-run decline in the share of defence in national output. In contrast, the share of some other state expenditures, such as education (a substitute?), showed a long-run upward trend at least until the mid-1970s. These share movements occurred under both Conservative and Labour governments. Strategic factors have also affected defence spending.

Strategic factors: the role of technical progress

The strategic determinants of military spending are reflected in the defence posture of the UK and its NATO allies. This posture emphasises deterrence through flexible response and forward defence, using a mix of nuclear and conventional forces. In this context, technical change affects both the equipment and force structures of the UK, its allies and the Warsaw Pact. As a result, UK defence expenditure has been influenced by changes in technology and relative factor prices with their effects on the military production function.

Defence is a classic example of technical change and substitution effects. Since 1945, nuclear weapons have reduced the traditional military advantages of large concentrated land and naval forces; guided weapons, cruise missiles and inter-continental ballistic missiles have replaced some of the roles of fighter, strike and bomber aircraft, artillery, anti-aircraft guns, battleships and cruisers; and jet transport aircraft which can fly out reinforcements quickly have meant that home bases have replaced many overseas garrisons. These technical developments have been reflected in strategy. There have been substitutions between nuclear and conventional forces, home and overseas bases, land-based aircraft and aircraft carriers, Europe and the rest of the world. The result of these substitutions has been changing roles and relative sizes of each of the Services. For example, during the 1950s, the RAF with its V-bombers and its nuclear deterrent, was expanded at the expense of the other Services; but in the 1960s, the Navy acquired this role with its Polaris submarines. Not surprisingly, there was inter-Service competition for a limited defence budget, with each Service acquiring tactical nuclear weapons and offering force structures which reflected government preferences.

Technical progress has increased both the costs and productivity of equipment. The cost of successive generations of equipment has been growing at an annual rate of 5–7 per cent in real terms (Gansler, 1989, p. 61 and Chapter 2, *Table 2.2*). Although more costly, today's military equipment is also more capable. A tank in 1961 cost 2.5 times its 1940 predecessor but its hitting power was 20 times greater. Similarly, one effective raid during the Second World War involved 560 Lancasters and almost 4,000 aircrew to deliver some 1,800 tons of bombs; the same raid in 1990 using more accurate modern weapons would need only 12 Tornados and 24 aircrew to deliver about 48 tons of explosives for the same results (*Cmnd 101-I, 1987*, p. 47). In the end, technical progress can render obsolescent a whole class of equipment and the associated forces. For example, tanks replaced cavalry, with implications for equipment orders and training programmes. Similarly, a successful SDI system might shift the balance between defensive and offensive forces to a greater emphasis on defence. Of course, the military-industrial complex is likely to favour new technologies which do not disturb their traditional roles and threaten established interest groups. Air Marshals will not want combat aircraft replaced by missiles and aircraft firms will not want aircraft to be regarded as obsolete. There is every incentive to resist new technologies which change the comparative advantage of each Service and to argue for balanced forces.

Technical change has also affected the demand for military manpower, particularly the role of conscription versus an all-volunteer force. In the UK, conscription ended in 1960 with an all-volunteer force achieved by 1963, leading to major changes in the relative costs of military manpower.

It was the increasing cost, complexity and skilled labour requirements of modern weapons which partly contributed to the end of conscription. Conscription was proving a relatively costly method of training manpower. It was argued that the more efficient solution required highly-skilled, experienced and consequently long-service regulars able to maintain modern weapons and use them effectively, so providing the Services with a worthwhile return on their substantial and rising training investments (*Cmnd 9691, 1956*). In this context, it takes the RAF three years to train a fast jet pilot at a cost of £3 million and a minimum of six years productive service is required to justify such training costs (*HCP 495, 1988,* p. 56).

The abolition of conscription increased the relative costs of military manpower. Economic theory predicts that there will be incentives to replace more expensive inputs with cheaper inputs. On this basis the introduction of an all-volunteer force will raise the relative costs of military manpower encouraging substitutions between equipment (weapons) and labour, as well as between Service personnel and cheaper labour inputs such as civilians. The effects of abolishing conscription on manpower and equipment are shown in *Figure 4.1*.

The economics of training in terms of its costs and benefits has some interesting implications for the forces, particularly where the Services provide skill training which has general marketability in the civil economy. Examples of transferable skills provided by the military include transport pilots, air traffic controllers, electronics engineers, computer

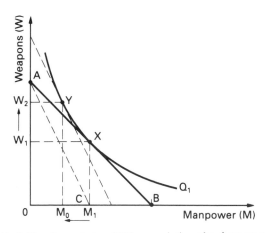

FIG. 4.1. Abolishing Conscription. With conscription, the cheapest combination of manpower and weapons to provide defence output Q_1, is shown at X. An all-volunteer force raises manpower costs, leading the iso-cost line to pivot inwards to AC (for a given defence budget). To maintain defence output at Q_1 requires a move to position Y, with a substitution of weapons for manpower and increased defence spending.

specialists, electrical engineers, vehicle mechanics and drivers. The forces might offer relatively attractive pay during training to attract recruits. Later, the Services might try to recoup their training investments by paying wages lower than the productivity of the newly-skilled workers. However, where training is transferable, such a policy is likely to attract recruits who when qualified will wish to leave for alternative more highly-paid civil occupations where firms have not borne the costs of training. In other words, such a policy will attract trainees but lead to a high loss rate of newly-skilled labour (Becker, 1964). Of course, the Services attempt to establish ownership or property rights in individuals through a contract for a specific period with compensation required for breaking the contract. However, even a legally-enforceable contract of a specific duration does not guarantee the productivity of the contract labour. Also, on completion of the contract, it might be beneficial to the armed forces to pay its skilled labour an attractive retainer to persuade personnel to sign-on for a further period rather than incur the costs of recruiting and training new and inexperienced staff. Indeed, with the likely recruitment problems in the 1990s, the armed forces might seriously consider the option of increasing the retirement age of their personnel. Not all tasks in the armed forces require young fit males capable of fighting in the front-line: some tasks could be performed by 65-year-olds, as occurs in private industry (*eg* coal-mining).

There is a further implication of technical progress which cannot be ignored. Technical progress amongst both allies and rivals makes it more difficult to predict accurately future developments in weapons, so increasing the emphasis on flexible general purpose forces rather than mission-specific weapons and force structures. For example, a new combat aircraft which will be costly might take 10 years to develop and it has to have an operational capability for up to, say, 20 years, giving a total time horizon of 30 years. Within this time-scale, the aircraft has to be sufficiently flexible to meet any new unforeseen technical changes which might occur, say, 15 years ahead. As a result of both costs and time scales, a new combat aircraft might have a multi-role capability rather than be dedicated to one mission. Uncertainty about the future has similar implications for force structures. For example, the UK defence budget describes the Navy and Air Force as general purpose combat forces, while the Polaris nuclear deterrent forces specialise in a specific mission (Chapter 3).

In defence, the emphasis on equipment performance and hence on technical progress (technological superiority) requires R & D expenditures on new weapons which, in real terms, are inevitably costlier to develop and produce. Admittedly, each new generation of equipment is better than its predecessor but often the increments of performance are achieved at massive cost. It is really worthwhile spending an extra £1 billion to achieve only a marginal improvement in performance? With a limited UK defence budget and rising unit costs for each new generation of equipment, only smaller quantities can be bought, so increasing the relative costs of the UK buying weapons from its domestic industry. In the USA, increasing unit costs have seen a substantial reduction in the purchases of fighter planes from over 2,000 units a year in the 1950s to some 300 in the 1980s, and forecasts of only one fighter plane a year in 2054 (Starship Enterprise: Gansler, 1989, p. 171). Similarly, in the UK, the RAF bought some 1,100 Hunter fighters in the 1950s, 281 Lightnings in the 1960s and 180 Tornado fighters in the 1980s. Increasingly, pressures of rising costs against a limited defence budget will require the forces to choose between quality and quantity. For instance, the RAF might have to choose between, say, 10 squadrons of advanced fighters and a mix of, say, 16 squadrons of high and medium performance fighters. There is an alternative choice, namely, international collaboration in the development and production of equipment. Since the 1960s, UK procurement policy has increasingly recognised that the costlier weapons will have to be developed in collaboration with other nations, mainly European, or purchased directly from the USA (see Chapter 9). Cost pressures resulting from technical progress means that defence spending cannot ignore economic factors.

Economic factors

Economic factors in the form of the performance and level of prosperity of the economy determine the resources which are available to pay for defence (*ie* the UK's ability to pay). Critics claim that UK defence spending is a burden in that it 'crowds out' valuable civil investment with adverse effects on the economy's international competitiveness. On this view, strong defences might actually weaken the economy which they are supposed to be protecting (Chalmers, 1985; Smith and Smith, 1983). Not everyone accepts the view that military spending is a burden. Admittedly, it has opportunity costs in the form of sacrifices of civil goods and services; but then defence is not unique and all economic activity involves sacrifices. In return, defence offer benefits in the form of security and protection (*cf* insurance policies and car seat belts). To its supporters, defence also offers potential technology benefits through promoting leading-edge technologies, advancing the frontiers of knowledge and providing spin-off for the civil economy. Furthermore, it provides jobs and contributes to the balance of payments through exports and import saving. Finally, for developing nations, defence spending might promote growth through its training of military manpower, the provision of an infrastructure (*eg* roads, communications) and the creation of a stable environment which promotes entrepreneurship and investment (Benoit, 1973; Kennedy, 1983).

Since 1945, the major UK political parties have recognised the economic determinants (burdens) of defence expenditure, including its effects on civil R & D, on investment, on the balance of payments and on the welfare state. For example, in 1956, Conservative government policy aimed to ensure that the cost of defence 'whether in terms of manpower, materials or money does not overload the economy' (*Cmnd 9691, 1956,* p. 6). Almost 20 years later, when Britain's economic performance had lagged behind that of its major European allies, the Labour government's 1975 Defence Review decided that 'resources must be released for investment and improving the balance of payments', and that 'the burden of defence expenditure should be brought more into line with that of our major European allies' (*Cmnd 5976, 1975,* p. 2). And in 1986, the Conservative government expressed a desire to release defence resources for civil work when it declared that 'necessary investment in defence R & D may crowd out valuable investment in the civil sector' (*Cmnd 101-I, 1987,* p. 48). Does the evidence support such beliefs?

Some commentators believe that Britain's high levels of military spending have had adverse affects on investment, technical progress, inflation, employment, growth and exports, resulting in a poor economic performance. Japan is often quoted as an example of an economy with a high growth rate and low defence spending. Elsewhere, a number of statistical studies based on a sample of industrial countries have shown that a change in the share of defence spending in national output tends to be associated with an equal, but opposite, change in the share of investment (Chalmers, 1985; Chapter 6; Smith and Smith, 1983, Chapter 4). However, other research work has produced different results. Some studies suggest that the empirical results are sensitive to a cross-section or time-series approach, to the nations selected for the sample, to the equation specification and to the time-period chosen for the analysis (Hartley and Hooper, 1990). A review of the arguments and the evidence for the USA found that the economic impact of military spending is only marginally different from that of other forms of Federal expenditure and concluded that 'the dispute over the economics of military spending is political, not economic' (Adams and Gold, 1987, p. 268).

A satisfactory evaluation of the opposing views and empirical results about the burdens or otherwise of defence spending needs to start from the underlying economic model. A model is needed which shows the causal factors relating defence spending to the major UK macro-economic variables, such as investment, growth and international competitiveness. All too often correlation is interpreted as causation and defence spending is regarded as the sole cause of Britain's poor economic performance. Nor is much attention given to the operation of labour markets and the economic impact of alternative public and private expenditures. For example, if defence R & D is cut what will happen to the resources released? Do they remain in the UK or emigrate; and if in the UK, do they work on civil R & D or move into non-technical jobs, or do they join the unemployed? Similarly, if defence spending is cut, what will be the likely economic impact of a rise in private expenditure or in state spending on, say, education, health, housing and the police? Some of these questions are related to the fundamental issue of the optimum size of the UK defence budget.

The point where defence expenditure becomes too high or an excessive burden depends on its 'price' in terms of the sacrifice of the other aims of government policy (*eg* growth, equity). Observation can quantify the maximum acceptable levels. In times of crises, such as the Second World War, society is willing to pay a high price for protection. In contrast, by 1957, following a period when defence expenditure had accounted for some 10 per cent of national output, the Conservative government announced that this share was too high. It was absorbing 7 per cent of the working population in the Services or supporting activities and 12.5 per cent of the output of the metal-using industries on which export trade depended. It also affected the general level of taxation and absorbed an 'undue' proportion of qualified scientists and engineers, as well as large forces overseas, with direct balance of payments effects (*Cmnd 124, 1957*, p. 2). By 1975, a Labour government was announcing a further planned reduction in the defence share to a target of 4.5 per cent to be reached by 1984: policy makers believed that defence was 'too costly' in terms of the sacrifices of industrial investment, exports, housing and medical services (*Cmnd 5976, 1975*). Interestingly, by the mid-1970s, emphasis was being placed on equity or comparability with our NATO allies in determining UK defence expenditure.

Questions always arise as to whether the UK spends too much or too little on defence. The optimum size of the defence budget is a controversial issue and various criteria have been suggested as guidelines for the UK. A popular rule-of-thumb suggests that UK defence spending should be proportionately similar to that of its major European allies, especially France and West Germany. In 1988, defence spending as a share of GDP was 4.3 per cent for the UK compared with 3.8 per cent for France and 3 per cent for Germany. A reduction to the German share would require the UK to cut annual defence spending by about £5.7 billion (1988 prices). There are, however, some obvious criticisms of basing the UK's defence budget on an arbitrary share figure related to that of its major European allies. The rankings of the three nations change according to whether defence burdens are measured by shares of national output, levels or *per capita* spending (*Table 4.2*). Moreover, France and Germany use relatively 'cheap' conscripts, so that money outlays understate the true opportunity costs of their military budgets (*eg* by about 0.5 per cent in 1988). Also, an approach which determines the UK's optimal defence budget on the basis of French or German military spending does not allow UK citizens to reveal their perceptions of the threat, their valuations of defence and whether they believe it is worth spending more or less on the defence of the UK. In principle, at any one time, the optimal defence budget will be the one which is preferred and chosen by society's representatives. In practice, the outcome is affected by the public goods nature of defence, free-riding problems and the limitations of the voting system as a means of expressing community preferences. Nonetheless, references to allies introduces alliances as a further determinant of UK defence spending.

Economic theory of alliances

NATO is an international voluntary club which specialises in providing a public good in the form of collective defence. Nations will join the club and remain members, paying the club fee, so long as membership is worthwhile. On this basis, NATO survives so long as it offers more protection and lower defence costs as compared with complete independence. Membership costs comprise a financial contribution to the funding of NATO's common infrastructure (*eg* airfields, communications, radar warning systems), a commitment of national forces to the alliance, acceptance of NATO defence strategy, including a commitment to the modernisation of forces, and the provision of bases for foreign troops (*eg* US forces in Europe and UK forces in Germany). For example, during 1980–84, the UK contributed some 10–12 per cent of NATO infrastructure costs compared with 23–27 per cent by both Germany and the USA. Moreover, in the late 1970s, NATO members agreed to increase real defence spending by 3 per cent annually, with the UK accepting this commitment for the period 1979–80 to 1985–86. The performance of NATO nations against the 3 per cent target varied widely, reinforcing controversies about burden-sharing (*Table 4.2*). In addition, the UK provides base facilities for US forces, especially air units. Finally, most of the UK's forces are committed to NATO, including substantial air and ground units located on the Central Front in Germany (Chapter 2, *Table 2.1*). In return for these expenditures and commitments, the UK and other NATO members benefit from collective defence, including the protection offered by US nuclear strategic forces. Under the North Atlantic Treaty, members agree to treat an armed attack on any one of them as an attack against all of them (Lunn, 1983).

Economic models of military alliances offer three policy-relevant predictions (Olson and Zeckhauser, 1966). First, the more defence a nation's allies provide, the less it tends to spend on defence (*Figure 4.2*).

TABLE 4.2. *NATO Defence Spending*

Country	Defence as share of GDP (%) 1960	Average 1973–77	1979	1988	Defence expenditure 1988 Total (US$M)	Per Capita (US$)	Average real growth in defence spending (%) 1979–85
Belgium	3.9	3.0	3.3	2.9	4,215	427	1.6
Denmark	3.1	2.3	2.3	2.2	2,336	455	0.3
France	7.4	3.8	3.9	3.8	35,909	646	1.4
Germany	4.6	3.5	3.3	3.0	35,369	578	1.3
Greece	5.4	6.3	6.3	6.6	3,465	347	2.2
Italy	3.7	2.5	2.4	2.4	19,148	334	2.5
Luxembourg	1.2	0.9	1.0	1.3	81	219	4.4
Netherlands	4.5	3.1	3.2	3.0	6,744	460	1.8
Norway	3.7	3.1	3.1	3.3	2,918	697	3.5
Portugal	4.5	4.9	3.5	3.1	1,261	123	1.0
Spain	–	–	–	2.2	7,319	188	–
Turkey	5.7	5.4	4.3	4.2	2,538	49	1.1
UK	7.3	4.9	4.7	4.3	34,913	614	2.5
Canada	4.9	1.9	1.8	2.1	9,906	384	4.0
USA	9.9	5.7	5.1	6.1	288,935	1,185	6.0

Sources: NATO (1984; 1976); Cmnd 675-I, 1989.

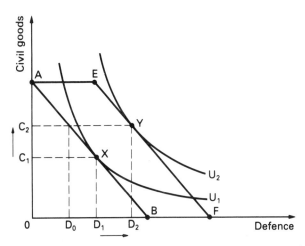

FIG. 4.2. Benefits of an Alliance. Initially, the nation operates on AB, maximising its level of satisfaction, utility or welfare (U_1) at position X consuming C_1 and D_1 of civil and defence goods, respectively. Membership of a military alliance provides extra security of AE and the country's new preferred position is Y where it is better off (U_2) with more civil and defence goods (C_2, D_2). However, the provision of alliance defence AE, allows the nation to reduce its own defence effort from D_1 to D_0 (free-riding) so that it consumes more civil goods at C_2 instead of C_1. Complete free-riding occurs at E.

Second, because the larger members of an alliance place a higher valuation on security and protection, they will usually devote larger shares of their national income to defence than smaller nations (see *Table 4.2*). Third, alliance defence output will always be sub-optimal; this is because independent states make defence choices on the basis of their individual national interests and not on the basis of the collective group interests. Substituting a political union with shared goals for an alliance would create incentives for the group to act optimally.

For the 1950s and into the mid-1960s, evidence supported free-riding in NATO, with the larger, wealthy allies (USA, UK, France, Germany) bearing a disproportionate share of the burden of common defence. This was the era of mutual assured destruction (MAD), with deterrence as an example of a pure public good. NATO's strategic nuclear umbrella could be extended to protect additional allies without diminishing the protection available to the nuclear allies so that free-riding was an obvious outcome. However, by the mid-1970s, NATO had adopted a policy of flexible response which placed a greater reliance on conventional forces with implications for the opportunities for free-riding (*Table 4.2*). This change has been recognised in new developments in economic models of alliances. A joint product model has been formulated in which an alliance produces more than one output, namely, deterrence, damage-limiting protection and private or country-specific benefits, each differing in their public goods content. In particular, a distinction is made between deterrent and protective or conventional forces. Unlike nuclear deterrence, conventional forces are not pure public goods since they are subject to 'thinning' as more territory has to be defended. In fact, conventional forces have characteristics of private (national) defence output with excludable benefits. The joint product model of alliances predicts that the amount of free-riding will be inversely related to the proportion of excludable defence outputs produced by the alliance arsenal. Alliances relying on protective and conventional forces are less likely to be characterised by free-riding and are more likely to share burdens in relation to the benefits received. In contrast, alliances specialising in deterrence will be characterised by substantial free-riding (Sandler, 1987).

For the purposes of developing a model, it is sufficient to recognise membership of NATO as a determinant of UK defence spending. However, the alliance effect is ambiguous, being negative if free-riding dominates and positive if the UK follows the pact leader. Elements of both influences appear to have been present since 1948. During the 1950s, the UK received 'gifts in kind' and US offshore purchases of UK equipment for its forces as well as the protection of the American nuclear umbrella. At the same time, the UK has usually devoted a larger share of its national output to defence than most of its NATO allies (*Table 4.2*). Estimates of the relationship between US and UK defence expenditure suggest that a one dollar rise in American military spending results in a 1.5 cents cut in British defence budgets, compared with reductions of 9.2 cents for West Germany and 7.5 cents for France. These same estimates also show that if the US allies raise their total defence spending by one dollar, the USA responds by reducing its military expenditure by 87 cents (1980 prices: Sandler and Murdoch, 1986).

Further problems arise in estimating the effects of the NATO alliance on UK defence expenditure. As already mentioned, potential enemies in the form of the threat cannot be neglected since it is often claimed that British military spending is related to that of the USSR and the Warsaw Pact. For the analyst, complications arise because it is difficult to isolate the separate effects of rivals and allies. Here, the point is that American and Soviet defence expenditures are likely to be positively associated with US spending interdependent with NATO and with the UK. The impact of the threat on defence spending has generated a major literature on the arms race. Indeed, arms race models which can be viewed as incorporating economic, political and strategic factors appear to offer a more satisfactory theoretical explanation of defence spending.

Arms race models

Arms race models start from the proposition that a nation's military spending is explained by an arms race, with nations arming in response to the threat which they believe, or perceive, to come from their potential adversaries or rival states. Recent and current examples of arms races include the US and Soviet superpowers, the Middle East, India and Pakistan, South America states, North and South Korea. The threat is reflected in either the level of military spending between potential adversaries or in their stock of armaments, or stocks of specific types of weapons (*eg* nuclear missiles). Research in this field is often based on the Richardson model of arms races which can be variously interpreted as a model of an arms race, as a model of war or as a model of dynamic interaction between nation states. Richardson related arms races to wars by considering the case where higher and higher levels of weapons in both nations eventually led to armed conflict.

The Richardson model of a two-nation arms race (nations X and Y) can be summarised:

$$\Delta X = a_0 - a_1 X + a_2 Y \qquad (1)$$

$$\Delta Y = b_0 - b_1 Y + b_2 X \qquad (2)$$

where ΔX, ΔY = the change in defence expenditure over time of the two nations, X and Y.

a_0, b_0 = grievance terms held by each nation. For example, this term might reflect the desire for revenge for past

The Economics of Defence Policy

wrongs and past defeats (*eg* Germany after the First World War).

a_1, b_1 = fatigue coefficients reflecting the costs or economic burdens of defence expenditure. The negative signs reflect the belief that over time as more resources are allocated to defence, a nation will increasingly find it 'too costly' to continue incurring such sacrifices of civil consumption (economics as the ultimate arms controller?).

a_2, b_2 = defence or reaction coefficients showing that each nation responds to the defence expenditure of its rival.

Clearly, the various grievance, fatigue and reaction coefficients can be interpreted as representing the political, economic and strategic determinants of defence spending. However, such an arms race model has been criticised extensively. Critics claim that it offers too simplistic an explanation of highly complex international relationships between nation states; that it is too static, failing to allow for the various coefficients changing over time; and that it neglects the behaviour of political parties, bureaucracies and interest groups in each state. Indeed, the Richardson model has been criticised for a 'black box' approach with its mechanistic responses to defence spending, without any consideration of the behaviour of agents in the system. Ultimately, though, the acceptability of a theory depends on its explanatory power: does it explain the facts? Empirical studies show that arms race models offer only limited explanations of defence spending: most of the empirical tests of the Richardson model have proved disappointing (Schmidt, 1987).

Arms race models are also useful in highlighting problems in making international comparisons of defence spending. Assessment of the threat requires reliable estimates of military expenditure and weapons stocks for the potential adversaries. For the superpowers, problems arise because of the secrecy surrounding USSR annual military spending. As a result, independent estimates have been made by the USA and by some Western agencies. With such estimates there are problems in obtaining reliable data on the size of Soviet forces, on military R & D and in converting expenditures in roubles (largely a domestic currency) into US dollars. Predictably, a budget-maximising Defence Ministry has every incentive to exaggerate the threat by adopting the worst-case scenario and over-estimating Soviet defence spending by applying US prices to USSR forces. This approach can be reinforced by calculations of the annual output of equipment, the introduction of new weapons and the imbalance of forces between NATO and the Warsaw Pact. An example is given in *Table 4.3* which shows that the Warsaw Pact has a large numerical superiority in conventional land and air forces in Europe.

TABLE 4.3. *NATO and Warsaw Pact Forces*

	NATO	Warsaw Pact	Ratio NATO to Warsaw Pact
Total armed forces (millions)	3.1	4.1	1:1.3
Total ground forces (millions)	2.21	3.09	1:1.4
Main battle tanks	16,424	51,500	1:3.1
Artillery	14,458	43,400	1:3
Anti-tank weapons	16,800	19,700	1:1.2
Attack helicopters	700	1,350	1:1.9
Combat aircraft	3,977	8,250	1:2.1
Nuclear-powered submarines	75	90	1:1.2
Conventional submarines	120	110	1:0.9
Surface ships	385	220	1:0.6

Note: Forces are based on the Atlantic to the Urals.
Source: Cmnd 675-I, 1989, Chapter 6.

The estimates of apparent superiority shown in *Table 4.3* need to be assessed critically. Are the comparisons on an identical basis? Quantity needs to be adjusted for quality differences. For example, there are differences in quality (productivity) between conscript and all-volunteer forces and equipment differs in its age and operational effectiveness. Similarly, some Soviet forces might be required for internal policing, others might be needed for non-European defence commitments and some might be earmarked for assisting the civil economy (*eg* harvesting). Also, it has to be recognised that there are possibilities of substitution between forces and that nations differ in their resource endowments so that they will use relatively more of those factors of production where they have a cost advantage. For example, if in nation X labour is relatively cheap, then X will use manpower-intensive forces. If nation Y estimates the value of X's forces at prices ruling in Y's economy where labour is scarce and hence costly, it will appear that X is spending highly on defence. Consider the following simplified example for the USA and USSR, shown in *Table 4.4* (Sivard, 1986, p. 44).

In the USA, capital is relatively cheap and manpower is relatively expensive, so that the US has a force of one man and four aircraft. In

TABLE 4.4. *Estimating Defence Spending*

	USA	USSR	Assumptions
I. Using USA Prices ($ costings)	1 man + 4 aircraft $100 $100	4 men + 1 aircraft $400 $25	aircraft = $25 men = $100
	$200 ─────────────▶ $425		
II. Using USSR Prices (Roubles costings)	1 man + 4 aircraft 10Rs 240Rs	4 men + 1 aircraft 40Rs 60Rs	aircraft = 60Rs men = 10Rs
	250Rs ◀───────── 100Rs		

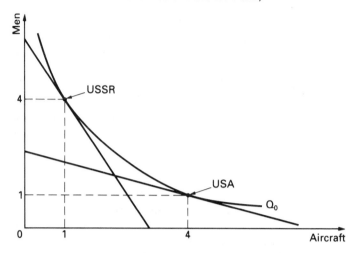

Fig. 4.3. Estimating Defence Spending. This example is based on *Table 4.4*. The curve or iso-quant Q_0 shows the various combinations of manpower and aircraft required to produce the defence output Q_0. The iso-cost lines reflect the relative prices of manpower and aircraft in the USSR and USA. The point of tangency between an iso-cost line and the iso-quant shows each nation's efficient position. The USA and USSR have adopted different force structures to produce the same defence output.

contrast, in the USSR manpower is relatively cheap and capital is relatively expensive so that the Soviet Union has a force of four men and one aircraft (these numbers of men and aircraft should be regarded as units, say, millions of men and thousands of aircraft). If the USSR forces are costed at US prices, it will appear that, in dollar terms, the Soviet Union is spending more on defence than America. However, if the USSR costs US forces using Russian prices, then in roubles costings the result is reversed, with American defence spending apparently exceeding that of the USSR. (*Table 4.4*). And yet, as shown in *Figure 4.3*, both nations could be identical in terms of defence output!

For our purposes, it is sufficient to stress the need for care when making international comparisons of defence spending. Nations have different comparative advantages and hence different relative prices for manpower and equipment, with prices affecting the quantities bought. Similarly, budget-conscious bureaucracies have every incentive to select the costing figures which show their nation to be at a disadvantage in the arms race. Indeed, the possibility arises that the methods used to estimate a potential adversary's defence spending might be a stimulus to the arms race and a barrier to arms control and disarmament.

Conclusion

Economic theory often analyses defence spending as a standard optimisation problem. The government chooses a preferred combination of military and civil goods which will give maximum welfare to the community subject to the constraints of the economy's available resources and the efficiency with which they are utilised (Chapter 2). Such an approach which embraces both demand and supply elements can be related to the policy model with its stress on political, strategic and economic determinants of defence spending.

The demand for military expenditure will be influenced by society's preferences, and its willingness to pay for defence will be affected by its perception of the threat and by the political composition of the government. Threats might take the form of actual involvement in conflicts or an arms race with potential enemies. Demand will be further influenced by household income levels, by the relative prices of military and civil goods, by spill-ins in the form of military expenditure by a nation's allies and by strategic doctrine (*eg* MAD v flexible response). Supply side factors comprise technical progress, economic growth and the economy's productive capacity. There are possible supply-side inter-relationships between defence spending, investment and growth. Also, on the supply side, technical progress and the efficiency with which defence equipment and military manpower markets operate will further affect the military production function (Hartley and Sandler, 1990, Chapter 1; Smith, 1990).

Empirical work on the determinants of military expenditure has been based on two contrasting approaches. One approach starts from a clearly-specified theoretical structure based on maximising the welfare of society subject to budget constraints. An alternative approach is based on a set of economic, political and strategic factors, the aim being to select the variables which give the best statistical fit. This *ad hoc* statistical approach has been criticised as measurement without theory. Interestingly, though, there are circumstances where the alternative approaches produce similar estimating equations (Smith, 1990). For our purposes, it is sufficient to suggest a model of UK military expenditure of the following general form:

$$M = f(SUM, AM, Y, W, P, D)$$

In this equation M is UK military expenditure in constant prices; SUM and AM are the real military spending of the USSR and the rest of NATO, respectively; Y is income as measured by real GDP; W is a dummy variable for UK involvement in wars such as Korea; P is a dummy variable for the politicial composition of the UK government; and D represents other dummy variables for factors such as Defence Reviews, the NATO 3 per cent commitment, the ending of conscription and changes in strategy (*eg*

NATO's adoption of flexible response). The threat is represented by Soviet defence spending. Alliance effects and the possibilities of free-riding are captured by the defence spending of all other NATO nations. A relative price variable for military and civil goods is excluded, usually because data are unavailable on the prices of military goods. Alternatively, it is argued that prices can be omitted from the equation provided that military and civil goods have been subject to the same rate of inflation (Sandler and Murdoch, 1986).

Empirical tests of the military expenditure model have used various forms, often focusing on shares of military expenditure in national output rather than levels, estimating linear or log-linear equations and using US defence spending to measure alliance effects. In some cases, dummy variables are added in *ad hoc* fashion and difficulties can arise in separately identifying demand and supply-side influences. Nevertheless, various results suggest statistically significant positive effects on UK military expenditure from the Korean war, the NATO 3 per cent commitment, and between levels of defence spending and income. Interestingly, the threat variable often appears not to have any significant effect, possibly reflecting measurement problems. American defence expenditure usually has a statistically significant effect on UK military spending, but contradictory evidence is available showing either positive or free-riding effects (Sandler and Murdoch, 1986; Smith, 1990). Further developments have suggested that models of military expenditure need to incorporate a specific role for the behaviour of agents in the political market, namely, voters, parties, bureaucracies and other interest groups which will seek to influence defence policy.

References

Adams, G. and Gold, D. A., 1987, 'The economics of military spending', in Schmidt, C. and Blackaby, F. (eds.) *Peace, Defence and Economic Analysis*, (Macmillan, London).
Becker, G., 1964, *Human Capital*, (NBER, New York).
Benoit, E., 1973, *Defense and Economic Growth in Developing Countries*, (Lexington Books, Mass.).
Chalmers, M., 1985, *Paying for Defence*, (Pluto, London).
Cmnd 9691, 1956, *Statement on the Defence Estimates*, (HMSO, London).
Cmnd 124, 1957, *Defence: Outline of Future Policy*, (HMSO, London).
Cmnd 5976, 1975, *The Defence Review*, (HMSO, London).
Cmnd 101, 1987, *Statement on the Defence Estimates*, (HMSO, London).
Cmnd 621, 1989, *The Government's Expenditure Plans 1989–90 to 1991–92*, (HMSO, London).
Cmnd 675-I, 1989, *Statement on the Defence Estimates 1989*, (HMSO, London).
Gansler, J., 1989, *Affording Defense*, (MIT Press, Cambridge, USA).
Hartley, K. and Hooper, N., 1990, 'The economic implications of US bases in Europe: costs and benefits to the UK', in Sharp, J. (ed.), *Europe After An American Withdrawal*, (SIPRI, Sweden).
Hitch, C. and McKean, R., 1960, *The Economics of Defense in the Nuclear Age*, (Harvard University Press, Cambridge, USA).
Hartley, K. and Sandler, T. (eds.), 1990, Introduction, *Economics of Defence Spending: An International Survey*, (Routledge, London).

HCP 495, 1988, *Statement on the Defence Estimates*, Defence Committee, (HMSO, London, June).

Kennedy, G. 1983, *Defence Economics*, (Duckworth, London).

Lunn, S., 1983, *Burden-sharing in NATO*, Chatham House Paper 18, (Routledge, London).

NATO, 1984, 1976, *Facts and Figures*, (NATO, Brussels).

Olson, M. and Zeckhauser, R., 1966, 'An economic theory of alliances', *Review of Economics and Statistics*, Vol. 48, August, pp. 266–279.

Sandler, T., 1987, NATO burden-sharing: rules or reality? in Schmidt, C. and Blackaby, F. (eds.), *Peace, Defence and Economic Analysis*, (Macmillan, London).

Sandler, T. and Murdoch, J., 1986, 'Defense burdens and prospects for the northern European allies', in Denoon, D. B., (ed.), *Constraints on Strategy*, (Pergamon, London).

Schmidt, C., 1987, 'Semantic variations on Richardson's armaments dynamics', in Schmidt, C. (ed.) *The Economics of Military Expenditures*, (Macmillan, London).

Sivard, R. L., 1986, *World Military and Social Expenditures*, (World Priorities, Washington, D.C.).

Smith, D. and Smith, R. 1983, *The Economics of Militarism*, (Pluto, London).

Smith, R., 1990, 'Defense Spending in the UK', in Hartley, K. and Sandler, T. (eds.), *The Economics of Defence Spending: An International Survey*, (Routledge, London).

CHAPTER 5

Economics, Politics and Public Choice

Introduction

Economists often propose policies such as greater consumer choice, more competition and free trade, all of which are designed to make people better off. Yet actual policy changes often involve substantial departures from the economists' ideal world. Industries are protected by regulations and tariffs, privatisation transfers monopolies from the public to the private sector, and defence equipment is often bought from higher-cost domestic firms. Why do governments frequently fail to exploit obvious opportunities for increasing society's welfare and making people better off? One possible explanation arises in the political market place where policy choices are made and implemented and which economists have traditionally regarded as a 'black box' so neglecting an important area of decision making.

Government decisions are likely to be the result of actions by various agents and interest groups in the political market, each acting in their own self-interest and seeking to influence policy in their favour. This chapter outlines the possible role of these agents and interest groups in formulating defence policy. The approach will be exploratory, showing how the public choice paradigm might be applied to the arguments used by different interest groups to influence the level and composition of UK defence expenditure, and the allocation of procurement contracts (*eg* Nimrod AEW v Boeing AWACS). What, for example, is the likely response (and success) of the armed forces and the domestic weapons industry to government proposals to reduce the level of defence spending and to change the 'mix' from nuclear to conventional forces? Does public choice analysis provide a framework for analysing the military-industrial complex? Debates about the desirability of UK membership of NATO, US bases in Britain, Trident, the purchase of foreign weapons and policy toward the defence industrial base cannot ignore the behaviour and influence of agents in the political market on the formulation of defence policy. Some of these agents represent barriers to proposed reductions in the level of military spending and to changes in its composition. Inevitably, questions arise as to who might gain and who might lose from a policy change and what arrangements, if any, will be made to compensate the potential losers? Clearly, those likely to lose will oppose any policy change, particularly if there are no arrangements for adequate compensation. Ultimately, society might regard a change as desirable only if the potential gainers are able to over-compensate the potential losers. Even so, the arrangements for transferring income between gainers and losers will be influenced by the agents in the political market.

The political market and public choices

The economist's approach to military spending stresses the 'public good' nature of defence and regards governments as maximising the welfare of society. With this approach, elected politicians and bureaucrats were assumed to pursue the 'public interest' and to implement the 'will of the people'. There are, however, problems in using the voting system to interpret society's preferences. Moreover, it cannot be assumed that in public office, politicians and bureaucrats will behave in a saintly fashion, completely ignoring the opportunities for self-interest which they pursue in their private lives. Public choice analysis applies the ideas of self-interest and exchange to the political process. This approach shows that choices about defence are made in political markets (Buchanan, 1986, Chapter 3).

Political markets resemble other markets in that they contain buyers and sellers pursuing their self-interest by undertaking mutually beneficial exchange within the rules determined by the constitution. The agents within the political market comprise voters, parties, bureaucracies and interest groups each of which will have preferences for alternative defence policies.

Voters act like consumers and are assumed to seek the maximum benefit from the policies offered by rival politicians and political parties. However, voters have only limited information and knowledge about such specialised topics as the threat, NATO, nuclear weapons, the defence contribution of British troops in Germany and the merits of buying British or foreign defence equipment. Where the collection of such information is costly, there are opportunities for producers and other interest groups with specialist knowledge to influence voters and political parties. For example, UK defence contractors can use their specialist knowledge to show that buying British is in the 'national interest', provides invaluable independence and makes a socially desirable contribution to jobs, high technology and the balance of payments. The opportunities for such groups to influence policy are reinforced by the limitations of the voting system as a means of accurately registering society's preferences.

Ideally, the individual tastes and preferences of large numbers of voters are recorded through the ballot box at elections. In the UK, however, votes are cast for a general package of policies (an election manifesto) in which defence policy is only one amongst a diverse set comprising economic, social, environmental, international and other policies between which voters cannot register the intensity of their preferences. Nor are voters provided with the necessary information to evaluate defence policy. The Official Secrets Act and 'national security interests' mean that voters are given little information about the contribution of different defence budgets to protection and the probability of survival in various conflict situations. Furthermore, voters cannot bind politicians to a clearly-specified set of policies, so that elected representatives have discretion in implementing their election promises. An elected party with, say, a commitment to abolish British nuclear weapons and withdraw from NATO can always delay the implementation of such commitments by claiming the principle of 'unripe time', the need for a thorough in-depth study and review of the issues, and the necessity of negotiating with their allies! All of which suggests that the limitations of the voting system as a means of accurately registering society's views on defence budgets and policies allows opportunities for governments, bureaucracies and other groups to interpret the 'national interest' and to influence UK defence policy. Ultimately, though, governments cannot ignore the need to be re-elected.

Economic models of politics assume that political parties are vote-maximisers (Downs, 1957). Like firms, parties offer policies in exchange for votes. Politicians are assumed to be self-interested, seeking the income, power and prestige which comes from holding office, rather than seeking office to carry out preconceived policies. Politicians have the choice of joining one of the UK's small number of established parties or forming a new party. For example, opponents of nuclear weapons and supporters of reduced defence spending have to decide whether to influence party policy by attempting to change the policies of an established political party (cf a take-over) or by creating a new party. Both solutions involve costs. Moreover, however attractive a specific defence policy might be to its supporters, it will never be implemented if the party fails to attract votes. The winning party at an election captures the entire market and forms the government. Its policies are implemented by bureaucracies.

Economic models of bureaucracies start by assuming that bureaucrats are budget-maximisers (Niskanen, 1971). In the UK defence market, the Ministry of Defence and the armed forces occupy a central role, with other Departments such as the Home Office, Employment, Trade and

Industry, and the Treasury concerned with civil defence and the jobs, technology and balance of payments implications of defence policy. A government can be viewed as buying protection from the Ministry of Defence which acts as a sole supplier of information and defence, with protection supplied by the Services specialising in air, land and sea forces, and each seeking to protect its traditional property rights. To maximise its budget, the Ministry of Defence can exaggerate the threat, under-estimate costs and formulate programmes which are attractive to vote-maximising governments (*see Figure 5.1*). Nevertheless, bureaucratic behaviour might be constrained by the activities of pressure groups and by the investigations of the National Audit Office and the Parliamentary Defence and Public Accounts Committees.

In formulating and implementing policies, governments and bureaucracies are subject to the activities of pressure groups. Such groups of producers and consumers will pursue their own self-interest by trying to influence policy in their favour through lobbying, advertising campaigns, sponsorship of politicians, consultancy reports, mass demonstrations and civil disobedience. The various interest groups will represent the potential gainers and losers from different defence policies. Producer groups of defence contractors will support a buy-British policy, they will demand protection from foreign competition and will seek favourable rules for regulating profits on defence work. Trade unions and

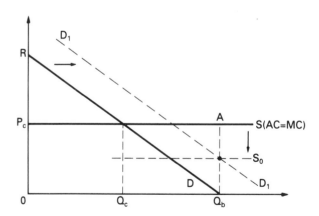

FIG. 5.1. A Budget-maximising Defence Ministry. Society's demand for defence is represented by D with S representing cost conditions where average and marginal costs are equal (AC = MC). The competitive output is OQ_c at price P_c. A budget-maximising bureaucracy supplies OQ_b for a budget of OP_cAQ_b: it covers its total costs and obtains a budget equal to the entire area under the demand curve (ORQ_b). In this example OQ_b is twice OQ_c (and $OP_c = P_cR$) and the output of the monopoly Ministry is 'too large'. However, the output OQ_b can be justified if demand is over-estimated (D_1) and/or costs are under-estimated (S_0).

professional associations with members in UK defence industries will also support domestic arms producers so as to protect the jobs and favourable income prospects of their members. An example occurred during the 1986 debate on the future of the Nimrod AEW project, when it was claimed that cancellation would involve writing-off £900 million of tax-payer's money, potential losses of 50,000 man years of work and exports estimated in excess of £2 billion over 15–20 years, as well as adverse effects on the future competitiveness of a number of areas of UK industry (GEC, 1986). Where defence projects are likely to be cancelled, it is not unknown for contractors to threaten major job losses and the closure of plants, especially in high unemployment areas and marginal con-stituencies. In 1965 a number of British military aircraft were cancelled (*eg* TSR-2). At the time, initial estimates suggested that cancellation would immediately result in 25,000 redundancies and the closing of five major plants. In fact, one year later, redundancies due to the cancellations totalled 7,000–8,000 and only one plant was closed (Hartley and Cor-coran, 1975).

Other pressure groups in the UK defence market represent specific consumer interests such as those in favour of disarmament (*eg* the Society of Friends); those opposed to nuclear weapons (*eg* CND); and those in favour of strong defences (*eg* Peace through NATO). Furthermore, a number of groups specialise in the independent evaluation of UK defence policy, so providing voters and politicians with an alternative source of information outside the state bureaucracy. Examples include university research centres, the International Institute for Strategic Studies and Jane's publications.

In addition to the agents in the UK political market, the international community has an interest in influencing UK defence policy. Examples include NATO, the United Nations and the Western European Union; foreign governments such as the USA and West Germany which will oppose reductions in UK defence spending; and foreign arms firms seek-ing British defence contracts.

A framework for identifying the various linkages within the political market, showing the different groups which will seek to influence UK defence policy, is given in *Table 5.1*. For simplicity, the focus is on the government but a more accurate representation would show a series of formal and informal linkages between the different agents. Producer and consumer pressure groups and foreign governments (*eg* USSR) will try to influence the opposition parties and voters (*eg* through advertising). Information is also required about the agents shown in the boxes and their behaviour: what happens within each organisation, how and why? The government will be based on a Cabinet with the Defence Ministers selected by the Prime Minister, each with different experience, qualifica-tions and motivation (*eg* Ministers with or without Service experience;

TABLE 5.1. *Mapping the defence political market*

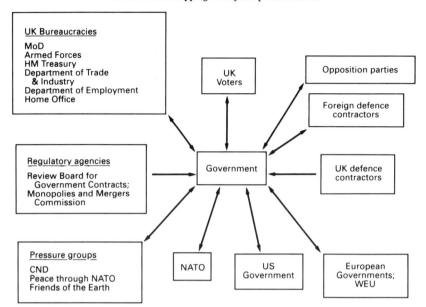

thrusters and sleepers). Information is also needed on the declared interests of elected politicians: are they directors or major shareholders in
defence companies or are they consultants to defence contractors raising
questions and participating in Parliamentary debates on defence policy?
Those who represent successfully a group's interest might be rewarded
through, say, the honours system, a directorship, or a lucrative consultancy. Further fears have been expressed that civil servants may be
influenced in their decisions by the prospect of employment in industry
or that there might be an 'undesirable cosiness between Crown servants
and the industries with which they deal' (*HCP, 392, 1988, p.v.*).

Predictions of public choice analysis

Public choice analysis embracing economic models of politics, bureaucracies, interest groups and regulation suggest five predictions relevant to
explaining UK defence policy. First, in a two party system, both parties
agree on any issues strongly favoured by a majority of voters. The result is
consensus politics, with party policies being vague, similar to those of
other parties and less directly linked to an ideology than in a multi-party
system. Throughout much of the period since 1945, both major political
parties in the UK offered similar policies on defence. For instance, the
economics of politics would explain the abolition of conscription as a

potential vote-winner, with both parties having an inducement to adopt similar policies favouring volunteer forces.

Second, although political parties attempt to differentiate their policies, movements towards the political extremes of *laissez faire* or collectivism are likely to be constrained by the potential losses of moderate voters. In the case of equipment procurement policy, this suggests that parties are unlikely to favour complete free trade or total protectionism. Political parties also tend to maintain consistent ideological positions over time, unless they suffer drastic defeats at which point they change their ideology to resemble that of the party which defeated them (Downs, 1957, p. 300). An example of such a major change occurred in 1989 with the Labour Party's policy towards nuclear weapons (unilateralism and multilateralism) and the adoption of a more 'credible' defence policy.

Third, the policies of democratic governments tend to favour producers more than consumers. Examples include supporting the defence industrial base and regulations which benefit producers rather than consumers (*eg* by guaranteeing the profitability of defence contracts). Producer groups dominate since they can afford the costly investments in specialised information needed to influence government and they have the most to gain from influencing policy in their favour. Also, the voters who are best informed on any policy issue are those whose incomes are directly affected by the policy change (*ie* producer groups), whereas such citizens are not as well-informed on policies that affect them as consumers. Professional associations and trade unions, for example, will oppose policies to import defence equipment pointing to the effects on technology, the balance of payments and jobs, especially in communities dependent on defence contracts. They will be less informed on the possible costs to the taxpayer of buying British, particularly since they benefit by spreading such costs amongst large numbers of taxpayers in the UK.

Fourth, there are political business cycles. Once elected, the governing party can use its policies to influence voter preferences, so increasing its chances of re-election. Popularity might be increased by an expansionary aggregate demand policy prior to an election (*eg* lower income taxes; higher public spending on roads, hospitals and schools). As part of such a policy, a military establishment which is 'vital' to a local community might be saved from closure: and orders for new equipment might be allocated to firms in marginal constituencies or in high unemployment areas. In 1985, MoD split an order for two frigates between Cammell Laird (Merseyside) and Swan Hunter (Tyneside) because of 'wider and relevant factors involved', at a cost to the defence budget of an extra £7 million (*HCP 37-I, 1985*, p. xxxv).

Fifth, bureaucracies aiming to maximise their budgets are likely to be too large and inefficient (*Figure 5.1*). To protect and raise their budgets, government departments which have a monopoly of specialist knowledge will use information to their advantage. Civil servants are experts: they have an infinite capacity for ingenuity and they can adjust and play any games. Fans of the television series *Yes, Prime Minister* will recognise the genre. Civil servants are specialists with technical information on the possibilities for varying output and for factor substitution. These possibilities, which could result in undesirable outcomes for vote-sensitive governments, might be too costly for any individual minister to police and monitor. In the circumstances, bureaucrats have an incentive to hoard valuable information and to erect a set of myths around their preferred policies.

For example, as a buyer of defence services, the government often lacks alternative sources of specialist knowledge to monitor and evaluate military plans, as expressed in operational requirements for new weapons and new force structures. It also lacks independent advice on the reliability of the cost estimates of new equipment, and on whether a new weapon is worthwhile in terms of its marginal contribution to national defence. Bureaucracies also have every inducement to under-estimate the costs of their preferred policies and new weapons systems. They can support 'optimistic' cost estimates and neglect life-cycle costs (impossible to estimate). Once started, defence projects are difficult to stop. They attract interest groups of scientists, contractors, unions and military personnel, each with relative income gains from the continuation of the work. Indeed, it has been claimed that one of the benefits of international collaborative projects involving government (*eg* Jaguar, Tornado) is that they are much more difficult to cancel!

Some applications

Public choice analysis offers some interesting insights and contributions to understanding the political process and policy formulation. Questions arise as to whether there is any evidence supporting the predictions of public choice analysis. Consider the case of cuts in military spending associated with Defence Reviews (see Chapter 4). A public choice approach identifies some of the agents most likely to oppose policies designed to reduce defence spending and to change its composition. It shows the type of arguments used by bureaucracies to protect budgets and how the armed forces and domestic defence contractors are likely to respond to cuts and programme cancellations. Such an evaluation also exposes to critical scrutiny some of the myths of defence and procurement policy. Ideally, though, public choice models need to be compared with alternative explanations of defence spending and policy formulation, aiming to discover which theory best explains the facts.

The UK Defence Reviews between 1957 and 1981 show at least three features which are consistent with public choice analysis. First, by aggregating modest annual savings in planned expenditure over a ten-year period, the armed forces and the Ministry of Defence can present an impressive picture of cuts, and a vote-sensitive government can show its supporters and the electorate that after a 'searching and thorough reappraisal of defence policy', it is taking 'firm, decisive action' to reduce military spending. Often long-term contractual commitments to military manpower and equipment projects make it difficult and costly to achieve substantial instant cuts. And, by offering sizeable future cuts, the armed forces and the Ministry of Defence can always hope for a change in government, or a change in the financial position, or a transfer of the problem to their successors!

Second, the armed forces are major interest groups which will seek to protect their traditional property rights and their prestige and glamorous high technology weapons projects which often give satisfaction to their users rather than to society seeking protection. Faced with cuts, the armed forces are likely to respond by cutting civilian manpower and economising on training, exercises, support functions and stocks, rather than sacrificing their major new equipment programmes. Admirals like aircraft carriers, generals prefer tanks and air marshals yearn for air superiority fighters. As a result, preferences for inputs are likely to differ between the Services. The capital intensive air force will be willing to sacrifice, say, personnel and its transport fleet rather than its latest combat aircraft. The labour-intensive army will aim to protect manpower as its most valuable asset, especially its élite combat forces, and it will sacrifice trucks for tanks.

Third, as a budget-conscious agency, the Ministry of Defence will oppose efforts to cut military spending. It will emphasise the dire consequences of cuts, pointing to the continuing threat from the Warsaw Pact, the emerging threat from international terrorism and the Third World, and the employment and social consequences of cancelling weapons projects and closing military bases in remote rural areas lacking alternative job opportunities. References will also be made to the loss of national independence, prestige and high technology, resulting in the UK becoming a nation of 'metal bashers'. Other Departments such as Employment, Trade and Industry and the Foreign Office are likely to support the arguments about jobs, technology and the international prestige of a world military power. Furthermore, some of these arguments might influence a vote-maximising government concerned about the electoral harm of cuts, particularly their impact on marginal constituencies. In turn, to protect itself and the armed forces against substantial cuts, the Ministry of Defence will promise future efficiency improvements in the form of competition, contracting-out, civilianisation, rationalisation and international collaboration (see Chapter 2). This suggests that Defence Reviews might have a 'shock effect' leading to efficiency improvements.

Some empirical tests of the shock effect hypothesis have concentrated on the manpower impact of Defence Reviews. It has been hypothesised that Defence Reviews will have a shock effect resulting in a once-and-for-all release of military and civilian manpower employed by the armed forces, the Ministry of Defence and the UK defence industries. With the possible exception of the Air Force, the evidence provided no support for a sudden shake-out of labour following a Defence Review (Hartley, 1987; Hartley and Lynk, 1983(a), and 1983(b); Lynk and Hartley, 1985).

Public choice analysis can also be applied to the debate about privatisation. Here, popular belief claims that a change of ownership from public to private improves performance. It is argued that in the private sector, the prospect of profits and the threat of take-over provides managers with incentives to remove organisational slack and to be efficient. In contrast, public sector managers lack efficiency incentives. Instead, in the public sector, policies are arranged to maximise votes, with managers subject to the detailed controls of Whitehall affecting their pricing, investment and location decisions. Also, departmental budgets are expanded so that bureaucrats benefit from better jobs, tenure, on-the-job leisure and higher salaries, and public sector trade unions have opportunities to pursue high wage claims, restrictive practices and over-manning. However, public sector organisations are not homogeneous and they include government departments, trading funds and public corporations. Trading funds are required to finance their operations commercially so that they might be expected to be more efficient than a government department. Defence provides an example in the form of the Royal Ordnance Factories (ROF) which in 1974 changed their organisational status from a government department to a trading fund (Dunsire, et al., 1988).

Empirical studies have examined the relationship between organisational status and performance in a number of UK defence industries. A public choice approach suggests that the performance of an organisation improves as its status is changed from a government department to a trading fund, and from a public corporation to a public joint stock company (privatisation). Three defence organisations were studied, namely, ROF, Rolls-Royce and British Aerospace. The study focused on the ROF change to a trading fund in 1974; on the 1971 movement of Rolls-Royce from the private to the public sector; and on the 1977 nationalisation of British Aerospace and its subsequent privatisation in 1981. At the time when the research project started in 1986, the privatisation of both ROF (1987) and Rolls-Royce (1987) were excluded because of the lack of sufficient data following the status change. Enterprise performance was measured by labour and total factor productivity and the results are shown in *Table 5.2*. It is recognised that empirical work in this area is fraught with difficulties. There are problems of the counter-factual, changes in enterprise objectives, the impact of other factors and the

TABLE 5.2. *Organisational status and productivity*

		Productivity (%)			
		Labour productivity		Total factor productivity	
Organisation	Status change	Before	After	Before	After
Rolls-Royce	1971 – from private to public ownership	−4.9	13.6	−0.4	4.7
ROF	1974 – government department to trading fund	11.8	1.6	1.3	4.6
British Aerospace	1977 – from private to public ownership	6.3	2.4	1.8	1.3
	1981 – from public to private ownership	2.4	7.8	1.3	3.3

Notes: (i) Productivity figures are for average annual growth.
(ii) Before and after refer to four years before and four years after the status change.

availability of a variety of performance indicators (Dunsire, *et al.*, 1988; Parker and Hartley, 1990).

The results for Rolls-Royce were contrary to expectations. The 1971 take-over by the state was associated with a substantial improvement in both labour and total factor productivity growth. This might be explained by the 'shock effect' of financial collapse, inducing management to remove organisational slack and over-manning, rather than to any beneficial effects of public ownership. The results for ROF were mixed. Contrary to the hypothesis, labour productivity growth fell following the change to a trading fund. However, once allowance was made for changes in all inputs, total factor productivity growth increased, thereby supporting the hypothesis. In the case of British Aerospace, nationalisation was associated with the predicted fall in productivity growth and privatisation with an expected improvement (*Table 5.2*).

The focus on defence industries raises a further aspect of public choice models, namely, the role of producer groups. By modelling the armed forces, the Ministry of Defence and defence contractors, public choice provides a basis for analysing the behaviour of the military-industrial complex. However, while producer groups have a major role in public choice analysis, few efforts have been made to operationalise the concept. Critics of military spending claim that defence contractors are a powerful and influential pressure group. On this basis, an analysis of the major UK defence firms and their market environment indicates that powerful producer groups have some of the following features:

(i) *Firm size and market structure.* Firms are large in both absolute and relative size. In 1989, the four largest defence contractors receiving over £250 million per annum from MoD were British

Aerospace (Aircraft, Dynamics, ROF), the General Electric Company (including Plessey), Rolls-Royce and Vickers Shipbuilding and Engineering. British Aerospace and GEC employed over 130,000 and over 150,000 people, respectively. The top four defence contractors were domestic monopolies or oligopolies with British industry receiving some 90 per cent of the MoD equipment budget.

(ii) *Dependence on defence business.* Some UK firms and industries are dependent on MoD contracts, so that their fortunes are closely linked with government decisions. In this context, MoD is a dominant customer for the UK ordnance, aerospace, shipbuilding and electronics industries, accounting for 60 per cent, 50 per cent, 40 per cent and 20 per cent of their output, respectively, in 1987.

(iii) *Location.* Vote-sensitive governments seeking re-election are likely to be influenced by firms located in marginal constituencies or in high unemployment areas (*eg* shipbuilding).

(iv) *Types of contracts.* Firms awarded non-competitive contracts (*eg* cost-plus or incentive contracts) will have close and continuous links with the Ministry of Defence procurement agents. Here it is possible that in the past the type of contract and the arrangements for regulating defence profits were the result of successful lobbying by producer groups, with both contracts and profit rules favouring producers. The introduction of a competitive procurement policy in 1983 changed the traditional 'cosy relationship' between MoD and the UK defence industries.

(v) *Lobbying activities.* This is another 'black box' which economists have neglected but it is a potentially important mechanism in the set of linkages in the political market. Defence contractors lobby as a group through specialist trade associations, such as those representing aerospace, electronics, engineering, naval equipment and defence manufacturers. Also, business appointments by staff leaving MoD and the armed forces provide defence contractors with valuable contacts and expertise in their search for more business.

Conclusion

Public choice analysis identifies the agents in the political market which will seek to influence defence policy. It shows how groups which will lose from cuts in military spending and from disarmament are likely to behave and the arguments which will be used to oppose such policies. The approach seems to offer a realistic description of the world. But descriptive reality and intuitive appeal are not sufficient for the acceptance of a theory. Does the approach offer any clear, testable predictions and does empirical testing support those predictions? More specifically, if there are alternative explanations of defence policy, it is necessary to determine whether the public choice approach is superior and out-performs existing models which ignore the political market.

To Marxists, military spending finances a permanent arms economy which allows demand to be expanded to absorb excess production, so sustaining profits. As a result, Marxists claim that military spending is necessary for the maintenance of capitalism as a viable system, both nationally and internationally (Smith and Smith, 1983). In contrast, standard economic theory analyses defence spending as an optimisation problem in which defence output is maximised subject to the available resources (Chapters 2 and 4). Alternatively, public choice analysis explains defence spending in terms of the maximising behaviour of governments, bureaucracies and interest groups. Analysts have the task of identifying alternative predictions from these different explanations or adopting an eclectic approach using elements from each model. Certainly elements of a public choice approach can be used to analyse procurement policy.

References

Buchanan, J., 1986, *Liberty, Market and the State*, (Harvester, London).

Downs, A., 1957, *An Economic Theory of Democracy*, (Harper and Row, New York).

Dunsire, A., Hartley, K., Parker, D. and Dimitriou, B., 1988, 'Organisational status and performance: a conceptual framework for testing public choice theories', *Public Administration*, **66**, 4, 363–388.

GEC, 1986, *Nimrod Airborne Early Warning: The Choice for Britain and the Future*, GEC Avionics, Herts, November.

Hartley, K., 1987, 'Reducing defence expenditure: a public choice analysis and a case study of the UK', in Schmidt, C. and Blackaby, F. (eds.), *Peace, Defence and Economic Analyses*, (Macmillan, London).

Hartley, K. and Corcoran, W., 1975, 'Short-run employment functions and defence contracts in the UK aircraft industry', *Applied Economics*, **7**, pp. 223–233.

Hartley, K. and Lynk, E., 1983a, 'Labour demand and allocation in the UK engineering industry: disaggregation, structural change and defence reviews', *Scottish Journal of Political Economy*, **30**, 1, February, 42–53.

Hartley, K. and Lynk, E., 1983b, 'Budget cuts and public sector employment: the case of defence', *Applied Economics*, **15**, 4, August, 532–540.

HCP 37-I, 1985, *Defence Commitments and Resources*, Defence Committee, House of Commons, (HMSO, London).

HCP 392, 1988, *Business Appointments*, Defence Committee, House of Commons, March (HMSO, London).

Lynk, E. and Hartley, K., 1985, 'Input demands and elasticities in UK defence industries', *International Journal of Industrial Organization*, **3**, 71–83.

Niskanen, W., 1971, *Bureaucracy and Representative Government*, (Aldine-Atherton, Chicago).

Parker, D. and Hartley, K., 1990, 'Organisational status and performance: the effects on employment', *Applied Economics*, forthcoming.

Smith, D. and Smith, R., 1983, *The Economics of Militarism*, (Pluto, London).

CHAPTER 6

Equipment Procurement Policy

Introduction: the policy issues

The Ministry of Defence is British industry's largest single customer. Through its Procurement Executive, it buys a variety of equipment ranging from such simple items as batteries and tyres to complex products such as main battle tanks, combat aircraft and nuclear-powered submarines (*eg* Trident). For 1990–91, equipment expenditure exceeded £8 billion representing some 39 per cent of the defence budget. Within the total spending on equipment, 36 per cent was for air systems, 34 per cent for sea equipment and 20 per cent for land systems, with corresponding implications for the defence industries supplying such equipment. In this context, 75 per cent of the equipment budget is spent in Britain, a further 15 per cent benefits UK industry through its participation in collaborative projects, and 10 per cent is spent overseas. In addition to its equipment budget, MoD also spent some £4.8 billion in 1990–91 on works, buildings, land and miscellaneous stores and services, giving a total annual procurement budget exceeding £12 Billion.

Inevitably, such large-scale spending by a single ministry creates controversy. There are pressures to buy British rather than foreign equipment (*eg* Nimrod AEW v. Boeing AWACS; UK v. foreign tanks) and to support jobs by buying from firms in areas of high unemployment (*eg* ship-building). The view also has been expressed that MoD purchasing should be used as an instrument of industrial policy. Popular criticism focuses on project management by the Ministry and on the performance of defence contractors. Critics point to inadequate monitoring by the Procurement Executive, leading to cost escalation, delays, unsatisfactory equipment performance and cancellations. Similarly, defence contractors are often accused of waste, high costs and excessive profits achieved in a business which is believed to be not very competitive (HCP 431, 1988). Since 1983, MoD has become more conscious of the need to obtain better value for money in equipment procurement. As a result, it has become a more demanding customer, with competition as the central element in its more commercial approach. Increasingly, firm or fixed-price contracts determined by competition are replacing cost-plus contracts.

This chapter provides an overview of the general issues raised by UK equipment procurement policy dealing with the choice set and the role of uncertainty. A more detailed analysis of alternative procurement policies involving standardisation, buying British and collaborative projects is presented in subsequent chapters.

A taxonomy: the choice set

Equipment procurement policy involves the Ministry of Defence and ultimately the Government in a related set of choices about what to buy, when, who to buy from and how. Decisions are needed on the following:

(i) *What to buy?* Equipment purchases require the selection of a project reflected in decisions about the performance requirements of a new weapon. For example, for a new combat aircraft, decisions are needed about its speed, range, weapons capability, and landing and take-off requirements, all of which will be related to the need to meet the future threat. The task of defining the initial operational requirement for new equipment starts with concept formulation, leading to a Staff Target.

(ii) *When to buy?* All projects have a life-cycle starting with research and development, through to production, followed by operational use in the armed forces. In the UK, equipment procurement involving development work usually passes through several stages involving concept formulation, feasibility study, project definition, full development, production, in-service operation and finally disposal (*eg* problems of disposing of nuclear-powered submarines). Choices have to be made as to when competition should end and selection both of a project and a contractor should occur. For example, in the early 1950s, the UK purchased a number of advanced combat aircraft off-the-drawing-board after only a design competition, with the successful bidder receiving a contract for both development and production work. Under MoD's new competition policy, rivalry is promoted at the feasibility, project definition and development and production stages in a project's life-cycle. Unlike the previous policy, design contractors cannot assume that they are guaranteed the first production order: they might be subject to competition for both the initial production work and for any subsequent production orders (including orders for spares during in-service operations). In this way, the Ministry can introduce and extend contestability into markets which were previously non-competitive (MoD 1987). However, if development and production work are undertaken by different contractors, problems arise in establishing and protecting property rights in new ideas, and transferring technology is not costless.

(iii) *Who to buy from?* A contractor has to be selected, using either competition based on price or non-price criteria (*eg* technical quality), or direct negotiation with a preferred supplier. In addition, in any competition, the Ministry has to determine the extent of the market. Should the competition be restricted to UK firms or should foreign firms be invited to bid? In this context in 1988, the Ministry declared publicly '. . . a greater readiness to consider non-UK sources where they are likely to offer greater value for money . . .' (*Cmnd 288-II, 1988*, p. 7). A further dimension of contractor selection involves a choice between the extremes of buying British or purchasing directly from abroad, or selecting an intermediate solution in the form of a joint project with another nation or producing foreign equipment under licence in the UK.

(iv) *How to buy?* A contract has to be selected ranging between the extremes of firm or fixed price and cost-plus contracts. Traditionally, cost-plus contracts were used for advanced technology work characterised by considerable uncertainty. However, under the new competition policy, MoD prefers firm price contracts where the contractor receives the contract price, no more and no less. For equipment programmes extending over several years, where there are uncertainties about inflation and exchange rate movements, fixed-price contracts are used where the price paid to the contractor reflects variations in an agreed price index (related to scheduled rather than actual dates if there is delay). Where possible, the Ministry seeks fixed price contracts for development work, so placing contractors at risk and giving them an incentive to control costs. Alternatively, where the development work cannot be defined clearly, a target price incentive contract is preferred, with the Ministry and the contractor sharing any cost savings or cost over-runs up to a maximum price beyond which the contractor assumes total liability. Finally, on non-competitive contracts a Review Board acts as a policing agency reviewing profit rates on defence work to ensure comparability with the return earned by UK industry. Also the Review Board adjudicates on individual contracts referred to it where actual profits or losses exceed agreed levels (*HCP 505, 1985*, p. 18).

Choice under uncertainty

Uncertainty dominates and complicates equipment procurement choices. What are the most appropriate market, institutional-organisational and contractual arrangements for coping with uncertainty? At one extreme, uncertainty is absent and the competitive model is applicable. The Ministry as a buyer knows what it wants; the products exist and are being bought and sold in something resembling a competitive market (*eg* vehicles). In such circumstances, the Ministry simply acts as a competitive buyer, specifies its requirements and invites competitive tenders. The lowest bid is selected and a firm price contract is awarded.

At the other extreme, the armed forces are not always certain about the type of product they wish to buy, particularly with high technology equipment (*eg* missiles, electronics, combat aircraft). Moreover, within the UK domestic market, there are often relatively few potential suppliers and there are no other buyers (*eg* aerospace, tanks). In this case, uncertainty occurs in a bilateral monopoly bargaining situation where both buyer and seller have opportunities for exercising bargaining power and discretionary behaviour in a non-competitive or imperfect market. The Ministry might have to choose a contractor and select a contract for a project which does not exist and which is likely to involve a substantial jump in technology or the 'state of the art'. For example, a modern combat aircraft might take 10 years to develop and will remain in service for a further 20 years, so that the Ministry has to anticipate a variety of technical developments as well as economic and political changes among both allies and likely enemies over a 30-year time horizon. Such advanced technology equipment is often associated with cost escalation and over-runs, time slippages, and major modifications, leading to allegations of contractor inefficiency, especially where the work is undertaken on a cost-based contract with no incentive provisions. Sometimes projects are cancelled, giving rise to further allegations of 'waste and incompetence' by both the Ministry and the contractor (*eg* Nimrod AEW).

Critics of MoDs project management can always be wise with the benefit of hindsight! There are, though, real difficulties in formulating policy rules for improving *ex ante* decision making under uncertainty. Usually, there are alternative methods of coping with uncertainty and economists are interested in identifying the costs and benefits of the various options. Decisions have to be made about the technical feasibility of an operational requirement for new equipment. Sometimes a new project builds on existing research knowledge and requires only an incremental step in new technology, so minimising risks and uncertainty. In contrast, if the armed forces seek to maintain technical superiority, they may demand major state-of-the-art advances in all spheres of a new equipment project (*eg* airframe, engine and avionics in a combat aircraft), so maximising risk and uncertainty! Either way, research and development work is required to obtain the information and knowledge needed to satisfy an operational requirement.

Acquiring information and knowledge is not without cost. It can be purchased at different points in a project's life-cycle, ranging from the initial design and development stage to the construction of a prototype and, ultimately, a production decision. Advanced technology equipment projects are the classic example of public sector choice under uncertainty. They can be bought 'off the drawing board', with only paper or design competition and the successful bidder receiving a contract for development and production work. This is believed to reduce the costs of competition but, at the same time, there are higher risks of technical failure as well as the removal of competitive pressure on the successful contractor. Alternatively, competition could be continued beyond the design stage through, say, the Ministry purchase of relatively cheap competing prototypes. In this way, the Ministry might postpone its final choice until it has more information on the actual performance of competing designs. An example was the US 'fly-before-you-buy' policy which was used to choose between competing prototype combat aircraft. In the competition for a lightweight fighter, Northrop and General Dynamics were selected as competing contractors, with General Dynamics awarded the contract for its F-16 aircraft. However, competitive prototyping is frequently rejected because it is believed to lead to delays and to involve higher development costs through competitive 'duplication'. But the critics implicitly compare an actual competitive procurement policy with an ideal (but never achieved) project, ordered off-the-drawing-board, which never encounters any technical problems, cost escalation, or delays! The general point remains. In buying advanced technology equipment, the Ministry has to choose the point in the life-cycle at which competition should cease and selection occur. And economists can make a contribution by showing that alternative policies involve different costs and benefits and, where possible, offering evidence on orders of magnitude (*eg* on the costs of competing prototypes and the magnitude of any delays (Hartley, 1983, p. 118). Of course, the Ministry's procurement choices can always be justified as offering good value for money!

The Ministry's buying power and value for money

As a monopsonist or a single buyer, MoD's procurement choices can have a major impact on UK industry. The Ministry can determine technical progress directly through its operational requirements for new equipment and, indirectly, through any technical 'spin-offs' which result from defence R & D. Its purchasing decisions can also determine the size of an industry, its structure, entry and exit, location and ownership; and, through regulation, it can directly affect prices, efficiency and profitability. In other words, the Ministry can determine the size, structure, conduct and performance of defence industries. For example, higher spending on defence equipment such as occurred during the Korean war, the Falklands conflict and the NATO 3 per cent era (1979–86) resulted in more orders for UK defence contractors, with implications for employment, profitability and inducements for new entry. Similarly, between 1958 and 1960, the government used its contractual powers to restructure the UK aircraft industry into a smaller number of larger firms (Hartley, 1965). Future prospects for the 1990s suggest a reduced threat, leading to lower UK and NATO defence spending, which is likely to be associated with further re-structuring in both the UK and European defence markets as well as exits from defence industries.

The Ministry's buying power raises questions about the aims of its procurement policy. The possibility arises that procurement contracts can be used to pursue other policy objectives which would then need to be included when assessing the purchased 'product'. Certainly this has happened in the past where equipment contracts have been used to pursue wider economic and social policy objectives concerned with jobs, technology and the balance of payments. Once such wider policy aims become part of the procurement choice and the purchased 'product', they make it difficult, if not impossible, to evaluate efficiency in procurement. Choices and decisions are always subjective and in the absence of a clearly-specified objective function, how is it possible to evaluate the efficiency of government procurement?

Under its new competition policy, MoD stresses that procurement choices are based on the need to obtain the 'best overall value for money' where this does not necessarily mean buying the cheapest equipment (MoD 1983; MoD 1987, p. 10). In addition to price, consideration is given to factors such as quality and reliability which will affect life-cycle costs, to delivery and export prospects, and to the need to avoid forcing prices so low that companies no longer find it worth bidding for MoD business. With this new approach, MoD now claims that its defence equipment choices are based on commercial criteria and not on wider economic and social objectives. Nonetheless, procurement officers have some discretion in interpreting 'best value for money'. Moreover, a commitment to a commercial approach by MoD fails to recognise the difference in employment contracts and in the system of incentives and penalties between public and private organisations. In the public sector, civil servants usually lack efficiency incentives and, in the last resort, the costs of poor performance are borne by the taxpayer. In contrast, poor performance by private firms is subject to the ultimate sanction of bankruptcy. Finally, even where MoD chooses equipment on commercial criteria, its decisions can always be over-ruled by the government, which will be concerned with wider policy objectives and, ultimately, its prospects of re-election. In this context, UK firms likely to benefit will lobby the government for new defence contracts, pointing to the strategic, economic, exchequer and social benefits of buying British. This raises questions about the choice of contractor and whether contracts favour producers rather than taxpayers.

The choice of contractor and the extent of the market

Selecting a contractor requires the Ministry of Defence to choose between open and selective competition, and direct negotiation with a preferred supplier. Applying the competitive model to tendering requires open competition with large numbers of bidders, the absence of entry restrictions and a clear product specification so that seller rivalry and buyer choice can be restricted to the price domain. In this model, the Ministry simply selects the lowest bidder and awards a fixed-price contract. Discretionary behaviour, including favouritism and corruption, is less likely. Departures from the model arise where non-price criteria, such as technical characteristics, quality, delivery and 'wider policy aims' enter the Ministry's choice set.

The Ministry of Defence and other public authorities often prefer selective to open competition. Since open competition is likely to result in lower prices, some explanation is required for the general opposition to this method. One possibility is that public buyers regard open competition as 'too costly': it involves substantial transaction costs for the buyer and it is believed to raise the costs of tendering for industry. Consider the transaction costs involved in organising an open competition and acting as a competitive buyer. The public agency will have to search for the 'best buy', which will be the lowest price, assuming there is a clearly-defined product. Search is not costless and it will require the public buyer to specify a product, or at least outline a broad requirement, so that contractors can submit meaningful bids. Lower prices might be obtained by approaching more firms, but searching will cease when its expected savings through lower prices equals the costs of obtaining the extra information (*ie* optimal search). The details of the competition have to be advertised, printed and distributed to potential bidders and enquiries have to be handled. When submitted, each bid has to be carefully assessed and checked, a selection procedure is required, and the bidders have to be informed of the outcome. Selective competition is believed to reduce some of these search and transaction costs since only a limited number of firms from an approved list and of known reliability are invited to tender. Also, contracts are often imperfect and cannot be completely specified, so the use of 'reputable' firms might minimise the Ministry's transaction costs. The successful contractor is the lowest bidder from the group of invited firms. Not only does this appear to reduce buyer search costs but it is believed to avoid the 'wasteful duplication' of estimating and tendering resources. Usually, only a few firms on the approved list will be invited to bid for a contract, the aim being to ensure that in the long-run all firms on the list have an opportunity to tender.

The supporters of selective competition claim that it is the simplest way of demonstrating that regard has been paid to the public interest. But simplest to whom – society, taxpayers, or the bureaucracy acting as the government's agent; and whose interpretation of the public interest is being used? What are the price implications and resource costs of selective, compared with open, competition? What about new entrants, X-inefficiency, and the likelihood of collusive tendering? Select lists might remain unchanged, so that there is neither new entry nor exit. It is also possible that the criteria required for entry on to an approved list will reflect a bureaucrat's preference for avoiding and minimising risks: hence governments as buyers are unlikely to be presented with information on the price implications of alternative risks associated with different contractors, including innovators. Nor can it be assumed that firms will be cost-minimisers when only a small group of approved enterprises are invited to tender and the buyer determines the invitation list. Indeed, selective competition resembles oligopoly with entry restrictions. It shows how governments can determine the extent of the market, so that any market failure is policy-created and policy-preferred. However, there are no costless solutions. The choice is between open competition, with lower prices and a belief of a greater risk of bankruptcy; or selective tendering, which is believed to reduce the risks of default but at a higher price. In each case evidence is required on the probability of bankruptcy and the magnitude of price differences. But open and selective competition is not the only method for contractor selection. Non-competitive and negotiated contracts are also used.

Negotiation occurs if a domestic monopoly exists and MoD is unwilling to open the UK market to foreign bidders (*eg* Trident submarines). In such cases, competition is encouraged at the sub-contract level. As part of its competition policy, the Ministry has encouraged more companies, especially small firms, to enter the defence market. MoD has created a Small Firms Advice Division, which advises small firms on how to enter the defence market, and it publishes a Contracts Bulletin which provides information on opportunities to tender (Hartley and Hutton, 1989).

Contractor selection also involves wider choice issues about entry and the extent of the market. In addition to encouraging new entrants from domestic suppliers, competition can be extended by opening the UK market to foreign firms. For example, while there are UK domestic monopolies in aerospace equipment (aircraft, helicopters, missiles and aero-engines), nuclear-powered submarines, tanks and torpedoes, these are all areas where rival suppliers exist elsewhere in the world market, particularly in Europe and the USA. In other words, a domestic monopoly can be subjected to competition by allowing foreign firms to bid for UK defence contracts. For the UK, with an established defence industrial base, the choice set can be illustrated by considering two extreme policy options. At one extreme, the UK could adopt the nationalist or complete independence solution and buy all its military equipment domestically. This would involve sacrificing the gains from international specialisation and trade (*cf* growing our own bananas). At the other extreme, the UK could 'shop around', acting as a competitive buyer, and purchase its weapons from the lowest-cost suppliers within the world market. This would mean buying more abroad, especially from the United States, with the attendant worries of 'undue' dependence on one nation and fears of an American monopoly. Opposition to such a policy would arise from domestic interest groups of defence contractors and trade unions, supported by bureaucrats with a preference for domestic suppliers, and vote-sensitive governments might believe that there are more votes in allocating contracts to national rather than foreign firms located overseas. Between these extremes, there are various intermediate policies.

The UK could undertake the licensed manufacture or co-production of foreign equipment. This is likely to be costlier than purchasing 'off-the-shelf' from the established supplier. But there are believed to be benefits through domestic jobs, the saving of both foreign exchange and research and development resources, together with access to new technology. Alternatively, Britain could participate in a joint project with other nations. Examples have occurred with aircraft, helicopters and missiles. Joint projects involve two or more nations sharing the R & D costs of a project and combining their production orders. In this way, a nation can retain a domestic industry while being involved in high-technology work which would be 'too costly' to undertake alone (see Chapter 9).

Contract types: firm and fixed prices

Once a contractor, either UK or foreign, has been selected, there remains the task of choosing an appropriate contract. There are two limiting cases, namely firm or fixed prices and cost-plus contracts, with various intermediate types offering different incentives related to, say, cost, or equipment performance or delivery dates. The Ministry favours firm or fixed price contracts and these can be determined by open or selective competition, or by negotiation. Increasingly, MoD's more commercial approach, where contractors are subject to greater risks and efficiency incentives, has meant a shift away from cost-plus contracting. The trends are shown in *Table 6.1*. The decline in the proportion of competitive contracts between 1986 and 1989 reflected major projects such as Trident and AWACS for which no competition at the prime contractor level was possible.

TABLE 6.1. *Types of Contracts*

Total value of MoD Headquarters contracts (£m)	1981–82 4606	1983–84 8580	1986–8 9310	1987–88 6541	1988–89 8443
Percentage shares of *value (%)* 1. Contracts priced by competition	23	22	39	30	28
2. Contracts priced otherwise by market forces	14	16	14	19	21
3. Contracts priced on initial or early estimate	40	37	20	32	42
4. Contracts priced on actual costs with cost incentives	2	10	20	12	5
5. Contracts priced on actual costs plus a percentage fee	21	15	7	7	4

Note: Contract types 3–5 are priced by reference to the Government profit formula.
Source: Cmnd 675-II, 1989; Cmnd 1022-II, 1990.

Firm prices are generally used for contracts of relatively short duration (*eg* up to two years). Where the work is long term, fixed price contracts contain escalation clauses allowing for variations in the prices of labour and materials. In this context, though, there are no obvious market failures preventing firms from bearing risks and estimating likely inflation rates over the period of the contract, whatever the length. Someone in the economy either in the private or the public sector has to bear risks and the process is not costless. Typically, fixed price contracts are used where the work required can be clearly specified and the uncertainties are removed, as in production work. The aim is to place the contractor at risk and provide the maximum efficiency incentives, both of which require the price to be agreed before the work begins. If the contractor beats a competitively-determined fixed price, he retains the whole of any extra profits or, in the opposite case, bears all the losses.

Problems arise with non-competitive fixed price contracts. Since competition is absent, the market cannot be used to determine prices, to provide competitive pressures for efficiency, and to 'regulate' profits through entry and exit. Instead, in non-competitive situations, prices and profits have to be negotiated. The Ministry's Procurement Executive is concerned with minimising the taxpayers' liability, so it aims to negotiate 'fair and reasonable' prices. For non-competitive fixed price contracts, these are prices based on *estimated* costs plus a government-determined profit margin. Such contracts assume that firms are profit-maximisers and that governments can estimate X-efficient costs.

The profit formula for non-competitive government contracts is administered by a Review Board for Government Contracts. This Board was created in 1968 as part of an agreement with industry, following the cases of excessive profits earned on UK defence contracts by Ferranti and Bristol Siddeley Engines. Under the 1968 agreement, the government's profit formula for non-competitive contracts is based on a target rate of return on capital designed to provide contractors with a return equal to the average earned by British industry. Higher profit rates are awarded for risk work and there are upper and lower limits on the profitability of non-competitive government contracts. In 1988, the target rate of return on capital employed was 21 per cent on an historic cost basis. The profit formula is based on both capital and costs of production and assumed an average cost to capital ratio of 2.55 to 1 in 1988. For risk contracts, the 1988 capital-based profit element was 11.3 per cent and the cost-based profit element was 4.4 per cent, and the corresponding figures for non-risk contracts were 8.6 per cent and 3.4 per cent, respectively, all on an historic cost basis (Review Board 1988).

Reflecting the concern about excessive profits on non-competitive contracts, the 1968 Profit Formula Agreement introduced three new features. First, the right of both parties to equality of information up to the time that prices are fixed (*ie* to ensure that the Ministry has as much information as the contractor). Second, the right of MoD to examine the outcome of individual contracts through post-costing investigations. Third, the right to refer a particular contract to the Review Board where the Ministry claimed that profits were excessive or where the contractor claimed an unconscionable loss. In 1984, excessive profits were defined as 37.5 per cent or more on capital and exceptional losses as 4.5 per cent or more on capital, with the Review Board able to determine any reimbursement by or to the contractor. After 1984, the trigger points for referring a contract to the Review Board were revised to situations where the out-turn costs vary from estimated costs by 10 per cent or more (Review Board 1987). On this basis, the Review Board is a regulatory agency responsible for policing and monitoring the profitability of non-competitive contracts with powers to re-negotiate any cases of excessive profits or exceptional losses. But how do excessive profits arise?

In principle, fixed price contracts specify the price to be paid for an agreed quantity and quality of product, together with delivery dates. A typical non-competitive fixed price contract will be based on estimated costs plus the Government's profit formula:

$$P_f = E_0 + \pi_g$$

where E_0 = total *estimated* expenditures for the required output. This total comprises direct labour, materials and bought-out parts (variable costs) and overheads (fixed costs). Direct labour costs might be estimated using a labour learning curve (*Figure 7.2*) and an agreed wage rate. Fixed outlays might be recovered by applying an overhead recovery rate to estimated direct labour costs.

π_g = the government-determined profit margin, calculated as a rate of return (r%) on capital employed (rK) or costs (rC).

With fixed price contracts, profits will exceed the government-determined margins whenever a firm's actual costs are *below* the original estimates. For example, if costs are estimated to be £100 million and the Ministry allows a profit margin of 10 per cent on costs, the firm will receive a lump sum payment of £110 million on completion of the work. An example is shown in *Figure 6.1*. If actual costs are, say, £90 million, its realised profits will be £20 million, which represents a return of some 22 per cent on cost or, if actual costs are £120 million, losses of £10 million will be incurred.

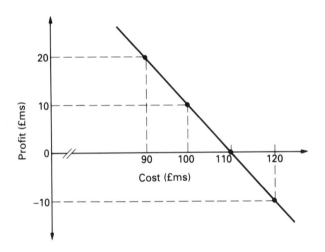

FIG. 6.1. Fixed Price Contracts.

Firms can reduce actual costs below the estimated level through two sources. First, they can raise efficiency. Second, there might be errors in the Ministry's cost estimates, so that the negotiated price is not based on X-efficient behaviour. As a result, the actual profits earned on fixed price contracts will be 'excessive' in the sense of exceeding the rate allowed by the Government's profit formula. The determinants of a firm's actual profits on fixed price work can be shown as follows:

$$\pi = \pi_g + s(E_0 - A_0)$$

where π = actual profits received by the contractor

πg = profit sum negotiated and agreed by the Ministry and the firm, based on the Government's profit formula

$s =$ the rate at which any difference between E_0 and A_0 will be shared between the firm and the government

$E_0 =$ estimated outlays

$A_0 =$ actual expenditures.

With fixed price contracts where $s = 1$, so that the firm retains the whole of any difference between estimated and actual outlays, $\pi > \pi g$ when $E_0 > A_0$. This provides a basis for determining excessive profits, especially if $E_0 > A_0$, not as a result of increased efficiency but due to inaccuracies in the Ministry's cost estimates. Such inaccuracies can result from the estimating techniques used by the Procurement Executive, differences in the information available to both parties, and their behaviour in the bargaining process. With non-competitive fixed price contracts, a firm wishing to increase its profits above the government-determined level has every incentive to maximise its estimated, and minimise its actual, outlays.

The 1968 Profit Formula Agreement sought to solve the problem of excessive profits through equality of information, post-costing and re-negotiation. Some of the results of the 1968 policy are shown in *Table 6.2*. Between 1980 and 1986, the MoD negotiated refunds on 14 per cent of contracts which were post-costed, with refunds representing under 1 per cent of the value of all post-costed contracts. Interestingly, though, for 1980's contracts which were post-costed, actual profit rates exceeded the target rate, leading the Review Board to conclude that for some years the profitability of non-competitive government contracts 'was appreciably higher than for British industry generally' (Review Board, 1987, p. 37).

Profit regulation of the type administered by the Review Board can affect the behaviour of defence contractors. Firms in imperfect and regulated markets have opportunities to pursue non-profit objectives, so

TABLE 6.2. *Review Board Performance*

	Contracts post-costed		Contracts on which trigger point exceeded		Contracts where MoD negotiated refunds			Average return on capital	
	Number	Value (£m)	Number	Value (£m)	Number	Value (£m)	Refund (£m)	Actual (%)	Target (%)
1980–82	230	843	48	95.5	27	52.5	3.2	23.6	21.1
1983	96	781	20	45	12	22.7	0.7	27.8	22.3
1984	70	653	24	303	17	291	20.1	35.3	22.9
1985	78	759	28	66	11	72	4.0	29.8	22.9
1986	67	459	20	33	9	44	2.5	40.1	25.2
Totals 1980–86	541	3,495	140	542.5	76	372.7	30.5	31.3	22.9

Note: Profit rates for 1980–82 and 1980–86 are averages based on post-costing of risk contracts.
Sources: Review Board 1987, 1988.

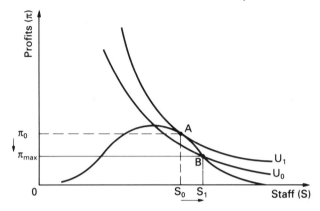

FIG. 6.2. Contractors and Profit Regulation. Utility depends on profits and staff expenditures S (*eg* number of secretaries). In the absence of profit restrictions, utility is maximised at point A. The introduction of a government profit constraint will restrict the firm to B, where utility is lower and increased staff expenditures are substituted for profits.

that procurement and regulatory policy formulated on the assumption of profit-maximising behaviour under competition might not produce the expected outcomes. An example is shown in *Figure 6.2* where a utility-maximising contractor is subject to a ministry-determined limit on profits. As a result, the firm has an incentive to substitute staff or other discretionary expenditures (*eg* luxury offices, company cars) for profits.

Cost-plus contracts

Advanced technology projects confront government procurement agencies with the classic problem of choice under uncertainty. They have to determine the optimal distribution of risks between the buyer and the contractor. In these circumstances, the traditional solution was some form of cost-reimbursement contract with the state bearing most, if not all, of the risks (*eg* Nimrod AEW). Under a cost-plus percentage profit contract, the firm recovers all its actual outlays regardless of their level, plus a government-determined percentage profit. Such contracts are believed to offer little or no efficiency incentives: they have been called 'blank cheque' contracts. Since the profit sum is directly related to costs, the contractor is almost encouraged to incur higher costs and to search for perfection! An example is shown in *Figure 6.3*.

Cost-plus contracts in non-competitive markets provide contractors with the financial framework for escalation in costs, time and quality. It is not unknown for defence equipment projects, especially those involving advanced technology, to cost substantially more than their original estimates, to be considerably delayed and to be 'gold plated'. Cost escala-

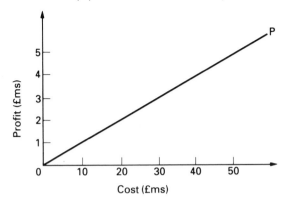

FIG. 6.3. Cost-Plus Contracts. With this form of cost-plus contract, profits (π) depend directly on the percentage profit rate (p) to be applied to costs (C), that is $\pi = pC$. In this example, $p = 10$ per cent. (0.1), so that an increase in costs from £20m to £50m raises profits from £2m to £5m.

tion factors of 2.0 or more are typical in development work on defence projects, with actual costs being twice the initial estimate, expressed in constant prices. One study of 12 UK defence development projects found real cost increases totalling £938 million, or 91 per cent since approval of the staff requirement and average delays of 19 months since the start of full development (NAO 1986). Other examples include the mechanised combat vehicle (MCV 80) with an original in-service date of 1980 which was delayed to 1988; the Alarm missile which by 1988 was some £260 million over budget and several years behind schedule; and the Nimrod AEW aircraft which was cancelled in 1986 with estimated delays in delivery of over eight years (see *Table 6.3*; also HCP 431, 1988).

The causes of escalation in its various forms can be shown using a

TABLE 6.3. *Nimrod AEW Cost and Delivery Estimates*

	Estimates at:		
	Start of project, 1977	1983	Cancellation, 1985–86
In-service date	Training release: May 1982	April 1984	Late 1990
Estimated cost	£319m (1976 prices)	£344.6m (1983 prices)	£882m already spent plus an extra £375m estimated to complete development (1985–86 prices)
Real cost increase	–	15%	165+%

Note: Late 1990 delivery would not have met initial operating capability.
Source: National Audit Office 1986.

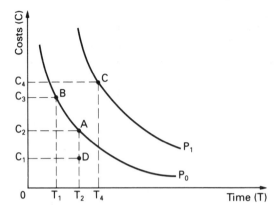

FIG. 6.4. Cost Escalation. Different levels of performance are represented by P_0 and P_1, with P_1 reflecting a higher performance (*eg* a faster aircraft) than P_0. The model shows that the planned performance of a project depends on inputs of costs and time.

trade-off relationship between costs and the time required to develop a given type of project. For example, the development of a new combat aircraft or a new missile can be achieved with different combinations of cost and time inputs. Faster development is costlier and an example of the trade-off is shown in *Figure 6.4*. Initially, the development of a new project is based on plans about its expected cost, time-scale and performance, between which there are possibilities of substitution. *Figure 6.4* provides an analytical framework which explains escalation in terms of urgency, modifications and unforeseen technical problems, together with contractor optimism and performance.

In *Figure 6.4*, a given performance P_0 might be initially estimated to cost C_2, requiring T_2 years to complete (position A). Actual costs can exceed estimates if a project is required earlier than planned. Urgency can lead to 'crash' programmes with more resources being required if the project (P_0) is needed earlier at, say, T_1 (position B). Furthermore, urgency might cause inefficiency in the Ministry's procurement agency, so further contributing to escalation. There could be 'hasty' decision making, 'inadequate' project specification, and relatively 'poor' Ministry financial control and estimation. Escalation can also be caused by unexpected project changes with modifications, alterations or improvements resulting in P_1 being purchased at cost C_4 and time T_4 (position C). Or a project might encounter unforeseen technical problems, especially if it involves a 'jump' in technical knowledge and hence substantial uncertainty; for example P_0 in *Figure 6.4* might be a band rather than a well-defined single line. This is a likely source of cost escalation if contractors and the Ministry tend to respond to uncertainty by submitting a minimum or most-optimistic cost estimate rather than a central point estimate from a range of feasible outcomes.

Consideration also has to be given to contractor behaviour as a possible cause of escalation. With a given performance (P_o), escalation might be due to the deliberate under-estimation of costs, say, C_1 instead of C_2 for duration T_2 (position D). Such behaviour might reflect the efforts of an income-maximising contractor to 'buy into' an attractive new programme by offering optimistic cost, time and quality estimates, thereby establishing a temporary monopoly. In competitive markets with firm or fixed price contracts, this optimism, especially in costs, would result in losses and possibly bankruptcy. But in non-competitive markets with cost-based contracts, a firm's optimism would be financed by the Ministry of Defence, so that the penalties for under-estimation might be absent. The situation could be reinforced by any budget-maximising aim of bureaucracies sponsoring the project, supported by interest groups of scientists and engineers with a preference for new technology and new designs: they would have an incentive to under-estimate costs. Once a contractor has been selected, then cost-based contracts are unlikely to deter modifications, ambitious technical proposals or X-inefficiency. As a result, firms might behave as though the actual (*ex post*) time-cost relationship is positive, which will be reflected in both cost and time slippages, with extra time being costlier.

Certainly there is substantial evidence of both contractors and MoD seriously under-estimating the technical risks, difficulties and costs of achieving an operational requirement. 'There was often a lack of realism by contractors, who had little incentive to act otherwise where cost-plus contracts were involved' (*National Audit Office, 1986*, p. 4). With the continual search for technical superiority in defence equipment, both the armed forces and contractors are encouraged to aim for the most advanced weapons – and cost-plus contracts mean that this process occurs regardless of costs! Moreover, the armed forces have little incentive to economise since they are not subject to clearly specified budget constraints and output targets (Chapter 2). The more performance requirements approach the frontiers of knowledge, the greater the additional costs of an increment of performance and the more uncertain are the cost estimates (McNaugher, 1989). An extra few miles of range for a combat aircraft might double its cost, with drastic implications for the numbers purchased. An example of the relationship between cost and performance requirements for defence equipment is shown in *Figure 6.5*. In response to this problem, MoD has introduced Cardinal Points Specifications supported by fixed or incentive price contracts to encourage greater realism by contractors in their cost estimates. Cardinal Points Specifications defines an operational requirement in very broad terms, leaving contractors to suggest the most appropriate solution. With this approach, it is

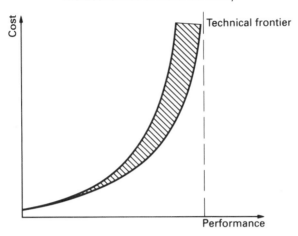

FIG. 6.5. Cost-Performance Curve. Costs rise rapidly as performance requirements approach the frontiers of existing knowledge. The hatched area also shows the increasing uncertainty of cost estimates as performance approaches the frontier.

claimed that procurement agencies are less able to 'gold plate' equipment and that the field for competition is widened, including the possibility of off-the-shelf purchases (*HCP 431, 1988*).

Cost-plus pricing in non-competitive markets is further criticised because it is believed to provide the financial basis enabling defence contractors to hoard labour, especially valuable scientists and technologists. This belief arises from the frequent observation that the cancellation of defence projects leads to employment reductions which are usually much less than the numbers involved on the project (*eg* TSR-2; Nimrod AEW). This suggests the hypothesis that cost-plus defence contracts are associated with labour hoarding and excess employment which is reflected in a sluggish employment response to cancellations and a relatively labour-intensive reaction to an increase in sales. In other words, it is predicted that employment behaviour in weapons markets will differ from that in a normal commercial environment. Empirical tests of this hypothesis require a model which identifies the major determinants of employment. The standard approach starts from a production function (*eg* Cobb–Douglas) and derives a model in which employment is determined by output, technology, and capital:

$$L = f(Q,A,K)$$

where L = employment, Q = output, A = state of technology, K = capital stock

The labour-hoarding hypothesis can be tested by estimating the relationship between employment and output, *ceteris paribus*. For cancellations and down-turns, the resulting elasticity of employment with respect to variations in output is predicted to be lower for defence contractors compared with civilian enterprises. In other words, the hypothesis can be tested by estimating employment elasticities for defence industries compared with other industries not dependent on government defence contracts. But empirical work is not without its analytical and statistical problems. There could be alternative explanations of sluggish employment behaviour by defence contractors. For example, the announced redundancy figures associated with the cancellations of weapons might be deliberate exaggerations, reflecting an attempt by producer interests, supported by budget-conscious bureaucracies, to influence the decisions of vote-maximising governments. Also, data might not be available and there are difficulties in obtaining accurate and reliable measures of technology and the capital stock. Nonetheless, statistical tests of the cost-plus and labour hoarding hypothesis for the UK aircraft industry found, at best, only limited support for the hypothesis (Hartley and Corcoran, 1975).

Continued concern about uncontrolled non-competitive costs and escalation in its various forms on equipment projects has resulted in MoD's shifting away from cost-plus contracting (*Table 6.1*). For development projects, MoD now favours agreeing early in its life either a fixed price or a maximum price with some form of incentive. Where the unknowns and uncertainties in a development project make it difficult to agree a fixed price, the Ministry prefers a target cost incentive contract with a maximum price, so limiting the taxpayers' liability (*National Audit Office, 1986; HCP 431, 1988*). A target cost contract is based on estimates and consists of an agreed target cost, a profit rate based on the target, and a sharing ratio whereby cost savings or losses are shared in a specified proportion between the Ministry and the contractor. For example, the target cost could be £100 million, the target fee £10 million, and the sharing ratio 80:20. If the actual cost equals the target, the firm receives the target fee of £10 million. If actual costs exceed the target, the firm bears 20 per cent of the extra cost, with adverse effects on its fee; and *vice versa* where actual costs are below the target. Similarly, with such a sharing ratio, the Ministry bears 80 per cent of any cost over-runs and receives the same percentage share of any cost savings. The Ministry's preference for a maximum price introduces an additional constraint and incentive into a target cost contract, and an example is shown in *Figure 6.6*. Of course, with a target cost contract and a bilateral monopoly bargaining situation, a contractor has an incentive to bargain for the maximum possible target cost and for a favourable sharing ratio. As a result, a firm's observed performance on an incentive contract might reflect its relative success in the bargaining process!

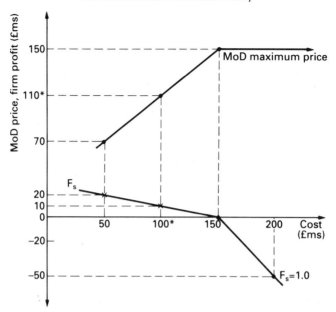

FIG. 6.6. Incentive Contracts. Assume an initial cost estimate of £100m and a target profit of £10m so that the target price to be paid by MoD is £110m. With an incentive contract, and a sharing ratio of 80:20 (Ministry share Ms = 0.8; firm share Fs = 0.2), if actual costs are £50m, the firms profits will be £20m; the Ministry will save £40m and pay the contractor £70m. If MoD's maximum price is £150m, its maximum liability for cost overruns is £40m beyond which further cost increases are borne solely by the firm (hence Fs = 1.0 beyond £150m).

Conclusion

The procurement of defence equipment raises an array of analytical, empirical and policy issues to which economists can contribute. It embraces the study of government and firm behaviour in various market and bargaining situations and the choice of the most appropriate contractual arrangements for coping with uncertainty. But the evaluation of procurement policy raises a fundamental issue: what criteria are to be used to evaluate MoD's project management and procurement performance? Is the model of a perfect or ideal project which encounters no technical problems and no slippages in costs and time-scales to be used? Or, is MoD's project management to be assessed against some average or typical UK project, or is it to be compared with foreign experience (eg France, USA)? Similar problems of criteria for comparison arise in relation to the efficiency of NATO as an organisation for providing defence forces and supplying defence equipment.

References

Cmnd 288-II, 1988, *The Government's Expenditure Plans 1988–89 to 1990–91*, HM Treasury, January (HMSO, London).

Cmnd 675, 1989, *Statement on the Defence Estimates 1989* (HMSO, London).

Cmnd 1022, 1990, *Statement on the Defence Estimates 1990* (HMSO, London).

Hartley, K. and Corcoran, W., 1975, 'Short-run employment functions and defence contracts in the UK aircraft industry', *Applied Economics*, 7, pp. 223–233.

Hartley, K., 1965, 'The mergers in the UK aircraft industry', *Journal of the Royal Aeronautical Society*, Vol. 69, No. 660, December.

Hartley, K., 1983, *NATO Arms Co-operation* (Allen and Unwin, London).

Hartley, K. and Hutton, J., 1989, 'Large purchasers', in Barber, J., *et al.* (eds.), *Barriers to Growth in Small Firms* (Routledge, London).

HCP 505, 1985, *Ministry of Defence: Production Costs of Defence Equipment in Non-Competitive Contracts*, National Audit Office, July (HMSO, London).

HCP, 431, 1988, *The Procurement of Major Defence Equipment*, Defence Committee, House of Commons, June (HMSO, London).

McNaugher, T., 1989, *New Weapons, Old Politics* (Brookings, Washington, DC).

MoD 1983, *Value for Money in Defence Equipment Procurement*, Defence Open Government Document, October (Ministry of Defence, London).

MoD 1987, *The Procurement Executive* (Ministry of Defence, London).

NAO 1986, *Ministry of Defence: Control and Management of the Development of Major Equipment*, National Audit Office, HCP 568, July (HMSO, London).

Review Board 1987, *Report on the Fifth General Review of the Profit Formula for Non-Competitive Government Contracts*, Review Board for Government Contracts (HMSO, London).

Review Board 1988, *Report on the Third Annual Review of the Profit Formula for Non-Competitive Government Contracts*, Review Board for Government Contracts, May (HMSO, London).

CHAPTER 7

NATO and Equipment Standardisation

Introduction: the policy issues

NATO is often criticised for being an inefficient organisation both in supplying defence equipment and in providing armed forces. The Allies are criticised for failing to agree on common tactics, common training and common weapons, with adverse effects on NATO's military effectiveness and an associated waste of resources. The estimates of wasted resources appear staggering. A pioneering study estimated the annual waste of Allied defence resources at more than $10 billion as a lower-bound estimate, with a more likely figure approaching $15–20 billion (1975 prices: Callaghan 1975, p. 37). Such figures reflect duplication in research and development, the cost penalties of short production runs and the duplication of support functions as each nation focuses on supporting its own armed forces (*eg* national defence ministries; national repair and training facilities; national stocks of spares). Examples of duplication in equipment programmes abound. There are 11 firms in seven different countries working on anti-tank weapons and 18 firms in seven countries making ground-to-air weapons (Houwelingen, 1984). Britain, France, the USA and West Germany each have major defence industrial capabilities in combat aircraft, helicopters, missiles, tanks and naval vessels. Such duplication and fragmentation of industrial effort has led to higher unit costs and less equipment purchased, resulting in structural disarmament (Callaghan, 1984).

A failure to standardise also has military penalties in that it reduces the operational effectiveness of NATO forces. With different weapons and equipment each Allied nation has to rely upon its own logistic support system for re-supply. Combat aircraft, for example, might be restricted to operating from their national air bases, unable to be refuelled, re-armed and serviced at airfields of other members of the Alliance. Currently, the air and naval forces of Britain, France and the USA operate almost 30 different types of combat aircraft. One estimate suggested that with standardisation, Allied military effectiveness could be enhanced by 30–50 per cent on average (Callaghan, 1975).

By failing to standardise, NATO is apparently incurring substantial economic and military penalties. With the likely future trends towards reduced defence spending, the search for improved efficiency becomes even more important. Economic analysis suggests that an efficient solution would require members of the NATO club to undertake mutually advantageous trade and exchange, based on the principle of specialisation by comparative advantage. Applied to the armed forces, this might mean the UK specialising in, say, naval forces and vertical take-off strike aircraft which would be provided to the whole of NATO, Germany specialising in armoured and tank forces, with the USA providing the strategic nuclear umbrella, electronic and space satellite surveillance. Of course, sovereign nations will be reluctant to sacrifice their independent balanced forces and to take the risks of relying upon other states to provide armed forces outside their specialism. Similar objections arise to applying the principle of gains from international trade based on specialisation by comparative advantage to the development and production of defence equipment in NATO nations.

While the search for standardisation embraces all aspects of the military production function (*ie* quantity and productivity of manpower, weapons and the efficiency with which these inputs are combined to produce defence output), this chapter focuses on the opportunities for cost savings within defence equipment markets. It shows how economists can analyse the arguments about equipment standardisation. Questions also arise about the size of any savings from standardisation and, if the savings are substantial, why they have not been exploited. As a starting point, an analytical framework is required for assessing the possible cost savings from equipment standardisation.

Cost savings from standardisation: an analytical framework

Inefficiency in NATO weapons markets is reflected in excessive product differentiation resulting in wasteful duplication of R & D and relatively short production runs, so that economies of scale remain unexploited. European defence industries are particularly criticised for being too small and too fragmented to be able to compete with the USA: hence the claim that weapons standardisation within NATO offers opportunities for cost savings in equipment procurement. At its simplest, it is argued that there would be major savings in R & D expenditure if, say, only one nation rather than three developed a new combat aircraft. Further savings would accrue through reduced unit production costs if all NATO nations combined their orders and purchased one type of equipment (*eg* aircraft, tank, missile).

The supporters of equipment standardisation claim three sources of cost savings:

(i) *Savings in R & D expenditures* due to a reduction in duplicate R & D. Also, large production orders for a given type of equipment enables fixed R & D costs to be spread over a greater output, so reducing unit R & D costs. For a new combat aircraft such as the European Fighter Aircraft, development costs are substantial at an estimated £6.6 billion (1988 prices), to be shared between four European nations. If two or more countries pursued separate national developments of a similar aircraft, each would have to bear R & D costs of over £6 billion: hence there are substantial savings from ending duplicate R & D.

(ii) *Economies of scale leading to lower production costs*: Compared with a variety of small-scale outputs, one large production run will lead to scale economies and lower production costs. On the three-nation Tornado, combined orders were some 900 aircraft, comprising 435 units for the UK, 375 units for West Germany and 100 units for Italy.

(iii) *Gains from international trade*: Further gains are expected if standardisation is associated with the creation of a free trade area in weapons. In this case each NATO member would specialise in those parts of the weapons development and production process in which it has a comparative advantage, so reaping the gains from international specialisation and mutually-advantageous trade and exchange. This suggests that a distinction is needed between the absolute cost savings associated with a greater scale of output within any nation; and the relative cost savings reflecting different comparative advantages between nations. *Figure 7.1* summarises the potential sources of cost savings.

In *Figure 7.1* each long-run average cost curve (LAC) shows the opportunities for economies of scale in production. Consider two nations, with A represented by cost curve LAC_2 and B by cost curve LAC_1. Initially, nation A (*eg* USA), is at the cost-output position C_2Q_2 on LAC_2 whilst country B (*eg* UK or France) is at C_3Q_1 on LAC_1. Each nation, and especially B, could achieve savings in unit costs if output were greater (*ie* by moving along its national cost curve). The point where each cost curve tends to become horizontal locates the minimum efficient scale (*mes*) or size of firm for a product within each nation: beyond *mes*, there are relatively few further cost savings. Evidence is required on the unit cost implications of operating below *mes* and where various NATO nations are in relation to *mes*. The advocates of equipment standardisation maintain

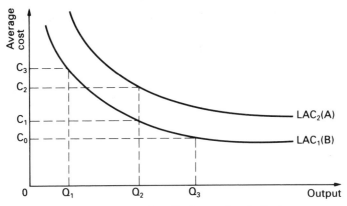

FIG. 7.1. Cost Savings from Equipment Standardisation.

that NATO defence firms are operating below *mes* and as a result are incurring substantial cost penalties (*eg* C_3 in *Figure 7.1*). But additional savings can be obtained by moving between cost curves. Nation B is the lowest-cost supplier and could produce Q_2 at C_1. If nation B specialised and produced both Q_1 and Q_2 equal to Q_3, its unit production costs would be C_0. There are potential cost savings for B of $C_3 - C_0$ and for A of $C_2 - C_0$.

A similar analysis can be applied to R & D, showing that a larger output will reduce unit R & D costs and that nations might have different comparative advantages in development work. R & D is a fixed total cost. Average fixed costs can be represented by a rectangular hyperbola showing a negative relationship between unit R & D costs and output. Nations are likely to have different comparative advantages in R & D, so resulting in different R & D cost curves. But which nations in NATO have a comparative advantage for which equipment? And would there be gains from international specialisation and separation of R & D and production work? The analytical framework of *Figure 7.1* shows that in estimating the likely savings from equipment standardisation, evidence is required on the cost advantages of operating at a larger scale *within* a nation (*ie* scale economies due to moving along a cost curve), and the relative position of cost curves *between* nations. So what is the evidence?

Some evidence

Unfortunately, economic studies of cost conditions in defence equipment industries throughout NATO are conspicuous by their absence. Nonetheless, published industrial and international trade studies can be used to provide broad orders of magnitude about the likely range of cost savings so providing some empirical content for the model outlined in *Figure 7.1*.

Industry studies provide evidence on cost-quantity relationships and minimum efficient scale (*mes*). Evidence on scale economies in Western Europe and North America suggests unit cost reductions of 10 per cent when output is doubled from 50 per cent of *mes*. But such evidence is subject to at least three qualifications. First, some defence contractors might be operating at less than 50 per cent of *mes* and this is most likely for highly-specialised equipment (*eg* tanks). However, the cost penalties of small-scale production can be exaggerated where there are military versions of civil products or where highly specialised weapons use standard components which are manufactured on a much larger scale (*eg* vehicle engines). Second, *mes* is not the minimum cost point and a doubling in scale to twice *mes* might further reduce unit costs by up to 5 per cent. Third, scale economies are a static concept which neglect the cost-reducing opportunities from learning-by-doing.

Learning curves show the extent to which unit costs decline with increases in *cumulative* output. For a number of activities (*eg* aircraft, machine tools, turbo-generators, marine diesels, shipbuilding, steel, refrigerators), labour learning curves with slopes of between 60–97 per cent have been observed. An example of an 80 per cent labour learning curve which is typical for UK aircraft manufacture is shown in *Figure 7.2*. Learning varies between nations, between industries and between different stages of the production process (*eg* assembly work compared with machining). For example, in the US aircraft industry, labour learning curves of 75 per cent are typical (Hartley, 1983, p. 193).

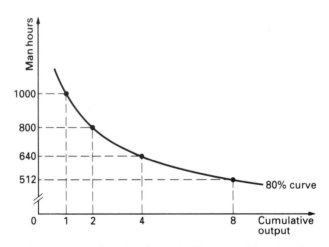

FIG. 7.2. An 80 per cent Learning Curve. An 80 per cent labour learning curve means that direct labour input declines by 20 per cent for each doubling in the cumulative output of a given aircraft – *eg* if unit 1 requires 1,000 man hours, unit 2 will require 800, unit 4 will require 640 (80 per cent of unit 2), and number 8 will need 512 man-hours.

Labour learning curves can be converted into unit production cost curves by assuming that the reduction in unit costs is about one-half of the reduction in direct labour costs alone. Thus, an 80 per cent labour learning curve results in a 90 per cent unit production cost curve, showing that unit costs decline by about 10 per cent for each doubling in cumulative output. It has been suggested that such experience is not unique to aircraft manufacture and is typical of a large number of industries (*Cmnd 7198, 1978*). If so, supporters of standardisation might claim an additional 10 per cent saving in unit costs from every doubling in cumulative output, always assuming that learning economies have not been included in estimates of scale curves.

Further gains are possible from specialisation and international trade on the basis of comparative advantage. These gains are likely if standardisation policies create a competitive market and free trade area in defence equipment within NATO. Evidence from international studies of comparative advantage, tariff protection and the gains from the creation of the European Community provide an indication of the possible cost savings from an Alliance free trade area. Such studies suggest that a NATO free trade area in defence equipment might lead to average cost savings of some 10 per cent, and this is likely to be a lower bound estimate (Hartley, 1983). Some of the price differences for European and US combat aircraft are shown in *Table 7.1*. For example, as an indication of the gains from trade, the British Hawk trainer is some 12 per cent cheaper than the Alpha Jet trainer.

TABLE 7.1. *Prices of European and US Military Aircraft*

Aircraft	Average 1985 prices ECUs millions
British Aerospace Hawk	7.5– 9.0
Dassault Breguet Alpha Jet	8.5–10.0
Mirage F-1	13.0–14.5
Mirage 2000	24.0–34.0
Panavia Tornado	39.0–48.0
General Dynamics F-16	23.0–33.0
Grumman F-14	38.0–48.0
McDonnell Douglas F-15	37.0–46.0
F-18	35.0–45.0

Note: Average programme unit costs including R & D, production, initial spares and ground support equipment.
Source: EC 1988.

To summarise, if equipment standardisation leads to scale economies, learning and the gains from free trade, it could result in unit cost savings in the region of 20–30 per cent (10 per cent from each source of cost saving). By applying these percentages to each NATO nation's expenditure on equipment, it is possible to obtain a broad indication of the impact on annual defence budgets. However, the analytical framework used to estimate such gains is based on a number of assumptions. Their specification indicates the limitations of the model and the associated estimates of cost savings. The major assumptions of the model (*Figure 7.1*) are:

(i) *The pricing policy for equipment.* An average cost or full cost pricing model is assumed with prices based on average costs, plus a profit margin. On this basis, reductions in unit costs will be reflected in lower prices. Otherwise the cost savings of larger scale will not benefit consumer nations through lower prices, with implications for the distribution of gains. Indeed, if standardisation restricts competition there are potential adverse effects through monopoly pricing, especially for spares. For example, consider the UK belief that US aircraft are cheap but you pay heavily for the spares: an argument which is often used for continued state support of an independent British aerospace industry.

(ii) *The internal efficiency of firms.* Firms are assumed to be technically efficient, with the cost curves in *Figure 7.1* representing cost-minimising behaviour. However, in non-competitive markets (aerospace, submarines, tanks, torpedoes) enterprises are likely to be characterised by organisational slack or X-inefficiency. Competition acts as a possible policing mechanism, inducing firms to minimise costs. If standardisation is associated with greater competition in NATO weapons markets, the resulting 'shock effect' leading to cost-minimising behaviour could be an additional source of cost savings. UK evidence shows that competition within national markets results in typical cost savings of 20 per cent (*HCP 399 1986, pxii*). However, if standardisation eliminates wasteful duplication, competition might be replaced by monopoly resulting in higher prices, inefficiency and a lack of dynamism.

(iii) *No dis-economies of scale.* However, a major expansion of firm size beyond existing experience levels might encounter managerial diseconomies. This is a particular problem for nations like country B (*eg* UK, France) in *Figure 7.1*. Will country B follow LAC_1 if output levels of Q_2 and Q_3 were to be feasible? For example, the UK and European aerospace industries have no experience of US production runs and there might be learning costs for a new entrant into the large-scale league. Learning curves in the UK aerospace industry, for instance, are reported to 'flatten out' after some 100–200 units, whilst learning seems to continue indefinitely in the USA. Moreover, if production is concentrated in a few localised plants, there could be dis-economies in transport and distribution. Evidence from mergers suggests that larger firms are not always associated with improved performance (Meeks, 1977). Any such dis-economies will *reduce* the estimated cost savings from standardisation.

(iv) *Adjustment periods and resource re-allocation.* To obtain the maximum cost savings from standardisation will require a re-allocation of resources to reflect each nation's comparative advantage in equipment development and production. Such a re-allocation will take time and might require government adjustment policies to 'improve' the allocative process, particularly in labour markets (re-training; labour mobility). Also, if standardisation concentrates output in a small-number of firms, an expansion of capacity will be required, with inevitable delays in the delivery of equipment during the adjustment process. In addition, the maximum savings are only possible when all NATO nations are in a position to change their stock of weapons. Even with complete agreement and harmony between governments on the most desirable form of standardisation(!), some 10–20 years is likely to be the minimum adjustment period.

(v) *Departures from the 'best' case.* Economic theory shows that a 'best' or optimum allocation of resources, as reflected in a competitive system, represents the maximum savings and benefits that can be achieved from standardisation. On this basis, all other standardisation policies, such as offsets, work-sharing, co-production and departures from competition, are likely to result in *smaller* savings than the maximum available. Often, such departures from the best case are explained in terms of a government's concern with wider policy targets, such as employment, high technology and the balance of payments.

The pot of gold paradox

A paradox is now apparent. There are claimed to be major cost savings from equipment standardisation (a pot of gold) and yet, apparently, NATO nations have failed to exploit these obvious opportunities for mutually-advantageous and beneficial exchange. If standardisation is as beneficial as claimed, why has it not occurred? Are there some obvious market failures preventing worthwhile international transactions or are the existing arrangements optimal reflecting preferred outcomes, particularly where it is recognised that all policies and exchange involve transaction costs?

The paradox is of further interest because the USA, as a major supporter of competition, free enterprise and capitalism, often finds itself advocating socialist solutions, in the form of rationalisation, collaboration and ending 'wasteful' duplication and competition in R & D. It is as though someone has re-discovered that houses, private cars, sports grounds, taxis and toilets are 'under-utilised' and that there would be massive cost savings if we all standardised and shared these commodities; but no one has asked whether the outcomes might be preferred by consumers. In other words, the standardisation debate tends to focus on the theoretical cost savings from longer production runs whilst ignoring the loss of consumer benefit which would be associated with reduced product differentiation.

Nations have different tastes and preferences for defence and varying comparative advantages in the production of equipment and the provision of armed forces. They differ in their views about the most efficient combinations of different types of equipment and manpower needed for achieving national 'protection'. Nations with worldwide commitments require equipment for operation in different regions, whereas some European countries might require weapons specialised for local conflicts. Also, a nation with an abundance of manpower will tend to have a comparative advantage in labour-intensive forces which will affect both the quantity and quality of equipment which it demands. Indeed, there is a potential confusion between standardisation and defence output. Standardisation sometimes appears as an end rather than a means to achieving the socially preferred end objective of peace, protection and the saving of lives (*ie* defence output). Moreover, complete standardisation involves a sacrifice of diversity in equipment and force structures, with adverse effects on NATO's ability to meet unforeseen threats. Nevertheless, it is likely that there is too much equipment differentiation within NATO, but reductions are not costless and complete elimination might not be worthwhile. Reduced product differentiation involves transactions costs as nations have to search for partners, bargain about common operational requirements and agree upon time-scales. In addition, any move towards a NATO free market in equipment will involve gains and losses for different national defence industries. The economic principle of compensation suggests that such a change would be socially desirable if the potential gainers were able to over-compensate the potential losers. But even if gains and losses could be measured, problems arise because of the difficulties of negotiating formal contractual arrangements for the payment of actual compensation between nations.

Three explanations can be suggested for the apparent failure of NATO nations to exploit the savings associated with equipment standardisation:

(i) The savings are not as great as claimed. Here, nations might have adopted various devices and sharing arrangements to reduce the cost barriers to independent procurement.

(ii) There might be substantial benefits from current arrangements which are at least equal to their costs. Independence, for example, might be regarded as worthwhile, with nations willing to pay the necessary price.

(iii) There could be major imperfections in weapons markets, preventing the exploitation of the gains from standardisation and these imperfections could be policy-created. Economic theory shows that if left to themselves, private markets might fail to work properly, adversely affecting community welfare. Barriers to international trade are a major source of market failure. Examples include tariffs, quotas, subsidies to domestic firms and preferential government-purchasing from national industries. Such barriers restrict the gains which could otherwise be obtained from standardisation and international trade. Thus, if markets are failing because of trade barriers, there is scope for state intervention to 'correct' such failures. However, this ignores the fact that many trade barriers are policy-created. Governments choose to impose tariffs and to award contracts to domestic firms so that governments are frequently the source of market failure. The economics of politics and public choice predicts that the policies of democratic governments tend to favour producers more than consumers (Chapter 5).

A public choice perspective

If international specialisation and trade in weapons raises economic welfare, how do we explain the present market structure and the likely constraints on the creation of a free market in defence equipment? One obvious explanation is that the majority of NATO members dislike the expected outcome of a free market. Since the USA is likely to have a comparative advantage in high technology goods, it is predicted that a free market would result in America specialising in the production and export of R & D intensive equipment, with the UK and Europe confined to 'metal-bashing'. For Europe, a free market is expected to result in much smaller defence industries with the resources re-allocated to alternative and more competitive sectors. Even so, the UK and Europe are likely to have a continued advantage in some areas of weapons technology (*eg* VTOL aircraft and sub-systems, helicopters, missiles). Nor must it be forgotten that the emotive business of 'metal-bashing' can be highly profitable and that the ultimate concern of business is with profitability rather than whether inputs are technology or production skills. However, as a market-improving policy, the focus on equipment standardisation might be criticised because it is confined to weapons rather than creating a NATO free trade area for all goods and services.

The general reluctance of NATO nations to accept the superior free market outcome can only result if defence is 'different' from other goods.

No one has ever suggested that the UK should, say, grow its own bananas to avoid undue dependence on foreign suppliers and to obtain the employment, strategic, balance of payments and technological fall-out 'benefits' of domestic production. Defence is different because individuals cannot express a preference for the commodity in the market place; they can only register their defence preferences in a general form at the ballot box, so that politicians and bureaucrats have discretionary power in interpreting the 'public interest'. Within a nation, alternative suppliers of defence services are absent and, for security reasons, governments are reluctant to provide information on the costs and effectiveness of alternative force structures and different procurement policies. For example, British voters are not supplied with information on the costs of buying weapons off-the-shelf from the USA compared with joint projects and licensed production. Instead, vote-maximising politicians and budget-conscious bureaucracies are likely to be influenced by producer interest groups (Chapter 5). Not surprisingly, to maintain the demand for a domestic weapons industry, there is every incentive for producers, bureaucrats and politicians to create a set of myths on procurement policy. Thus, it is alleged that the UK needs a defence industry for 'independence', for advanced technology and jobs. There is the myth that competition in weapons markets is impossible and that US weapons might be 'cheap but you pay for the spares'. Some of these propositions might be valid; the worry is that many are long on emotion and short on economic analysis and evidence.

The economics of politics and public choice can modify the standard predictions of comparative advantage. Foreign defence orders are unlikely to attract votes for domestic politicians. In a vote-conscious market, governments have an incentive to ensure that any foreign orders are 'compensated' with domestic work to satisfy producer interest groups (especially where there are state-owned defence industries). Such offsets and work-sharing are likely to be supported by domestic bureaucracies since they lead to higher budgets and opportunities to exercise discretionary power. These political bargains are unlikely to be based on comparative advantage. For US weapons built in Europe, some 25 per cent co-production might raise costs by about 10 per cent. Similarly, with advanced technology weapons, UK governments and interest groups will tend to prefer joint projects with Europe rather than with the USA. The US political market is also likely to favour domestic projects, with a reluctance to become involved in international collaborative ventures, especially in R & D work (the US would lose technology). Nationalism and the desire for an independent technical capability is not costless and it is a major constraint on the extent to which NATO can create a free trade area in weapons. If governments believe that nationalism contributes to votes, they are unlikely to favour market-improving policies. Why should they, when the potential beneficiaries are widely-dispersed consumers compared with the more localised producer groups whose income depends on domestic defence orders. Certainly, the numbers employed in European defence industries are substantial as shown in *Table 7.2*. Such groups will obviously oppose policies likely to harm their income and employment prospects and they have every incentive to create a set of myths about standardisation and equipment procurement policy. Here, economists can contribute by critically evaluating such myths and by providing information on the costs and benefits of alternative procurement policies. Sensible public choices require an information framework which identifies the consequences of alternative decisions and the magnitude of likely trade-offs involved in different policies.

TABLE 7.2. *European Defence Industries*

	Arms spending as proportion of defence spending (%)	Percentage of arms production for export (%)	Employment (000s)	Defence share of manufacturing employment (%)
Belgium	14.7	72.6	18.5	2–3
France	23.3	36.5	300.0	6.5
FR Germany	25.5	9.7	200–250	2–3
Italy	22.6	59.2	83.0	1.3
Netherlands	28.7	45.3	11–12.5	1.2
UK	29.1	34.2	405.0	7.2

Note: Data are for 1983.
Source: WEU, 1986.

A framework for choice

In purchasing defence equipment nations have four broad policy options. These range between the extremes of complete independence (nationalism) and buying everything from overseas, and the intermediate solutions of international collaboration involving joint development and production, or some variant of licensed production. The relationship between unit costs and output determines the cost implications of each option and indicates the magnitude of any domestic benefits required to justify a particular policy. Clearly, the more nations buy each other's equipment, the greater the extent of standardisation: hence national independence is a major barrier to equipment standardisation.

For European nations, complete independence is costly, involving the sacrifice of the potential gains from international specialisation and trade, resulting in a failure to standardise. With independence, a European nation has to bear the costs of developing modern weapons and, in the absence of exports, its production runs will be relatively small. Moreover, each new generation of weapons is costlier in real terms than its predecessors.

Not surprisingly, the quantities purchased have tended to decrease so that the high R & D costs have to be spread over a smaller output, and there are fewer opportunities for scale and learning economies. This is especially the case with combat aircraft. In the UK, a typical production run for the RAF is 200–300 units (*eg* Harrier, Hawk) at the rate of two to five aircraft per month. In contrast, US production runs for its air forces vary between 1,000 and 3,000 units (*eg* F-15, F-16, F-18), produced at rates of 12–30 aircraft per month. Such outputs allow the US aerospace industry to exploit learning economies and this is reflected in the unit prices for off-the-shelf purchases by foreign buyers. For example, if the UK had purchased its Phantoms off-the-shelf directly from McAir, their unit prices might have been some 23–43 per cent lower: this is also an indication of the possible gains from standardisation in combat aircraft. These examples raise two policy questions. First, how can European nations afford to support domestic defence industries, particularly in high technology areas? Second, what are the alleged benefits from the retention of a domestic defence industry and what valuations are placed on such benefits? These issues are examined in more detail in Chapter 8.

Nations can adopt different policies to respond to cost barriers. France, for example, has retained a degree of independence through large-scale exports of combat aircraft (*eg* Mirage). Alternatively, joint projects can be undertaken, with two or more nations sharing both the development and production work. This option which contributes to standardisation is considered in detail in Chapter 9.

Another policy option is some form of licensed production, including co-production or industrial collaboration (*eg* F-104, F-16, AWACs). These involve the domestic manufacture of another country's equipment either wholly or in part. This option usually results in higher unit costs than if the output had been purchased directly off-the-shelf from the original manufacturer. Higher costs for the licensed or co-producer result from the loss of learning economies, shorter production runs, duplicate tooling and the costs of transferring technology. In return, the co-producing nation saves substantial R & D resources which would have been required for an independent project and there is some standardisation of equipment. Also, a domestic defence capacity is maintained, the balance of payments is protected, jobs are created and there are benefits from access to new production technology. An indication of the valuation placed on such 'social benefits' can be obtained by estimating the extra costs of licensed production compared with off-the-shelf purchases. For example, the F-16 co-production programme resulted in an extra 34 per cent cost penalty for the Europeans compared with a direct purchase from General Dynamics, USA (Rich, 1981).

In choosing its 'best' or preferred equipment procurement policy, a government has to know the costs of the options and their implications for the pursuit of other policy targets. *Table 7.3* presents a general information matrix or programme budget which shows policy makers the consequences of alternative decisions and the magnitude of trade-offs; it is illustrative rather than comprehensive. Four broad policy options are shown, although the list could be extended to include further variants. Possibilities include single or multi-nation production of sub-systems, or a direct buy with offset or work-sharing arrangements on the same programme or over a 'package' of projects. Each option will require a choice between a European, US or other partner or supplier. Alternatively, within NATO, there could be competing development projects between, say, US and European consortia, with the winner manufactured on a co-production basis throughout the Alliance. *Table 7.3* shows that for a given type of weapon and each policy option, information is required on:

(i) *Features of the equipment to be acquired*: For each type of equipment, say, combat aircraft, warship or tank, the requirement needs to be specified in terms of performance, delivery dates and quantity. Often equipment is not identical and choices are required between weapons differing in performance and delivery dates, as well as costs.

(ii) *The expected life-cycle costs of the equipment*: Life-cycle costs comprise acquisition costs, namely, R & D and production, and in-service costs comprising repair and maintenance, operations, training and post-design modifications. For a combat aircraft with a 15-year life, total life-cycle costs might exceed twice the initial acquisition costs (Kirkpatrick, 1983). Similarly, maintenance costs are about 30 per cent of the total life-cycle cost of a weapon system. Indeed, if the RAF could improve by a third the reliability of the next generation of aircraft, the resultant saving, over the life of the new aircraft, would be sufficient either to purchase an extra 100 aircraft or to fund the UK's share of a collaborative development programme for its successor (Truelove, 1987). Cost data are required for each policy option. The extra costs of each policy, compared with not buying from the least-cost supplier, need to be expressed in terms of the implications for numbers, possible delays in delivery and quality, all of which will affect defence output.

(iii) *The expected life-time benefits of the alternatives*: In principle, the Ministry of Defence should be concerned with defence objectives, with other government departments responsible for wider economic and social objectives. NATO will obviously be interested in collective defence and in the contribution of equipment choices to

TABLE 7.3. *A Choice Framework*

Policy	Features of equipment			Total price		Contribution to NATO standardisation	National economic benefits		
	Performance	Numbers	Delivery	Acquisition	Life-cycle		Jobs	Technology	Balance of payments
1. Complete independence									
2. International colla-boration in R & D and production									
3. (a) Licensed production									
(b) Co-production									
(c) Work-sharing									
4. Buy from abroad									

standardisation. However, nations with an established defence industry usually wish to retain their domestic capability for its contribution to independence, security of supply, its responsiveness to national military requirements and for its wider economic benefits in terms of jobs, technology and the balance of payments. While the list of benefits appears impressive and persuasive, there is considerable scope for critical evaluation. The exact nature of the benefits has to be specified; it needs to be recognised that such benefits are not costless and that the resources involved in defence industries have alternative uses; and evidence on the size of the benefits is also required. These issues are examined in Chapter 8.

References

Callaghan, T. Jr, 1975, *US–European Economic Co-operation in Military and Civil Technology*, September (Georgetown University, USA).

Callaghan, T. Jr, 1984, 'The structural disarmament of NATO', *NATO Review*, 3, pp. 21–26, June.

Cmnd 7198, 1978, *A Review of Monopolies and Mergers Policy* (HMSO, London).

EC, 1988, *The European Aerospace Industry: Trading Position and Figures*, February (EC Commission, Brussels).

Hartley, K., 1983, *NATO Arms Co-operation* (Allen and Unwin, London).

HCP 399, 1986, *Statement on the Defence Estimates 1986*, Defence Committee, June (HMSO, London).

Houwelingen, J., 1984, 'The Independent European Programme Group', *NATO Review*, 4, pp. 17–21, August.

Kirkpatrick, D., 1983, 'Costing aircraft projects', *Air Clues*, MoD, London, January.

Meeks, G., 1977, *Disappointing Marriage: A Study of Gains from Merger* (Cambridge University Press, London).

Rich, M. *et al.*, 1981, *Multi-national Co-Production of Military Aerospace Systems*, Rand, R-2681, Santa Monica, California, October.

Truelove, O. J., 1987, 'Aircraft reliability', *Air Clues*, November (MoD, London).

WEU 1986, *Armaments Sector of Industry in Member Countries*, January (Assembly of Western European Union, Paris).

CHAPTER 8

The UK Defence Industrial Base

Introduction: what is the policy problem?

In the 1990s, the UK will face some difficult defence choices, the outcome of which will affect not only the size and composition of the armed forces but will also have major implications for the future of the UK's defence industrial base. Pressures from arms control, a declining defence budget and possibly a smaller share for equipment suggest a pessimistic future for defence contractors (Chapter 2). Since the mid-1980s, business prospects have also been affected by MoD's competitive procurement policy and by the fact that between 1985 and 1995, the purchase of Trident will absorb almost 10 per cent of the available funds for new equipment (HCP 479, 1985). Such a market environment will force defence contractors to reassess their future income prospects, leading to mergers, take-overs and diversification into other defence and civil activities, entry into overseas markets, as well as exits from the industry. What should be the government's response to such changes in the size and structure of the UK's defence industrial base? Should it intervene and, if so, what would be the purpose of intervention? Or should it leave the industry's fate to be determined by market forces? The answer is important since the defence industrial base and the efficiency with which it provides equipment are major inputs into the protection of the UK.

Critics of UK defence industries point to fraud, waste, inefficiency, poor productivity, expensive and unreliable equipment, often delivered late and way over budget (HCP 431, 1988). During the 1980s, controversy surrounded major equipment choices such as the decisions to buy Trident and the European Fighter Aircraft, to cancel the British Nimrod AEW aircraft and to buy US Boeing AWACS aircraft, and the decision to develop a UK tank rather than buy off-the-shelf from Germany or the USA. There was also concern about privatisation, foreign take-overs, the future of the Westland Helicopter Company and its involvement in European collaborative projects, and the GEC–Siemens bid for Plessey (HCP 518, 1986; Cmnd 676, 1989). Further worries have been expressed about competitive tendering damaging the defence research base and threatening some contractors with bankruptcy. All of these criticisms raise questions about government support for the defence industrial base, its efficiency, ownership and structure: issues which are central to economics, particularly industrial economics. In examining these issues, this chapter starts by describing UK defence industries as part of weapons markets; it considers the concept of the defence industrial base, its benefits and costs, and reviews the economic arguments about buying British or importing defence equipment.

UK weapons markets: demand and supply

Weapons markets comprise buyers and sellers. On the demand side of the market, the UK government is a sole purchaser of the equipment needed for its armed forces. Other nations also enter the UK market as buyers of British defence equipment. Between 1983 and 1989, annual exports of UK defence equipment varied between £781 million and £2,408 million, with the major customers being the Middle East and North Africa (*eg* Al Yamah contract to supply aircraft and other equipment to Saudi Arabia). As a major purchaser of defence equipment, the Ministry of Defence can use its buying power to influence the size, structure and performance of the UK arms industry (Chapter 6). In 1990, the Ministry's Procurement Executive employed 33,000 people. About 75 per cent of the Ministry's equipment budget is spent in the UK, 10 per cent is spent overseas and the balance benefits British industry working on collaborative projects. In 1990–91, some 36 per cent of the equipment budget was spent on air systems, 34 per cent on sea systems, 20 per cent on land systems and the balance on general support (*Table 8.1*). However, between 1986 and 1990, both the real defence budget and the share going to equipment declined.

On the supply side of the market, the UK defence industry comprises almost 10,000 companies involved in the R & D, production, repair and maintenance of defence equipment, for MoD and overseas governments. Some industries are dependent on sales to MoD, with the Ministry purchasing about 60 per cent of the output of the UK ordnance industry, 50 per cent of the UK aerospace industry's output, 40 per cent of the output of British shipbuilding and 20 per cent of the output of the UK electronics industry (Cmnd 9763-I, 1986; Taylor and Hayward, 1989). However, one study concluded that the official statistics consistently under-estimated the scale of resources committed to defence electronics in the UK. Between 1983 and 1985, MoD accounted for at least one-third of the domestic sales of the UK electronics industry, for about one-third of its R & D expenditure and for over 90 per cent of state-funded electronics R & D. Furthermore, defence electronics accounted for about

20–25 per cent of MoD equipment expenditure, much of it concentrated in a few specialist product areas, namely, airborne radar, sonar data handling, torpedoes and army radio-products where there are less obvious opportunities for technology transfer to the civil sector (Walker, 1988). R & D also forms a substantial part of defence equipment procurement, through which it can have a major impact on technical progress in specific parts of the UK economy. Much of the research programme is undertaken in the government defence research establishments which specialise in air, land and sea systems, chemical defence, radar and signals, and nuclear weapons. These research establishments employed over 14,000 staff in 1989, and they enable MoD to act as an intelligent customer for defence equipment. Plans exist to create a Defence Research

TABLE 8.1. *UK Defence Industries*

	£m current prices	
	1978–79	1990–91
1. Total MoD equipment procurement (£m current prices)	3,303	9,325
2. MoD expenditure on defence R & D	1,028	2,465
of which:		
military aircraft	332	720
guided weapons	105	384
other electronics	126	365
ship construction and underwater warfare	81	368
3. MoD expenditure on production and repair	2,275	6,859
of which:		
air	884	2,254
sea	751	2,385
land	521	1,407
4. Industrial analysis of MoD expenditure in UK:		
Aerospace	1,089	2,176
Electronics	429	1,754
Shipbuilding	354	680
Ordnance, small arms, ammunition	297	723
Other mechanical and marine engineering	99	671
Petroleum products	239	295
5. MoD expenditure on works, buildings, land, stores and services	1,178	4,146
6. Exports of UK defence equipment	393	2,408
Total procurement in UK of equipment and other items by MoD and overseas buyers	4,874	15,879

Notes: (i) For industrial analysis and exports, latest figures are for 1988–89.
(ii) There was a change in the SIC between 1978 and 1988, which affected marine engineering – classified under shipbuilding in 1978–79.
(iii) Export figures are for defence equipment exports identified by Customs and Excise: there are additional exports where it is not possible to distinguish between military and civil goods from official records.
(iv) The final totals relate only to items 1 + 5 + 6. For 1990–91, the export figures are for 1989.
Source: *Cmnd 8212, 1981; Cmnd 1022, 1990.*

Agency in 1991 based on the non-nuclear establishments. This executive agency will have greater managerial freedom, a sharpened customer–supplier relationship and a greater incentive to market its human and physical capital (*Cmnd 675-I, 1989*, p. 33; Dunsire *et al.*, 1988). In contrast to research, most of the defence development work is undertaken by private industry and is focused on aircraft, missiles, electronics, ship construction and underwater warfare (*Table 8.1*).

The UK has a distinctive defence industry which has the capability to design, develop and produce a complete range of defence equipment, including high technology items such as combat aircraft, helicopters, missiles, nuclear weapons, nuclear-powered submarines, aircraft carriers and tanks. But independence in high technology equipment is costly. Typical ratios of development to unit production costs are 100 or over for combat aircraft and 1,000 for guided weapons (Pugh, 1986, p. 346). Since development costs are fixed and independent of the numbers produced, a small production run will have to bear all these costs. For example, development costs of £1,000 million will add £1 million to unit production costs over an output of 1,000 units, but will increase average production costs by £10 million for an output of 100 units. Thus, nations with the capability to develop a complete range of defence equipment, particularly high technology products, will usually have large defence budgets allowing them to buy weapons in substantial numbers, thereby spreading fixed development costs over a large output (Chapters 7 and 9). By 1990, the MoD's ratio of defence R & D to production expenditure had improved from 1:2 in 1979–80 to about 1:3. However, the prospects of future cuts in defence equipment expenditure must inevitably place at risk the UK's independent capability in a complete range of defence equipment. Signals have already emerged. To ensure that defence does not pre-empt an excessive share of the nation's scarce technological resources, MoD aims to achieve a gradual and continuing reduction in the real level of defence R & D over the period 1988–98. Instead, MoD will place greater emphasis on international collaboration and off-the-shelf procurement (*Cmnd 601, 1989*, p. 7). Defence contractors can respond by seeking collaborative business, by increasing exports of military equipment or by entering civil markets.

Within the UK defence market, companies vary in specialism and size. Some specialise by product group or Service. For example, Westland specialises in helicopters which it supplies to all three Services; and in 1986, MoD provided almost 60 per cent of the company's business (ACOST 1989). Others specialise in supplying equipment to one Service such as submarines or warships to the Navy (*eg* Vickers Shipbuilding; Yarrow) or land equipment and tanks for the Army (*eg* Vickers plc). Recently, though, the search for growth and profitable opportunities in a defence market which has been budget-constrained has resulted in mergers and take-overs within the UK and the EC. Examples include the British Aerospace acquisition of Royal Ordnance and the GEC–Siemens take-over of Plessey. The result has been larger defence contractors some of which are diversified groups with a range of military and civil activities. For example, GEC acquired Yarrow Shipbuilders in 1985 and Plessey in 1989 so that it now manufactures a wide range of defence equipment (*eg* avionics, radar, communications systems, torpedoes, warships) together with major civil interests in power systems, telecommunications, consumer goods, office equipment, printing and medical equipment. In 1988, GEC employed some 147,000 people. Similarly, British Aerospace manufactures military and civil aircraft, missiles, ordnance equipment and motor vehicles, with some of these activities resulting from the acquisition of Royal Ordnance in 1987 and the Rover Group in 1988. Total employment for British Aerospace in 1988 exceeded 131,000 people.

TABLE 8.2. *Major UK Defence Contractors*

Contractors paid £250m or more by MoD	
British Aerospace (Aircraft, Dynamics, Royal Ordnance, Rover) The General Electric Company (including Yarrow and Plessey) Rolls-Royce Vickers Shipbuilding and Engineering	
Contractors paid £100–250m by MoD	
Boeing Aerospace	Hunting
Devenport Management	Racal Electronics
Ferranti	Thorn EMI
FKI Babcock	Vickers plc
GKN	Westland

Note: Based on 1988–89.
Source: *Cmnd 1022-II, 1990.*

In addition to substantial restructuring, there have also been significant changes in ownership. During the 1980s, the major state-owned defence firms were privatised. These included British Aerospace, Rolls-Royce, Shorts, Royal Ordnance, the warship builders, and the introduction of private commercial management into the Royal Dockyards. The belief is that, *ceteris paribus*, a change from public to private ownership will improve enterprise performance as reflected in productivity, exports, innovation and, ultimately, profitability. Critics of privatisation doubt that an ownership change alone will improve performance. They raise doubts about the capital market as an efficient policing mechanism and point to the possibility of manager-controlled firms pursuing objectives other than maximum profits (*eg* luxury offices, company cars). It is also stressed that an improvement in performance requires competition and rivalry in product markets, otherwise there are dangers of a private monopoly replacing a public monopoly. Doubts about the success of privatisation in defence markets are reinforced where there are restrictions on take-overs, including foreign ownership, where profits are regulated and where firms believe that they can rely upon a guaranteed and protected domestic market (Dunsire et al., 1988).

Any analysis of UK defence contractors is complicated by data problems. Most defence firms have military and civil business involving UK and overseas customers. Generally, company reports and accounts only provide information on broad aggregates such as annual total sales, numbers employed and company profitability, with no breakdown of such data by major military and civil product groups for domestic and overseas customers. British Aerospace is an example of a company which provides more detailed data, as shown in Table 8.3. In 1988, defence business accounted for some 46 per cent of employment, 53 per cent of sales (including 60 per cent overseas) and contributed most of the profits. Even so, some of the British Aerospace figures for military product groups do not separate MoD from overseas customers.

TABLE 8.3. *British Aerospace 1988*

	Sales (£m)			Trading Profit (£m)	Employment
	UK	Overseas	Total		
Military aircraft and support systems	412	1,247	1,659	195	28,800
Weapons and electronic systems	817	524	1,341	176	32,000
Commercial aircraft	160	758	918	(49)	23,500
Motor vehicles	735	444	1,179	35	42,300
Property development and construction	5	378	383	17	3,800
Space systems	25	108	133	12	1,900
Other enterprises	4	22	26	1	1,300
Company funded product development				(76)	
TOTAL	2,158	3,481	5,639	311	133,600

Source: BAe, 1988.

Further information on companies in the UK defence electronics market is available from the Monopolies and Mergers Commission Report on the take-over bid for Plessey from GEC and Siemens (*Cmnd 676, 1989*). This Report provides both useful market data and raises interesting questions about the implications of mergers for competition policy. Data on the GEC and Plessey shares of UK defence sales in avionics, underwater systems, radar and communications systems are

TABLE 8.4. *GEC, Plessey and the UK Defence Electronics Market*

	Annual sales (£m):			GEC – Plessey share of UK sales (%)
	GEC	Plessey	Total MoD	
Avionics	130	20	430	35
Underwater systems	190	90	300	93
Radar	190	50	330	73
Radio and communications	65	150	300	72

Note: Sales figures are annual averages over the period 1983–88.
Source: *Cmnd 676, 1989.*

shown in *Table 8.4.* UK competition policy defines a monopoly where one firm supplies 25 per cent or more of the market. On this basis, the merger of GEC and Plessey created or increased a monopoly situation in all four product markets. Indeed, the aggregate share figures conceal wide variations in different sub-markets. For example, within the underwater systems group, GEC accounted for 99 per cent of the UK torpedo market, whilst Plessey accounted for 94 per cent of mine-hunting equipment. Similarly, GEC had a 100 per cent market share for army and naval tracking radar and Plessey supplied 71 per cent of strategic radio for the Army. Not surprisingly, the 1988–89 GEC–Siemens bid for Plessey was criticised for its adverse effects on competition. In 1986, the Monopolies and Mergers Commission reported on a previous bid for Plessey by GEC only. It concluded that the merger would be against the public interest mainly because of its adverse effects on competition in the UK defence electronics market, leading to increased costs for MoD and a reduced technical innovative choice. However, in its 1989 Report, the Monopolies and Mergers Commission felt that the involvement of Siemens and other changes resulted in a completely different situation. Nonetheless, the Commission continued to be concerned about the adverse effects of the merger on competition in parts of the UK defence electronics market, and about the national security implications from the presence of a foreign-owned company (Siemens) in the UK defence industrial base. It concluded that with appropriate undertakings by GEC and Siemens, the adverse effects of the merger would be remedied or prevented (*Cmnd 676, 1989*). There are other examples of monopoly (Faltas, 1986).

Within the UK defence market, the sectors involving high technology and costly equipment are dominated by domestic monopolies. These comprise aircraft and missiles (British Aerospace), aero-engines (Rolls-Royce), helicopters (Westland), ordnance and small arms (Royal Ordnance now owned by British Aerospace), tanks (Vickers), submarines (Vickers Shipbuilding and Engineering Ltd) and torpedoes (GEC: see *Table 8.2*). Economists associate monopoly with high prices, output restrictions, inefficiency, a lack of dynamism and continued excessive profits. In principle, MoD could make such monopolies contestable by inviting foreign firms to bid for UK defence contracts. However, proposals to introduce more foreign competition into the UK market will encounter massive opposition from defence contractors and other groups likely to lose from such a policy. Potential job losses especially in high unemployment areas and marginal constituencies will be used to persuade vote-sensitive governments to buy British (Chapter 5).

Defence industry employment

Jobs are often claimed to be one of the benefits of UK defence spending. In addition, to assess the likely employment impact of possible future cuts in defence budgets, it is necessary to know the number of jobs involved and which regions are especially dependent on equipment spending. In 1988, MoD defence expenditure supported 480,000 jobs, with exports resulting in a further 150,000 jobs. Interestingly, the long-run trend has been downwards from a total of 740,000 jobs in 1980–81 to 630,000 in 1988. Within this total it is noticeable that, despite a period of growth in real defence spending, MoD-created jobs have declined substantially. This might be due to general efficiency improvements and labour-saving technical progress. Also, after 1983–84, MoD introduced a new competitive procurement policy and efficiency programme which might be a further explanation of the declining employment, particularly the 'shake-out' between 1985 and 1987 (*Table 8.5*).

Over 50 per cent of direct industrial jobs dependent on MoD equipment expenditure are located in the prosperous south of England (south-east and south-west), and a further 24 per cent in the north. Northern Ireland, Scotland and Wales, which traditionally are high unemployment areas qualifying for regional aid, account for a mere 12 per cent of these jobs. Also, some towns and areas are heavily dependent on defence industries. Examples include Barrow (Trident), Bristol, Brough and Preston (British Aerospace), Liverpool (Cammell Laird), Tyneside (Swan Hunter) and Yeovil (Westland). While employment is important to society, ultimately the performance of the UK defence industries will be reflected in whether the equipment supplied to the armed forces represents good value for money.

Competition and value for money

Before 1983, MoD equipment procurement policy was characterised by support for UK industry ('buy British'), non-competitive cost-plus or cost-based contracts, with firms bearing none of the risks of the project. Examples of industrial inefficiency and project failures are readily available. The Nimrod AEW aircraft was cancelled with cost escalation

TABLE 8.5. *Employment in UK Defence Industries*

	1978–79	1980–81	1985–86	(000s) 1986–87
Due to MoD equipment expenditure				
direct	220	230	200	170
indirect	180	190	160	140
Due to MoD non-equipment expenditure				
direct	100	100	85	85
indirect	80	80	70	70
Total due to MoD expenditure	580	600	515	465
Due to exports				
direct	70	75	60	55
indirect	60	65	50	45
Aggregate totals	710	740	625	565
UK defence expenditure:				
constant 1987–88 prices (£m)	15,413	16,593	19,570	19,456

Direct employment due to MoD equipment expenditure 1986–87

	000s	(%)
North	16	9
Yorks and Humberside	4	2
North West	21	12
East Midlands	9	5
West Midlands	7	4
East Anglia	3	2
South West	21	12
South East	70	40
England	151	87
Scotland	17	10
Wales	2	1
N. Ireland	4	2
UK	174	100

Source: Cmnd 657-II, 1989.

exceeding 2.0 and the aircraft unlikely to achieve its required performance until the mid-1990s compared with an original in-service date of 1982 (Chapter 6, *Table 6.3*). In 1988, the British Aerospace Alarm missile was some £260 million over budget and several years behind schedule. Although the RAF preferred the American Harm missile, the British Alarm was chosen because of the desire to foster a strong home-based missile technology, the judgement that Alarm had more scope for development and the fact that it would support more jobs in the UK aerospace industry (*HCP 431, 1988*). A 1985 study of warships concluded that 'in terms of the prices paid for warships, the evidence on warship builders' productivity, the out-turn on MoD contracts and the profits made by warship builders in the past suggest that the MoD have not always received good value for money' (*HCP 423, 1985*, p. 5). During the 1985–86 debate on the future of the Westland helicopter company it was claimed that the European helicopter industry was characterised by 'over-production, over-manning, and lack of profitability' and that Westland also wished to enter the commercial helicopter market to have the discipline of making it more 'customer-conscious and more cost-conscious' (*HCP 169, 1986*, Q484, Q576). Another example is the GEC Foxhunter radar for the RAF Tornado F-2 aircraft which was over two years late on initial delivery and some four years late on expected final delivery (*HCP 371, 1988*). Finally, an MoD study found cost escalation in real terms of almost 70 per cent from initial estimates and some 30 per cent after the start of full development (MoD 1988).

In 1983, MoD introduced a new competitive procurement policy designed to change the traditional dependency relationship in which defence business was regarded as 'lucrative, not very competitive and a cosy relationship' (*HCP 431, 1988*, pp. vi, xxvi). Accordingly, MoD has placed emphasis on being a more demanding customer introducing and extending competition, encouraging new entrants (*eg* small firms), resorting to a greater use of firm or fixed price and incentive contracts rather than cost-plus contracting, and shifting risks from MoD to industry. As part of this new commercial and competitive policy, MoD has moved away from specifying its requirements for equipment in considerable detail. Instead, requirements are defined in broad terms, leaving the contractor to determine how best to meet the criteria (Cardinal Points Specification). As a result, MoD is now more willing to consider the incremental costs of equipment requirements (*HCP 104, 1987*, p. xii). The major features and some examples of the results of the new competition policy are shown in *Table 8.6*. The policy is also likely to have contributed to improved export performance.

MoD's competition policy appears to have been successful in terms of improving the efficiency of UK defence contractors and achieving cost

TABLE 8.6. *MoDs Competition Policy*

Main Features	
(i) Competition – at development stage ⎫ – at production stage ⎬ – at sub-contract level ⎬ – from foreign firms ⎭	resembling economists models of market forces, rivalry and contestable markets
(ii) Competitively-determined firm or fixed price contracts	
(iii) Incentive contracts with maximum price for development work	
(iv) Cardinal Points Specification	

Results: examples of cost savings from competition	
Harrier GR5 airframe fatigue testing	70%
Magnetic Anomaly Detection System	65%
Tucano trainer aircraft simulator	40%
Air defence simulator	40%
S10 respirator	40%
Tank thermal imaging systems	20%
Four minehunters	10%

Source: *Cmnd 344 1988*.

savings for the armed forces. Nonetheless, the Ministry's competition policy is faced with some major problems:

(i) Difficulties arise in obtaining reliable estimates of the savings from competition. In the absence of repeat orders for identical items, estimates of savings will depend on the accuracy of MoD's cost-estimating relationships: large savings may reflect bad estimating!

(ii) The meaning of competition and the probability of bankruptcy. For MoD, what constitutes competition? The Ministry does not provide evidence on the number of firms which bid for contracts, the opportunities for new entrants, or the extent of entry and exit from selected lists. Further opportunities for savings might be available if MoD were more willing to allow firms to offer a range of alternative solutions, the aim being to obtain *competitively-determined* cost information on increments of performance. Of course, within a competitive system some firms make mistakes and the ultimate sanction on poor performance is bankruptcy. However, MoD accepts a major constraint on its competition policy: 'the Ministry were not in the business of putting . . . companies out of existence' (*HCP 104, 1987*, p. vii). In addition, vote-sensitive governments might be unwilling to allow a major contractor to go out of business, particularly if it is located in a marginal constituency.

(iii) The competitive process can be affected through business appointments of staff from MoD and the armed forces. The possibility arises that public servants might be influenced in their decisions by the prospect of employment in industry and there are fears of an 'undesirable cosiness between Crown servants and the industries with which they deal' (*HCP 392, 1988*, p. v). Between 1975 and 1986, nearly two-thirds of all applications from MoD civil servants and from the armed forces to take up outside appointments were for posts with defence contractors, particularly in the electrical, electronics and engineering sectors (*HCP 392, 1988*, p. xii).

(iv) In the long run, competitive pressures might lead to exits from the UK defence industry and the creation of domestic monopolies, necessitating a greater willingness to invite foreign firms to bid for MoD contracts. There are also worries that over time, firms will respond to competitive pressures by shifting some of their costs to their non-competitive defence contracts (*HCP 431, 1988*).

(v) Domestic monopolies dominate the high technology and costly equipment programmes. For example, between 1983 and 1988, GEC's proportion of non-competitive MoD contracts exceeded the national average, as shown in *Table 8.7*. Interestingly, many of the

TABLE 8.7. *MoD Contracts for GEC*

	Percentage of MoD contracts by value (%):									
	1983-84		1984-85		1985-86		1986-87		1987-88	
	GEC	Total MoD	GEC	Total MoD	GEC	Total MoD	GEC	Total MoD	GEC	Total MoD
Competition	7	22	2	26	30	38	27	38	7	30
Market forces	20	16	19	19	21	25	18	14	17	19
Non-competitive	73	62	79	55	49	37	55	48	76	51
Total value (£m)	525	8,580	1,462	8,217	724	7,523	865	9,309	548	6,541

Source: *Cmnd 676, 1989.*

examples of cost savings from competition refer to relatively small systems (*eg* minehunters, sonars, respirators; *Table 8.6*). MoD has now recognised the domestic monopoly problem and in 1988 declared a greater willingness to purchase equipment from overseas sources where they are likely to offer 'greater value for money'. The threat of foreign competition is likely to increase the contestability of those UK defence sectors dominated by domestic monopolies. There are, though, potential conflicts between competition policy leading to foreign purchases and support for the UK defence industrial base with its apparent benefits in terms of security of supply, jobs, technology and the balance of payments. Indeed, MoD has admitted that there are security, physical and political constraints on encouraging overseas competition and that 'it would be a long process before the market in defence equipment became as open as in other areas' (*Cmnd 676, 1989*, p. 70). All of which raises questions about the meaning of the defence industrial base, who needs it and why?

What is the UK defence industrial base?

As became apparent during the 1986 debate on the Westland helicopter company, there are few clear public policy statements on the meaning of the defence industrial base. The 1984 *Statement on the Defence Estimates* referred to the UK's needing a 'strong indigenous defence-industrial base, as was illustrated vividly during the Falklands crisis' (*Cmnd 9227-I, 1984*, p. 17). But what is meant by a 'strong indigenous defence industrial base'; why is such a base required and by whom; what is its minimum size and industrial composition (*ie* which industries); and what are the costs of supporting such a base? Similarly, the Defence Committee's 1986 Report on Westland referred to 'those industrial assets which provide key elements of military power and national security and ... thus demand special consideration by government' (*HCP 518, 1986*, p. xxxvii).

However, these 'essential, key national assets' have rarely been specified. Indeed, over the single issue of Westland, differences of view emerged even between members of the same government!

In evidence on Westland given to the Parliamentary Defence Committee in 1986, Michael Heseltine, then Defence Secretary, believed that it was essential that the UK had a helicopter industry and he also referred to the need for a capability in air and sea platforms. In contrast, Leon Brittan, then Trade and Industry Secretary, felt that the defence interest was satisfied so long as helicopter spares could be obtained. Norman Lamont, as Minister of State for Defence Procurement, admitted that the Ministry did not have a series of contingency plans for each of its suppliers 'getting into trouble'; and the Prime Minister's view on Westland was that there was no defence interest that called for a rescue operation by the public sector (*HCP 518, 1986*, pp. xi–xii). The Westland affair also revealed a further aspect of the debate, namely the desire to create a European defence industrial base. If there is a lack of clarity about a UK defence industrial base, the potential confusions are even greater at the European level where nationalism is likely to dominate policy decisions.

There are at least three possible definitions of the defence industrial base:

(i) *It could be defined as all UK firms receiving Ministry of Defence contracts.* This includes companies supplying complex equipment such as Trident submarines and Tornado aircraft as well as firms providing boots, furniture, buildings, fuel, food and torch batteries (Taylor and Hayward, 1989). However, this list does not include merchant shipping, or civilian air and land transport and communications, all of which are often deemed vital for defence needs. Nor does it include exporters of military equipment which also contribute to a UK-based defence capability. Nevertheless, a broad definition of the defence industrial base will be advocated by those interest groups of politicians, bureaucrats, contractors, unions and professional associations likely to benefit from such an approach.

(ii) *It could be defined as a minimum core of key national assets*, which is considerably smaller than the complete range of UK defence contractors. Examples might include the need to maintain capabilities in high technology equipment such as air and nuclear systems. Often these are domestic monopolies. In addition, even if the key national assets can be defined, there are still questions as to whether these should be confined to a limited research and development capability or whether a production capability is also essential.

(iii) *A free market view* could be taken, in which the UK defence industrial base would be determined by market forces, and would comprise those activities in which the UK has a comparative advantage internationally, together with its general industrial capacity. Such a defence industry would be considerably smaller than the current size, especially for equipment which is supplied by domestic monopolies. This definition recognises the need for an efficient procurement policy which economises on costly equipment. It is also possible that future wars might be of short duration in which the greatest contribution from industry might consist of its 'surge capacity' in the form of its flexibility, adaptability and responsiveness to emergency defence needs. If necessary, this free market approach could be modified to allow for an MoD interest in preserving key national assets. MoD might be required to specify a premium showing its maximum willingness to pay for some clearly-defined strategic assets. For example, following an international competition, MoD contracts might be awarded to the lowest fixed price bidder, after allowing for a maximum premium or tariff to favour a limited group of essential UK suppliers. Such a procedure would be a departure from a blank-cheque approach where MoD effectively supports key assets regardless of their cost. This competition plus premium policy would identify the true costs of supporting key national assets. It would also require the armed forces to think more carefully about the military benefits of a defence industrial base. From a fixed budget, how much extra are the Services willing to pay for a domestic source of supply? More spent on buying British means less available for other items in the defence budget (Hooper, 1989).

By the late 1980s, MoD's competition policy meant that, in principle, it was somewhat more willing to allow the defence industrial base to be determined by market forces. MoD aims

> to buy British whenever it is sensible, economic and consistent with our international obligations to do so, and thereby foster a strong defence industry competing successfully in world markets as well as our own. But we buy overseas when the advantages of cost, timescale and performance outweigh the long-term benefits of procuring the British alternative (MoD 1987, p. 3).

These developments have been reinforced by MoD's decision gradually to reduce spending on government-funded defence research and development (*Cmnd 675, 1989*). Here, it is also worth mentioning a military view which suggests that, unless a large peacetime investment were to be made in raw materials, part-manufactured items and dormant production lines,

> it is difficult to imagine how, with increasingly complex technology implying long lead-times, industrial production could significantly benefit the war effort. The most that can be expected of industry, therefore, would be a short-term acceleration of output of items already on

production or overhaul lines, plus increased production of an unsophisticated stores (Alli-stone, 1986, p. 86).

The complete opposite to a free market approach is a 'Fortress UK' policy whereby the UK would have the capacity to produce all the defence equipment needed to protect itself. The enormous costs of such a policy have ruled it out for the UK (and even for the USA). Nonetheless, supporters of a 'strong defence industrial base' (whatever this means?) advocate substantial intervention by MoD to retain a range of domestic capabilities for armaments production. It is claimed that such support provides invaluable military and economic benefits to the UK. What are these benefits and what has to be sacrificed to achieve them?

The benefits and costs of a defence industrial base

Emphasis is often given to the military and strategic benefits of a defence industrial base. These take the form of independence, security of supply and responsiveness in emergencies and war, the ability to be an informed buyer, together with the need to provide equipment specially designed for the requirements of national forces. In addition, there are claimed to be wider economic benefits from awarding defence contracts to British industry. Defence industries are presented as high technology, high value-added and labour-intensive. They contribute to jobs, the balance of payments and innovation, and form one of the more successful parts of the 'vital manufacturing fabric of our economy'. An opposing view suggests that defence claims scarce, high technology resources needed by British industry, so reducing both the level and efficiency of industrial investment and adversely affecting the economy's competitiveness and growth rate (Kaldor, Sharp and Walker, 1986).

Much of the debate about the defence industries is dominated by special pleading, myths and nationalism, and economists wishing to evaluate the arguments have to consider their underlying economic logic and the available empirical evidence. Each argument needs to be critically evaluated. For example, national independence is both costly and an illusion when the UK is involved in collaboration, technology transfers, imports of specialised components and materials, and relies upon the USA for its so-called independent nuclear deterrent (Hartley, Hussain and Smith, 1987). Also it has to be recognised that there are alternative and often better ways of achieving national economic benefits in the form of jobs, technology and exports. For example, more jobs might be created if defence spending were reallocated to education, health, housing and roads. Or, where overseas equipment is acquired by MoD, UK jobs might be protected through an offset agreement as occurred with the purchase of Boeing Chinook helicopters and AWACs aircraft.

The decision to buy Boeing AWACS rather than the British Nimrod

AEW aircraft involved a commitment by Boeing to place offset work with UK companies worth 130 per cent of the value of the AWACS purchase price, equivalent to over $1.5 billion (1987 prices: *HCP 286, 1989*). Boeing estimated that the AWACS offset agreement would create some 4,500 new jobs in the UK in the first year and 40,000 new jobs over five years (*ie* an annual average of 8,000 jobs over five years). Indeed, when the decision was announced in 1986, MoD estimated that the job losses resulting from the cancellation of Nimrod would be equalled if not exceeded by job gains in firms all over the country resulting from the Boeing offset proposals (*HCP 286, 1986*, p. xv). There are, though, problems with offset agreements. Difficulties arise in ensuring that work is placed with UK defence industry rather than industry in general; that the work is high technology; and that offsets represent new work rather than work which would have come to the UK anyway (*HCP 286, 1989*).

Questions also arise as to whether the wider economic benefits from a defence industrial base should be the concern of the Ministry of Defence or the responsibility of other government departments. Such a reallocation of responsibilities would require the Ministry of Defence and the armed forces to define the assets which they regard as vital to the UK's security, to identify the military benefits of their preferred defence industrial base and their willingness to pay for these benefits. As a result, the armed forces would have to consider more carefully equipment choices and trade-offs. Buying British means that equipment is produced locally or tailor-made to national requirements but, if it is more expensive and involves delays in delivery, the services will have to protect the UK with fewer new weapons and older equipment. However, there is always the possibility that without fixed budgets and clearly-specified output targets, the armed forces will prefer to buy British simply because it might offer them greater opportunities for gold-plating and for obtaining equipment which satisfies the users rather than protecting the UK.

The military and economic benefits of a UK defence industrial base are not free gifts. Some UK equipment is more expensive and involves delays in delivery. Examples have included the torpedo programme, the cancellation of the Nimrod AEW and the considerable delays with the Alarm missile (*HCP 431, 1988*). The decision to incorporate a British engine and avionics into the UK buy of Phantom aircraft raised unit costs by at least 23–43 per cent and possibly by as much as 100 per cent compared with buying the US model off-the-shelf (Hartley, 1985, p. 180; Healey, 1989, p. 272). In contrast, the purchase of the Hercules transport aircraft off-the-shelf from the USA meant that it cost only one-third of the price of the British alternative and entered service at least four years earlier (Healey, 1989, p. 272). The costs of buying British were expressed most dramatically by Mr Heseltine in 1986 when he stated that '. . . there is practically nothing you cannot buy cheaper from the United States of

America because they have huge production runs, huge research programmes, funded by the taxpayer . . .' (*HCP 518, 1986*, p. xli). This also
raises the more general question of whether UK defence industries are
efficient and how efficiency might be measured.

Assessing efficiency

In analysing any industry, economists are centrally concerned with its
efficiency. Efficiency has two related aspects. First, technical or X-
efficiency which involves the lowest-cost method of supplying a given
quantity and quality of output. Second, allocative efficiency which is
concerned with the choice of the most appropriate output in both its
quantity and quality aspects. This requires an assessment of whether the
current output in both quantity and quality is worthwhile and whether
small changes in either direction might be even more worthwhile. What
are the costs and benefits of a slightly smaller or slightly larger UK
defence industrial base?

Industrial economists assess efficiency by applying a structure-
conduct-performance framework. With this approach the performance of
an industry depends on its structure. Two polar market situations are
contrasted, namely, perfect competition and monopoly. In this static
model, perfect competition produces technical and allocative efficiency.
Perfect competition is characterised by large numbers of relatively small
firms and free entry into the industry. Against the benchmark of perfect
competition, monopoly is regarded as undesirable since it results in
higher prices, a lower output and an inefficient allocation and use of
resources. However, monopolies and mergers might be socially acceptable (in the public interest) if they provide compensating benefits in the
form of technical progress and the economies of large-scale operations.
Applying this approach requires that the efficiency of the UK's defence
industries be measured on the basis of their structure, conduct and performance, using the following indicators:

(i) *Structural features* as reflected in:
  (a) *Concentration ratios* which measure the proportion of an
      industry's output produced by the largest firm or the top 3–5
      firms. But simple concentration ratios need modifying to allow
      for MoD's countervailing buying power and for the ease or
      difficulty of entry into the industry.
  (b) *Entry conditions.* Are there barriers to entry such as govern-
      ment preferential purchasing or tariffs and import controls
      preventing new domestic and foreign rivals bidding for UK
      defence contracts?
  (c) *Economies of scale.* Efficiency will be affected by the extent to

which defence firms are exploiting all the available economies of scale, including learning economies. For some industries, the UK market is only able to support one or a few firms able to exploit most of the worthwhile scale economies. In such cases, the price of efficient scale might be monopoly or oligopoly.

(ii) *The conduct of firms* as reflected in advertising, sales promotion, product differentiation and research and development, all of which reflect non-price competition.

(iii) *Performance* as reflected in profitability (are profits 'excessive'?), organisational slack or X-inefficiency, technical progress and, ultimately, economic efficiency. In principle, economic efficiency can be measured by comparing the relationship between prices and marginal costs or the costs of producing an extra unit of output. On this basis, an efficient outcome arises where prices equal marginal costs, assuming such costs are at their lowest attainable levels: an outcome achieved under perfect competition.

The structure-conduct-performance approach is useful in identifying some of the major determinants of efficiency in UK defence industries. Two factors are important. First, the extent of rivalry (contestability and competition); and second, the scale of output which determines the extent to which UK defence firms are exploiting learning and scale economies (Chapter 7).

The structure-performance framework also provides a basis for developing a set of performance indicators for assessing the efficiency of defence industries. Here, it has to be recognised that there is no single, unique indicator. Instead, a variety of indicators can be formulated, using hard and soft data, many of which will be suggestive and indicative rather than conclusive. Possible performance indicators for defence industries in the UK and elsewhere include:

(i) *Cost-benefit analysis* which seeks to identify and quantify the costs and benefits of a larger or smaller UK defence industrial base.

(ii) *Concentration ratios*: are defence industries monopolistic or competitive: Domestic monopolies exist for a number of UK defence industries (*eg* aerospace, nuclear-powered submarines, ordnance, tanks, torpedoes).

(iii) *Profitability* measured by the rate of return on capital. Government regulation of defence profits makes it difficult to use profitability as a performance indicator. However, comparisons might be made between the profitability of military and civil business, especially within the same firm (Chapter 6, *Table 6.2*).

(iv) *Any government protection for UK defence industries* as measured by government preferential purchasing, subsidies, tariff protection and guaranteed profits. Are UK defence industries more heavily protected compared with the rest of the economy (*eg* agriculture)?

(v) *International competitiveness*, measured by exports, imports and shares of home and world markets. Improvements in international competitiveness will be reflected in a rising share of both home market sales and world exports.

(vi) *The extent of competition for defence contracts and the type of contracts.* Efficiency is likely where there is rivalry for contracts and where the successful bidder is awarded a competitively-determined fixed price contract. It follows that inefficiency is likely the smaller the number of firms bidding for a contract, and where the winner is awarded a cost-plus contract. Since 1983, MoD's competition policy has resulted in efficiency improvements reflected in cost savings varying from 10–70 per cent (*Table 8.6*).

(vii) *Labour productivity and labour hoarding.* Comparisons of labour productivity can be undertaken between different defence firms within the UK; between defence and civil industries; and between defence and civil firms in different countries. Problems arise in ensuring that labour productivity is measured on a standardised basis (value-added if possible); that output and the product mix is standardised; that allowance is made for other factor inputs; and further difficulties arise in using official exchange rates for international comparisons. Labour hoarding might also be used as a supporting indicator of efficiency or the lack of it. On this view, the employment behaviour of defence contractors is expected to differ from that of commercial firms operating in civil markets (Chapter 6).

(viii) *Economies of scale and learning economies.* Ideally, evidence is needed on the minimum efficient scale (*mes*) of operations for various types of defence equipment; the relationship between *mes* and the size of the home market; and the cost implications of operating below *mes* (Chapter 7).

(ix) *Time scales for development and production.* The time required from the start of development work to first deliveries to the armed forces is a further crude indicator of efficiency. Comparisons need to be made between different projects within a nation and between different countries. For instance, on military aircraft projects, typical US development time scales might be some two years shorter than for the UK (Elstub, 1969; Hartley, 1972). However, in the absence of cost data, such evidence is inconclusive as an efficiency indicator.

(x) *Performance against contact specification.* This requires evidence on slippages in cost, time and in equipment performance. The data need to be compared against other national projects of similar complexity and with foreign experience. Nor does it follow that all slippages, escalation and 'gold-plating' are undesirable (Chapter 6).

(xi) *Some general indicators at the economy level.* Two possibilities are:
  (a) To compare nations with and without a defence industry and their macro-economic performance measured by unemployment, inflation, international competitiveness, and growth rates (Chapter 4; Kaldor *et al.*, 1986).
  (b) To assess the extent of civil spin-off from defence R & D. Comparisons can be made between different defence companies and between the UK and other nations. The whole area of defence R & D and spin-off has attracted considerable controversy in the UK and merits further attention.

Defence R & D and spin-off

Supporters of a strong UK defence industrial base often stress its economic benefits in promoting high technology activities and in providing valuable spin-off to the civilian economy. However, defence R & D employs scarce resources which have alternative uses. It is often asserted that defence R & D deprives the civil sector of scarce scientific resources, that the industries and firms dependent on defence work perform badly in international markets and that there is too little spin-off from defence R & D to the rest of the economy (ACOST 1989). Similar worries have been expressed by the UK government which '. . . shares the underlying concern of those who fear that necessary investment in defence R & D may crowd out valuable investment in the civil sector . . .'; and that '. . . it would be regrettable if defence work became such an irresistible magnet for the manpower available that industry's ability to compete in the international market for civil high technology products became seriously impaired' (*Cmnd 101-I, 1987*, p. 48).

To economists, the controversy over defence R & D raises analytical and empirical questions which can be summarised as follows:
  (i) Does defence R & D 'crowd-out' civil R & D? Why and what is the evidence?
  (ii) Has the UK's commitment to defence R & D enhanced or impaired its international competitiveness – *eg* are defence-intensive industries and companies experiencing a loss of market share, especially in high technology sectors (*eg* aerospace, electronics)?
  (iii) Does the UK fully exploit the possible spin-off from defence R & D? If not, why are markets failing?
  (iv) If defence R & D has been detrimental to the UK economy, do

any such adverse effects reflect some unique and distinctive features of military markets? For example, are UK industries and companies with a large proportion of their R & D funded by MoD more or less profitable than those without a significant defence business; and does profitability affect a firm's innovativeness? Or, is it the case that defence R & D and defence contracts (*eg* cost-plus) have, in the past, tended to reduce a firm's innovative drive? Has the situation changed following MoD's competitive procurement policy?

These are all issues which have emerged in popular debates about defence R & D. Such issues need to be subjected to rigorous and independent scrutiny, critical evaluation and empirical testing. Their analytical basis needs to be explored, predictions need to be derived and formulated into testable hypotheses, and the hypotheses need to be tested.

Central to the debate is the often-asserted proposition that the level and share of resources devoted to defence R & D has a detrimental effect on the performance of the UK economy, particularly on growth and international competitiveness. The analytical basis of the proposition needs to be explored. In principle, there are three related and possible links between defence R & D and economic performance:

(a) *The operation of R & D markets.* Beliefs about 'too much' defence R & D and 'too little' spin-off need to start from a general understanding of how R & D markets work and how well they work (*ie* market failure). R & D can be considered as a market for information and knowledge. This approach shows the importance of property rights (ownership) which cannot be ignored in debates about spin-off. It also shows that buyers and sellers of knowledge need information on what is available, where to find it, and what is demanded, all at a set of prices. R & D is undertaken in a variety of organisations in different sectors and industries organised in different ways and pursuing various objectives. Failure to transfer information at reasonable cost between groups (spin-off), may reduce the productivity of the national R & D effort. However, information is not a 'free good', floating throughout the economy and potential users need to know what is available and how profitable its use is likely to be. The transfer of R & D results between military and civil sectors is usually emphasised, but little evidence exists on transfer within the civil sector between one use and another (*eg* is the civil sector better at spin-off?).

(b) *Characteristics of the defence market.* It is believed that the UK defence market dominated by the MoD does not make the best use of R & D resources in the same way as other markets (but how well do these other civil R & D markets work?). This may reflect the monopsonistic nature of the market, the traditional lack of competition, the traditional support for UK defence firms and the past use of cost-plus contracts. The defence market environment might have encouraged companies to pursue non-profit objectives such as the acquisition and retention of R & D resources, particularly manpower. Also, defence work might create a set of attitudes towards R & D which are appropriate for military requirements and which permeate other sectors where such attitudes might be less appropriate and less marketable (a culture of dependency rather than enterprise). Recently, though, MoD has introduced new policy initiatives which could improve the operation of defence R & D markets. First, MoD now pursues a competitive procurement policy with a greater use of competitively-determined fixed price contracts. Second, Defence Technology Enterprises Ltd has been created to encourage private industry to exploit technology originating in MoD research establishments.

(c) *A more general problem facing the UK economy.* The possibility has to be recognised that concern over the UK's performance in R & D might be part of a wider problem of the UK's general economic performance as reflected in international comparisons of labour productivity, growth and shares of world trade. The problem might not be specific to defence markets and might reflect wider issues affecting the whole economy, such as entrepreneurial attitudes towards risk-taking and competition. Such an approach has at least to be recognised in relation to the alternative assertions implying that all the problems of the UK economy are due to too much spending on defence R & D (Chapter 4).

For the UK, a 1989 study of defence R & D provided two pieces of evidence relevant to the policy debate. First, it found that evidence for the 'crowding out' or pre-emption of civil resources by defence R & D is often anecdotal and inconclusive. There was, though, support for the related argument that UK companies have often concentrated their efforts on obtaining the benefits from R & D in the relatively protected defence market. Second, in relation to spin-off, it was estimated that in 1986–87 less than 20 per cent of government defence R & D was aimed at technologies which have a potential for application in both defence and civil sectors (ACOST 1989, Chapter 3). There are further worries about the spin-off argument. It raises questions about whether the aims of defence R & D are to achieve defence or wider economic objectives; whether direct state support of civil R & D would promote more marketable products; and whether the frequent assertions that spin-off is difficult to measure might reflect the fact that there is nothing to be measured!

Conclusion: imports or domestic equipment?

This concluding section reviews the policy issues surrounding the debate about whether UK governments should intervene to maintain a strong defence industrial base or let the base be determined by market forces. Certainly the market solution would be a logical development of the various Conservative government's policies of the 1980s. Effectively, the choice is between domestic equipment and imports.

The debate about policy towards the defence industrial base often contains a mixture of general propositions about free trade and protectionism and about imports and manufacturing, and *specific propositions* about the implications for UK defence industries and defence policy. This distinction is maintained in this section which presents a review of the opposing arguments and concludes with some questions for policy makers.

I Free Trade Versus Protection: A General Review of the Issues

A The case for free trade and the market approach

(i) Under certain assumptions, a country can maximise its GDP by relying upon comparative advantage with economic agents buying from the cheapest source either domestically or in the world market.

(ii) In a capitalist system, properly functioning competitive markets will determine the allocation of an economy's resources, with governments restricted to the role of correcting major market failures (*eg* monopolies and externalities such as pollution, etc.).

(iii) A different version of the free market approach (Austrian version) recognises that economies are characterised by ignorance, errors and uncertainty and that firms (entrepreneurs) bear the risks of searching for profitable opportunities. It accepts that while private markets can fail to work properly, governments can also fail in their efforts to improve the operation of the economy (Chapter 5).

(iv) In a completely free market, it is assumed that all prices, including wages, always adjust to clear all markets quickly, if not instantly (*ie* markets for goods, labour, land, capital, money and foreign currency). However, some free market economists (*eg* Hayek) accept that actual markets are not characterised by instant adjustment and equilibrium, but instead show continuous change: individuals will change their plans in response to price signals but they will always be uncertain as to whether the changes are permanent.

B An alternative view and the case for protection

(i) Critics of free markets raise doubts about how well they actually work, especially questioning the time required to adjust to changes and their implications for the whole economy. Worries are expressed that a free trade and free market policy will lead to substantial and continuing unemployment, with further fears of a continuous, vicious downward spiral for the economy. Also, it is pointed out that there exist major barriers to international trade and that non-price factors (*eg* delivery, quality, reliability) are often important in determining international competitiveness.

(ii) One view regards output, quantities and unemployment rather than prices and wages as the means by which the economy adjusts to change (Keynesians). With this approach, increased imports have an immediate adverse effect on domestic income, output and employment, and on the balance of payments.

(iii) Protection of domestic producers is often advocated as the solution to rising unemployment due to foreign competition. The immediate result of protection is higher domestic output and more domestic jobs, but at the expense of either consumers or taxpayers (through higher prices or through subsidies to domestic producers). Over time there can be direct retaliation as well as foreign trade multiplier effects causing overseas nations to reduce their imports (*ie* UK exports).

C Some specific issues

(i) *Does the UK pursue free trade with the rest of the world?*
   (a) The UK is an open economy, much more so than other major trading nations such as Japan and the USA; and since 1966, the degree of openness has increased, as evidenced by the rising import share of the UK home market.
   (b) It has been suggested that the greater liberalisation of world trade in the 1960s had beneficial consequences for economic progress generally, although critics might question the direction of causation (Morris, 1985, p. 477). References are sometimes made to the experience of relatively small economies such as Hong Kong, Netherlands and Singapore which have both high incomes and are dependent on international trade. Other studies have estimated that the net benefits of the UK's entry to the EEC represented a gain of no more than one per cent of national income.
   (c) Studies of the job implications of foreign trade suggest that the net effect of trade requires workers to change jobs rather than

to lose them. This reflects job losses due to import penetration being offset by increased exports (although involving different goods).

(ii) *Do we need to worry about imports?*

(a) Imports reflect beneficial trade and exchange based on comparative advantage. Voluntary transactions are only undertaken so long as they are beneficial to both parties (*ie* mutually-advantageous).

(b) A freely floating exchange rate is the mechanism for adjusting to an import and, hence, balance of payments problem. It is also possible that a trade deficit could reflect expenditure financed by borrowing by households and firms which is either temporary or because borrowers have profitable prospects – in which case, a government might not be concerned about the current external deficit. However, imports might become a problem if the UK continually fails to adjust to its changing comparative advantage. In this case, questions arise as to why UK producers are failing to respond to changing demands and opportunities in world markets.

(c) One obvious and immediate response of UK firms to cheaper imports is to reduce prices in the domestic market. This is a short-run response but, to survive in the long-run, domestic manufacturers either have to increase efficiency or seek alternative profitable opportunities in the UK and world markets. For example, the UK cigarette companies have responded to changing demands for cigarettes by seeking new markets for their products and by diversifying into completely different activities.

(iii) *Does it matter if the UK runs down its manufacturing base?*

(a) At the outset, it has to be recognised that markets in the UK and the world are characterised by *change and uncertainty*, so that a nation's comparative advantage is not fixed in perpetuity. Historically, the UK had a comparative advantage in textiles, railway equipment and, more recently, in motor cycles. Changing markets, technologies and competitiveness have resulted in the decline of these traditional sectors in the UK and the emergence of new industries such as aerospace, electronics and information technology.

(b) The broad principle of comparative advantage is a sound basis for a nation's trading policy. The question then arises of identifying the products in which the UK has, or can create, a comparative advantage: such choices can be made by free markets or by governments. Given the failure of UK governments to 'pick the winners' (*eg* British Leyland, Concorde), public policy might concentrate on correcting major market failures and ensuring that markets are contestable. Properly functioning private markets would then be left to take the risks of searching for profitable opportunities and 'finding the winners'.

(c) Mention must be made of the view that other countries such as France and Japan are associated with industrial strategies and economic planning which is claimed to have been successful in 'picking winners'. If so, questions arise as to why UK governments, civil servants and producers have been less successful (*HL 238, 1985*).

II Defence Specific Effects

A A free market procurement policy

(i) For defence equipment the implications of a free market approach to procurement policy are:

(a) In purchasing, governments should act like a normal commercial customer in a competitive market and seek competitive bids with the aim of buying its preferred product from the cheapest supplier (*ie* competition in both price and quality). For defence equipment, this will require genuine rivalry and contestability for UK defence contracts – a policy which would obviously conflict with the traditional support for a strong domestic defence industrial base (*Cmnd 9227-I, 1984*, p. 17).

(b) Much more defence equipment would be imported – *ie* more than the 10 per cent currently imported. The effects are likely to be greatest for those industries which are domestic monopolies, namely, aerospace, helicopters, nuclear-powered submarines, tanks and torpedoes. The former Secretary of State in 1986 stated that '. . . there is practically nothing you cannot buy cheaper from the United States of America . . .' (*HCP 518, 1986*, p. xi); but US equipment might be too simple or too complex for UK requirements.

(c) There is no need to worry about imports – the exchange rate and other prices and wages in the economy will always tend to adjust to clear all markets (*ie* removing all shortages and surpluses). Cost savings through importing more defence equipment would either allow a given defence budget to buy more kit, or would allow greater government civil or private spending. Resources released from UK defence industries would be available for employment elsewhere in the economy.

(d) It must be remembered that the majority of the UK's annual imports are generally free of specific restrictions and subject only to a common external tariff: hence to place on MoD a special burden of saving imports would be inconsistent with general policy.

(e) An example illustrates the case for a free trade and free market approach to defence procurement. Consider a situation where MoD has to choose between imported equipment costing £1 billion and a UK product costing £1.2 billion. If these are minimum supply prices, a decision to import results in a gain to national income (and possibly to the defence budget) of £0.2 billion. In this situation, UK defence producers as the best judges of their future income prospects are unwilling to undercut foreign suppliers because they estimate that £1.2 billion represents the alternative-use value of their resources – *ie* either through undertaking future defence work or doing something else. This example is based on a number of assumptions which need to be recognised by policy-makers:

(i) The behaviour of UK defence contractors depends on their expectations about future business prospects. For example, they might not believe that a UK government will buy from abroad. If so, the government has to decide whether to change their expectations (*eg* by buying from abroad as with AWACS).

(ii) Associated with (i) above, UK prices might reflect domestic monopoly behaviour so that they are not minimum supply prices: hence, the threat of competition (contestable markets) might lead UK firms to cut their prices to match foreign suppliers.

(iii) Firms incur costs in moving into alternative markets: such costs might be lower for large diversified conglomerates with both military and civil activities.

B The implications for the defence industrial base

(i) The defence industrial base provides over 600,000 jobs particularly in the south of England.

(ii) A free market approach to procurement will result in a smaller but more efficient defence industrial base, specialising in those activities where UK defence producers are competitive (it is comparative advantage and not absolute advantage which is crucial). The resulting size and composition of the defence industrial base will depend upon whether and how quickly, UK defence producers can adjust to open competition. In addition, further supply could be provided from the economy's general industrial capacity (*ie* outside the defence industrial base).

(iii) Under a free market approach, competition and market forces would determine the ideal size and composition of the defence industrial base. However, if the military believe that there is a core of industrial capability which is essential for the defence of the UK (and which would not exist under a free market policy), then they need to specify clearly the central core and be required to pay for it from their fixed budgets. Wider considerations such as employment, technology and the balance of payments should be the concern of other Departments and not MoD.

C Importing and the resources released

(i) What are the employment effects at national and local level? The size of any national employment effects will depend upon the scale of imports, how quickly the UK adopts such a policy, and whether any savings are spent on defence or on other activities. Any change in policy is likely to be gradual and incremental and related to major procurement decisions (*eg* a new combat aircraft, or new torpedo or new AEW aircraft). If so, the effects are more likely to be local resulting in less domestic defence orders for particular contractors, some of which might be concentrated in certain regions or towns (*eg* Barrow, Bristol, Yeovil, etc.). However, reliable estimates of the local employment effects depend upon which contractors are likely to be affected, their location, their competitiveness, their response to the loss of future business and the availability of alternative employment in local labour markets. Despite the data limitations, some broad indications of possible effects are as follows:

(a) UK estimates suggest that for every job created by military final demand, 1.5 jobs might be created by an equivalent amount of government civil expenditure.

(b) Defence contractors have considerable experience of adjusting to reduced business as reflected in the adjustment problems following the Second World War, the Korean war and successive Defence Reviews. Such experience shows that the economy is capable of adjusting and adapting to a reduced volume of defence business. More generally, the experience of contraction and subsequent recovery of UK manufacturing production since 1979 is a general example of producers' resilience – although such resilience might require a large 'shock effect' and can be costly. At the local level, and in spite of the prophets of doom and gloom, it is not unknown for towns and local communities to be remarkably resilient and to adjust successfully to the loss of defence orders and factory closures. In addition, there are trade union studies showing the feasibility of conversion for arms producers (Kaldor, *et al*, 1979).

(c) MoD has expressed concern that defence R & D may crowd out valuable R & D in the civil sector. The worry is that defence R & D might attract too many of Britain's scarce scientists and technologists, seriously impairing the economy's ability to compete in world markets for civil high technology products (*Cmnd 101-I 1987*, p. 48).

(ii) Importing and its effects on the exchange rate:

(a) Forecasting exchange rates is notoriously difficult. Indeed, a free market approach regards the exchange rate like any other price as an adjustment mechanism and not a policy objective.

(b) Our tentative estimates indicate that importing up to 20 per cent of defence equipment appears to have little noticeable effect on the exchange rate. With half of procurement met by imports, a fall in the exchange rate of up to one per cent may occur (from an initial rate of £1=$1.60).

(iii) The impact of defence spending on economic performance. The choice between buying British and importing will be partly influenced by the likely impact of defence and civil spending on the UK economy. Some studies show that there is no clear evidence that military expenditure is a burden on the economy; nor does it have a unique relationship with economic performance (*ie* compared with civil spending: Chapter 4).

D Importing: its benefits and problems

(i) Historically, there have been examples where imported equipment has been cheaper, more reliable and available sooner – *eg* aircraft (AEW v. AWACS) and torpedoes. Despite the efficiency improvements following MoD's current competition policy, it is unlikely that the UK has a comparative advantage in the complete range of its existing defence industries. An obvious check on the competitiveness of UK defence firms is to subject them to foreign competition for MoD contracts.

(ii) If the UK defence industrial base is reduced through importing, are there potential problems of monopoly supply? Clearly, there are no costless solutions but in assessing the possible monopoly problem, the following points need to be considered:

(a) Already, a number of UK contractors are domestic monopolies, operating at a small scale and often inefficiently.

Also, if current competition policy eliminates rivals, the long-term result might be more domestic monopolies.

(b) The USA supports more than one supplier of most types of defence equipment. There are also other suppliers elsewhere in the world market (*eg* France, Italy, Japan).

(c) As a large buyer, the UK can exercise countervailing power.

(d) It is not envisaged that the UK deference industrial base will be eliminated completely. The aim of a free market approach would be for the UK to specialise on the basis of its comparative advantage. Indeed, over the years, the UK has chosen to import some costly high technology equipment – *eg* Polaris, Trident, AWACS and has been prepared to accept any monopoly problems!

(e) Most markets are potentially contestable and over time there can be new entrants so inducing efficient behaviour by existing monopolies. This requires a government commitment to creating and maintaining contestable markets.

Questions for policy makers

A free trade and free market approach will lead to an efficient procurement policy and will maximise GDP. If a free trade and free market policy is rejected for *military* reasons, then policy towards the defence industrial base will depend upon MoD's answers to the following questions:

(a) Why is a defence industrial base required and what contribution does it make to the protection of the UK? Buying more expensive British equipment means less protection for the UK.

(b) What is the minimum size and composition of the defence industrial base?

(c) How much are MoD and the armed forces *willing* to pay for the defence industrial base and how much do they *actually* pay?

(d) What are the implications for the defence of the UK if the defence industrial base were, say, 10, 20 or even 50 per cent smaller?

Of course, many of these policy questions are not unique to the UK and have arisen in all nations with a substantial defence industrial base, particularly countries such as France, West Germany, Sweden and the USA. Within Europe, one policy solution has been to favour collaborative projects as a means of maintaining and creating a defence industrial base capable of competing with the United States.

References

ACOST 1989, *Defence R & D: A National Resource* (HMSO, London).
Allistone, M. J., 1986, 'From trip wire to flexible response', *Air Clues*, **40**, 3, RAF Magazine, Ministry of Defence, London, pp. 83–86, March.
BAe, 1988, *British Aerospace*, Annual Report and Accounts, London.
Cmnd 8212, 1981, *Statement on the Defence Estimates 1981* (HMSO, London).
Cmnd 9227, 1984, *Statement on the Defence Estimates 1984* (HMSO, London).
Cmnd 9763, 1986, *Statement on the Defence Estimates 1986* (HMSO, London).
Cmnd 101, 1987, *Statement on the Defence Estimates 1987*, Vol. I (HMSO, London).
Cmnd 344, 1988, *Statement on the Defence Estimates 1988* (HMSO, London).
Cmnd 601, 1989, *The Government's Expenditure Plans 1989–90 to 1991–92*, Ministry of Defence (HMSO, London).
Cmnd 1022-II, 1990, *Statement on the Defence Estimates 1990* (HMSO, London).
Cmnd 676, 1989, *The General Electric Company plc and Siemens AG and The Plessey Company plc*, Monopolies and Mergers Commission, April (HMSO, London).
Dunsire, A., Hartley, K., Parker, D. and Dimitriou, B., 1988, 'Organisational status and performance', *Public Administration*, **66**, 4, pp. 363–388.
Elstub, 1969, *Productivity of the National Aircraft Effort*, Ministry of Technology (HMSO, London).
Faltas, S., 1986, *Arms Markets and Armament Policy* (Martinus Nijhoff, Lancaster).
Hartley, K., 1972, 'Development time scales for British and American military aircraft', *Scottish Journal of Political Economy*, **XIX**, 2, pp. 115–134.
Hartley, K., 1985, 'Defence procurement and industrial policy', in Roper, J. (ed.), *The Future of British Defence Policy* (Gower, London).
Hartley, K., Hussain, F. and Smith, R., 1987, 'The UK defence industrial base', *Political Quarterly*, **58**, 1, pp. 62–72.
Healey, D., 1989, *The Time of My Life* (Michael Joseph, London).
Hooper, N., 1989, 'Defending the defence industrial base', *Economic Affairs*, **10**, 1 October–November, pp. 12–15.
HCP 423, 1985, *Ministry of Defence: Design and Procurement of Warships*, National Audit Office, June (HMSO, London).
HCP 479, 1985, *The Trident Programme*, Defence Committee, July (HMSO, London).
HCP 169 and 518, 1986, *The Defence Implications of the Future of Westland plc*, Defence Committee, July (HMSO, London).
HCP 104, 1987, *Control and Management of the Development of Major Equipment*, Committee of Public Accounts, February (HMSO, London).
HCP 371, 1988, *Annual Statements on Major Defence Projects*, Committee of Public Accounts, March (HMSO, London).
HCP 392, 1988, *Business Appointments*, Defence Committee (HMSO, London).
HCP 431, 1988, *The Procurement of Major Defence Equipment*, Defence Committee, June (HMSO, London).
HCP 286, 1989, *The Working of the AWACS Offset Agreement*, Defence Committee, May (HMSO, London).
HL 238, 1985, Report from Select Committee, *Overseas Trade*, House of Lords, July (HMSO, London).
Kaldor, M. et al., 1979, *Democratic Socialism and the Cost of Defence* (Croom Helm, London).
Kaldor, M., Sharp, M. and Walker, W., 1986, 'Industrial competitiveness and Britain's defence', *Lloyds Bank Review*, No. 162, October, pp. 31–49.
MoD, 1987, *The Procurement Executive*, Ministry of Defence, London.
MoD, 1988, *Learning from Experience*, Ministry of Defence, London.
Morris, D. (ed.), 1985, *The Economic System in the UK* (Oxford University Press, 3rd edition).
Pugh, D., 1986, *The Cost of Seapower* (Conway, London).
Taylor, T. and Hayward, K., 1989, *The UK Defence Industrial Base* (Brassey's, London).
Walker, W., 1988, *UK Defence Electronics: A Review of Government Statistics*, PICT Policy Research Papers, ESRC, London, August.

CHAPTER 9

Evaluating International Projects

Introduction

International collaboration is dominated by myths and emotion, lacking independent analysis, critical evaluation and empirical evidence. To its supporters, all collaboration is good and more is desirable, regardless of costs. Critics point to excessive technical sophistication, bureaucracy and delays in decision making, leading to uncompetitive products, the loss of valuable national technology to rivals and, ultimately, to the loss of national independence. There are few analytical and empirical studies by economists of international collaboration. In particular, there is a need to evaluate the performance and competitiveness of joint ventures and the reasons for success or failure. This chapter focuses on developing a framework for evaluation. It presents a survey of issues, outlines the criteria which might be used to evaluate international collaborative projects, considers some testable hypotheses and reviews the available evidence. Stress has to be given to the sheer difficulties of making reliable generalisations from a small data set and the dangers of generalising by focusing on the favourable or unfavourable experience of one specific collaborative project! Ultimately, the chapter aims to discover what we know, what we do not know and what we need to know for an informed public policy towards collaborative programmes.

Why collaborate?

Europe's high technology industries especially in defence equipment (*eg* aerospace, electronics) are frequently criticised for the wasteful duplication of costly research and development and for relatively short production runs resulting from a dependence on a small domestic market (Chapter 7). International collaboration is often presented as the appropriate solution, leading, so it is claimed, to the eventual creation of a European-wide set of advanced technology industries which would be internationally competitive. However, there have been few independent and authoritative economic studies and evaluations of European experience with collaborative programmes. Surprisingly, in view of the frequent official references to the benefits of collaboration, especially its cost savings, there is an absence of publicly-available information, particularly from governments, on the magnitude of the benefits and savings (HCP 626, 1984).

Collaboration can be viewed as an international transaction resembling the formation of an international club, with countries and firms joining so long as membership is expected to be worthwhile. With collaborative defence equipment projects, governments create the club; they determine the rules for entry and exit, they set the entry fee and they distribute the benefits of membership through agreements to share work between club members and their national producers. Not surprisingly, club rules will reflect the behaviour of 'actors' in each nation's political market place. Governments will be concerned with votes, bureaucracies with their budgets and firms will be seeking contracts. Often, the result of such political bargaining is a government-created, protected and regulated market for an international cartel of each nation's major contractors. On this view, a country will join an international club for defence, economic, industrial or political benefits which it believes cannot be attained at reasonable cost by other means, such as independence (Hartley, 1986).

There are at least four economic pressures for international collaboration in defence equipment. First, limited defence budgets and the social pressures for greater expenditure on civil goods and services. Second, rising weapons costs. For aircraft, real unit costs are rising at 8–10 per cent per annum and the trend is towards fewer new projects and greater gaps in time between launching new projects (Yates, 1987). Third, the increasing costs and risks of independence. Fourth, the desire to protect jobs and national technology, including the desire to acquire high technology from partners (recognising that a price has to be paid for such benefits).

The facts on international projects

Various definitions of international programmes and packages are available reflecting different forms of contractual relationships between two or more nations. Countries might agree to arms co-operation at various stages in the life cycle of defence equipment, commencing with feasibility studies through to development, testing, production, sale and maintenance. The life cycle approach suggests the following classification system for international arms co-operation programmes (see *Table 9.1*):

(i) Joint feasibility studies such as the NATO Frigate Replacement and the NATO helicopter for the 1990s (NH 90).

(ii) Joint development work as on the EH 101 helicopter, the Trigat missile and the European Fighter Aircraft.

(iii) Joint development and production such as the Jaguar and Tornado combat aircraft. Arrangements for export sales can differ, with partner nations being completely free to market the equipment overseas or restricted to certain regions or subject to unanimous decisions. Difficulties can arise in international competitions where one of the partners has to choose between marketing a joint venture or supporting a national project (*eg* Dassault Mirage versus Jaguar).

(iv) International sharing of production work. This takes a number of forms:

    (a) Licensed production of another nations equipment such as the European manufacture of US Sidewinder air-to-air missiles and of US F-104 aircraft.

    (b) Co-production of another nation's equipment as with the F-16 European co-production programme. Co-production involving American companies allows a foreign nation a share of US orders, a share of its national production and a share of exports. Traditionally, with licensed production, the foreign nation builds for its own domestic orders only.

    (c) Work-sharing, industrial collaboration and offsets. These are different names for work-sharing, whereby a nation purchasing foreign equipment obtains some production work, usually on its own order (although it could be on a completely different project). Examples include the NATO and UK purchases of AWACS and the UK purchase of US Phantom aircraft.

(v) International sharing of a single project or of a family of weapons. The above life-cycle classification can be extended to a package or family approach whereby nations agree to share development and/or production work on a number of weapons projects. Examples include the Anglo-French helicopter package, ASRAAM and AMRAAM advanced short to medium-range air-to-air missiles.

In general, the European nations have considerable experience in the joint development and manufacture of defence equipment, especially aircraft, helicopters and missiles. In contrast, US defence industries favour international collaboration through sharing production work (but not design and development). Economic factors in the form of the high costs of advanced technology defence equipment and the scale of national orders partly explain these differences between Europe and the USA. But, political factors in the form of the desire for independence, security of supply and the jobs, technology and balance of payments benefits

TABLE 9.1. *Major Collaborative Projects*

	Status		No. of partner nations	Participating nations
	Initial study or development stage	In-service		
1. Aircraft				
Alpha Jet – trainer/light attack		✓	2	France, WG
Goshawk – trainer	✓		2	UK, USA
Transall – transport		✓	2	France, WG
AMX – light attack	✓		2	Italy, Brazil
Eurofighter	✓		4	UK, WG, Italy, Spain
Harrier II – attack		✓	2	UK, USA
Jaguar – attack		✓	2	France, UK
Tornado – interceptor/ strike		✓	3	UK, WG, Italy
2. Helicopters				
Gazelle – light utility		✓	2	France, UK
Lynx – multi-role		✓	2	France, UK
Puma – medium transport		✓	2	France, UK
EH 101 – naval; utility	✓		2	Italy, UK
A 129 – light attack	✓		4	Italy, UK, Neth., Spain
PAH 2 – combat	✓		2	France, WG
NH 90 – transport; naval	✓		5	France, Italy, Neth., UK, WG

3. Missiles				
Martel – air-surface		✓	2	France, UK
Otomat – anti-ship		✓	2	France, Italy
ANS – anti-ship	✓		2	France, WG
Roland – surface-air		✓	3	France, USA, WG
HOT – anti-tank		✓	2	France, WG
Milan – anti-tank		✓	2	France, WG
TRIGAT – anti-tank	✓	✓	3	France, UK, WG
ASRAAM – short range air-to-air	✓	✓	3	UK, WG, Norway
Short-range anti-radar	✓	✓	7	Belgium, Canada, Italy, Neth. UK, USA, WG
LRSOM – long-range stand-off	✓		3	UK, USA, WG
4. Land Equipment				
Multiple-Launch Rocket System – Phase II	✓		4	France, UK, USA, WG
FH70 Howitzer	✓	✓	3	Italy, UK, WG
SP70 Howitzer	✓		3	Italy, UK, WG
5. Naval Equipment				
NATO Frigate Replacement	✓		8	Canada, France, Italy, Neth., Spain UK, USA, WG
PARIS Sonar		✓	3	France, Neth., UK
Sea Gnat Decoy System	✓		3	Denmark, UK, USA

Notes: (i) B = Belgium; C = Canada; D = Denmark; F = France; It = Italy; Neth. = Netherlands; Nor. = Norway; Sp = Spain; UK = United Kingdom; USA = United States of America; WG = West Germany

(ii) Data based on 1985–86. SP70 now cancelled; UK now withdrawn from NH 90 and NATO frigate.

Sources: *Cmnd 9430* (1985); Taylor (1989).

associated with protecting a national defence industrial base are important (Chapter 8).

Table 9.1 summarises the status of the major collaborative projects (31 projects) undertaken by the mid-1980s. The focus is on projects involving European states in joint development or joint development and production; licensed and co-production packages are not included. This table shows the status of projects, the number of partners and the list of participating states. A number of generalisations emerge:

(i) The list of projects can be used to provide an indication of the scale and type of equipment which some governments are no longer willing to undertake as independent national ventures and where international collaboration is believed to be worthwhile. The list is dominated by aerospace equipment, namely various types of aircraft, helicopters and missiles. Some of these are costly projects in terms of both R & D and production outlays. For example, for the UK the Tornado programme is estimated to have cost £11.1 billion; the Harrier GR5 programme will cost £1.5 billion; the EH101 helicopter will cost £835 million for development and the development costs of the European Fighter Aircraft are estimated at some £2.2 billion (1988 prices: *Cmnd 675-II, 1989*).

(ii) For the sample, the number of partner nations varied between two and eight with a median of two and an average of almost three. Significantly, the collaborative projects actually in-service have involved only 2–3 partner nations.

(iii) The states most extensively involved in the sample of collaborative projects were the UK (22), followed by France (18), West Germany (18) and Italy (11). The UK is involved in collaboration in a complete range of air, land and sea systems. In terms of numbers, France has a relatively greater involvement in collaborative helicopters and missiles while West Germany has a substantial involvement in missile programmes. These variations partly reflect the extent of each nation's domestic defence industrial base, its desire to maintain a high technology capability and its 'willingness and ability to pay'.

(iv) The types of equipment *not* listed in *Table 9.1* cannot be ignored. The obvious examples are in naval and land equipment, especially tanks and armoured vehicles. The absence of more collaborative ventures for such equipment can reflect the fact that cost pressures on such equipment are not yet sufficiently great to persuade nations to sacrifice their independence. More generally, national governments and national producers might be unable, unwilling or reluctant to reach a mutually acceptable and worthwhile international agreement. In this context, however, it has to be recognised that the major European arms producing nations (France, UK, the Federal Republic of Germany, Italy) are already extensively involved in collaborative ventures for aerospace equipment.

(v) It can be seen that the European nations, particularly, France, Italy, the UK and West Germany, are involved in a variety of inter-locking relationships. For example, France and the UK have collaborated on aircraft and helicopters; France and West Germany on aircraft, helicopters and missiles; UK, West Germany and Italy on aircraft; the UK and Italy on helicopters; and France, the UK and West Germany on the Trigat missile. From the dates shown in *Tables 9.2 and 9.3* it seems that from the early projects of the mid-1960s, there has been a general trend towards more European collaborative ventures, many in aerospace.

Aerospace as a case study

In analysing collaboration, a study of aerospace is attractive for a number of reasons:

(i) It involves a high-technology sector and one where collaboration is seen as a means of creating an internationally-competitive European aerospace industry. Is it the case that collaboration promotes international competitiveness?

(ii) There is a substantial experience of international collaboration involving Concorde, Jaguar, Tornado, the European Fighter Aircraft, UK-French helicopters, EH101, Trigat, etc. Has collaboration been more or less successful for high technology military projects (*eg* Tornado) compared with civil programmes (*eg* Airbus)?

(iii) International collaboration has taken various forms ranging from the sharing of R & D and production work (*eg* Tornado), to co-production (European F-16s), work-sharing and offsets (*eg* Boeing AWACS, UK Phantoms). How far have these different forms offered technical benefits to the participants and have they generated jobs and balance of payments benefits?

(iv) International collaboration has involved the UK in partnership with a range of other European nations (France, West Germany, Italy, Spain), with the USA (Harrier) and with Japan (aero-engines). Different partner nations involve different firms. Is there any relationship between success or failure and the type or size of companies involved in collaboration and the range of a firm's diversified interests?

(v) There have been a variety of organisational arrangements from joint management committees, prime-contractor and sub-contractor relationships, new international companies (*eg* Airbus Industrie, Panavia, EHI) and competing consortia. It would be interesting to test the relationship between organisational form and the success or otherwise of a collaborative project.

(vi) The European Space Agency (ESA) has been recommended as an appropriate model for European collaboration. It involves collaboration in risky and costly high technology and ESA's research programme is 'managed very flexibly, rationalises European technological competence through sensitive bidding arrangements, enables ideas to be sought from outside member nations and makes good use of existing centres of excellence in Europe' (Vredeling 1986 vol. 1, p. 12). Indeed, ESA is regarded as a 'particularly good example of a successful co-operative European endeavour which in its field has matched, and even surpassed, the impressive achievements of the US' (*Ibid*, vol. 2, p. 127). What is the evidence for such a statement and, if it is accepted, why is ESA successful?

The benefits of collaboration

European collaboration is often presented as a solution to US competition in high technology. Supporters of European collaboration claim a variety of benefits which provide indicators for assessing the performance of joint programmes (success or failure). The benefits are as follows:

(i) Cost savings for both R & D and production (including the production of spares – *ie* effects on life-cycle costs). Partners can share the costs and risks of R & D on high technology projects and, by combining their national orders to achieve a longer production run, they can obtain economies of scale and learning. In the ideal model of collaboration, two equal partners on an aircraft programme would share R & D costs equally and a doubling of output would reduce unit production costs by about 10 per cent (Hartley, 1983; 1986; 1988). An example is shown in *Figure 9.1*.

(ii) The creation of a European industry able to compete with the USA in high technology and so avoid Europe becoming a nation of 'metal-bashers'. In aerospace, it is claimed that collaboration allows Europe to undertake advanced aerospace projects which would be too costly on a national basis. With such a policy, Europe can continue competing in high technology aerospace products (including spin-off for its economies), while retaining a European defence industrial base and preventing a US monopoly.

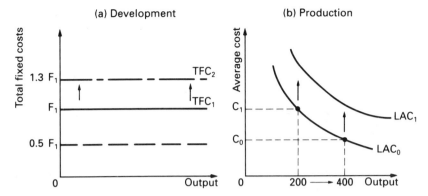

FIG. 9.1. Economics of Collaboration. R & D costs are shown as TFC in diagram (a); unit production costs are shown by the long-run average cost curve LAC in diagram (b). Comparing a national venture with a joint project, ideal collaboration leads to an equal sharing of R & D costs ($0.5F_1$) and a saving in unit production costs of C_1–C_0 as output is doubled from 200 to 400 units. Actual collaboration results in inefficiencies (premia) reflected in departures from the ideal case as shown by TFC_2 and LAC_1.

'A strong element in the UK's approach to collaboration has been the desire to develop an effective European alternative to what it has been feared would otherwise become US domination of the armaments market' (*HCP 626, 1984*, pp. 5–6).

(iii) General economic benefits in the form of domestic jobs (some being high value-added), balance of payments benefits (exports and import savings) and the industrial and Service benefits which result from production being spread over a longer period.

(iv) Political and military benefits associated with creating a united Europe, demonstrating the cohesion and credibility of the Alliance and contributing to greater standardisation of defence equipment. It has also been suggested that collaborative programmes are much more difficult to cancel – although some would view this as a cost rather than a benefit!

(v) Other benefits include claims that collaboration leads to greater technical rigour, to a pooling of knowledge and a competitive stimulus from the partner nations (*eg* rivalry between scientists) and the greater funding available in the R & D stage compared with a national project may enable equipment to enter service before it is nearly obsolescent.

The costs of collaboration

Collaboration has some disadvantages and costs leading to departures from the 'ideal model'. Where governments are involved, substantial transactions costs arise as partner nations seek to establish property rights in the joint venture. Bargaining between partner governments, their bureaucracies and customers (*eg* armed forces) together with lobbying from interest groups of scientists, engineers and contractors can lead to inefficiencies. Critics claim that inefficiency in collaboration arises from:

(i) The work sharing arrangements, with work allocated on political, equity and bargaining criteria and not on the basis of competition. On aerospace projects, each partner will require a flight testing centre and its own final assembly line. Some critics have suggested the *incompetence principle*, whereby work is allocated to the least competent partner! Claims are also made of major losses in valuable technical knowledge to partner nations as well as severe restrictions on overseas sales of the joint venture. Examples have arisen where the costs of collaborative projects have been increased substantially by the unilateral actions of one or more partners.

(ii) Administrative costs reflecting duplicate organisations, frequent committee meetings and delays in decision making. Joint ventures have often been criticised for management by committee.

(iii) Difficulties in harmonising requirements and delivery schedules and the need to make compromises (Hartley, 1983; 1986). Often national replacement schedules together with industrial and political ambitions have meant that collaborative aircraft programmes were characterised by a new airframe, a new engine and a new weapon system – a combination which maximises the chances of delay!

Evidence on work-sharing and organisational arrangements, including the arrangements for government monitoring of joint programmes is shown in *Table 9.2* and *Table 9.3*. Critics claim that as a result of these 'inefficiencies', collaborative programmes take longer to develop and involve higher costs than a national project, all of which will adversely affect their international competitiveness. Questions also arise about the different forms of organisation for collaborative projects and their contribution to success or failure. Examples include prime contractor and sub-contractor models; joint companies; competing consortia; the type of companies involved in collaboration and whether they have a range of diversified interests (*eg* Aerospatiale, Agusta, British Aerospace). Consideration needs to be given to whether competing consortia offer more efficient solutions to collaboration.

The need for evidence

Despite frequent official pronouncements on the benefits of collaboration, there is a surprising lack of evidence in the field. Evidence is needed on both the benefits and costs of collaboration. How large are the cost savings compared with both a national venture and with importing from the lowest cost overseas supplier? Also are there any inefficiencies due to work-sharing arrangements in both R & D and production, bureaucracy, duplication, and compromises? Does the square root rule still apply (*ie* where joint R & D costs are equal to the square root of the number of partner nations)? Is there an optimum number of partners (*eg* bilateral v. tri-lateral v. four nations: Jaguar, Tornado, EFA)? Does collaboration lead to more ambitious technical advances, reflecting the aspirations of scientists in the partner companies and nations and resulting in cost escalation and longer development times? Is R & D work allocated on the basis of each partner's comparative advantage and what about technology transfer including the possible loss of technology to future rivals? Collaboration also involves some interesting intellectual property rights problems. There are issues concerning the sharing of technology between partners (both firms and governments), the flows of technology between partners, to other projects in the partner companies and to firms in the rest of the economy (spin-off) – all compared with a national venture. Are particular forms of organisation for collaboration more or less conducive to promoting spin-off? There is no lack of questions, only a shortage of answers. How can economists evaluate collaborative projects?

Criteria for assessment: performance indicators

Major problems arise in assessing the performance of international collaborative ventures, especially those involving joint R & D and production work (*eg* Tornado). Difficulties arise because there is only a limited population of joint projects, involving different partner nations and various organisational arrangements (*Tables 9.2* and *9.3*). Also, within the small population international projects are heterogeneous, involving trainer and transport aircraft, various types of combat aircraft; helicopters, missiles and other land and naval equipment (*Table 9.1*).

There is also the problem of the counter-factual. What would have happened in the absence of a collaborative venture? For instance, in the absence of Tornado, would the UK have built an identical aircraft, purchasing the same quantity in the same time-scale? Care also has to be taken to ensure that comparisons are made between an *actual* collaborative venture and an *actual* national project rather than some *ideal*, problem-free national programme. Here, further difficulties arise since there are relatively few national programmes and they are unlikely to be of a

TABLE 9.2. *Examples of Collaborative Organisations: Aircraft*

Project	Partner Nations	Major companies and work share (%)			
		Airframes		Engines	
1. Alpha Jet	France	Dassault-Breguet	(50)	SNECMA: Turbomeca	(5(
	W. Germany	Dornier	(50)	MTU; KHD	(5(
2. Transall	France	Aerospatiale	(50)	Rolls-Royce (UK): SNECMA	
	W. Germany	MBB	(50)	MTU; FN-Herstal	
3. AMX	Brazil	Embraer	(29.7)	Rolls-Royce (UK)	
	Italy	Aeritalia	(46.7)		
		Aermaachi	(23.6)		
4. Eurofighter	UK	British Aerospace	(33)	Rolls-Royce	(33
	W. Germany	MBB	(33)	MTU	(33
	Italy	Aeritalia	(21)	Fiat	(2)
	Spain	CASA	(13)	SENER	(13
5. Harrier II	UK	British Aerospace		Rolls-Royce	(75
			(40–50)	Pratt-Whitney	(25
	USA	McDonnell-Douglas			
			(50–60)		
6. Jaguar	France	Dassault-Breguet	(50)	Turbomeca	(5(
	UK	British Aerospace	(50)	Rolls-Royce	(5(
7. Tornado	UK	British Aerospace	(42.5)	Rolls-Royce	(42.5
	W. Germany	MBB	(42.5)	MTU	(42.5
	Italy	Aeritalia	(15)	Fiat	(15

Notes: (i) NEFMA is NATO European Fighter Management Agency.
(ii) NAMMO is NATO MRCA Development and Production Management Organisation, with NAMMA as the executive Agency.
(iii) Date of start based on the announcement of a joint requirement by the partners; although Harrier II date is for first flight of modified prototype.
Source: Taylor (1989).

similar type. Furthermore, there are different policy aims. Partner nations in a collaborative venture are likely to have different policy objectives and to differ in their willingness to pay for the various benefits from a joint programme. Finally, collaboration forms only one variable in a complex model. All other relevant factors in determining success or failure have to be held constant, such as the complexity of the programme, the extent of market contestability, the type of contract, the size of firms, the previous experience of collaboration and of the technology.

In assessing international collaborative ventures, the criteria for success often focus on inputs rather than end-outputs. Reference might be made to the number of partner nations involved in collaboration or to the fact that a joint programme has been completed. But number of partners and

TABLE 9.2. *continued*

Arrangements for:		Location of final assembly	Date of start
Buying	*Development and production*		
National governments	Dassault is main contractor / Dornier is industrial collaborator	France / W. Germany	July 1969
National governments	Aerospatiale = wings; doors; fairings / MBB = fuselage; tail surfaces	France	1977
National governments	Co-ordination and monitoring by Joint Management Committee	Brazil / Italy	March 1980
NEFMA	Two new joint companies: (a) Eurofighter for airframe (b) Eurojet for engines	UK / W. Germany / Italy / Spain	July 1984
National Governments	McAir to undertake 60% of work on US orders and 50% of work on UK orders; balance to British Aerospace	UK / USA	November 1978
Governments created an official Jaguar Management Committee	Creation of joint company SEPECAT but no separate staff	France / UK	May 1965
Programme guided and monitored on behalf of 3 governments by NAMMO with NAMMA as its executive agency	Creation of two new international companies with separate staffs: (a) Panavia Aircraft (b) Turbo-Union for engines	UK / W. Germany / Italy	1968

completion are not necessarily evidence of economic success in terms of efficiency, marketability and profitability.

Given these qualifications, various criteria and indicators can be used to assess the performance of collaborative ventures. Some of these performance indicators can be formulated into testable hypotheses. In principle, the range of possible performance measures embrace *planned* and *realised* economic, technical and political criteria such as:

(i) Profitability. However, difficulties arise where defence profits are subject to government control, where markets are non-competitive and where there are hidden subsidies, protection and preferential purchasing.

TABLE 9.3. *Examples of Collaborative Organisations: Helicopters and Missiles*

Project	Partner Nations	Major companies and work or ownership share (%)		Organisation of development and production	Date of start
HELICOPTERS					
1. Gazelle, Puma Lynx	France UK	Aerospatiale; Turbomeca Westland; Rolls-Royce		(i) Anglo-French helicopter package involving 3 types (ii) Prime contractor – sub-contractor relationships (iii) Westland as prime contractor for Lynx (70%); Aerospatiale as sub-contractor (iv) Aerospatiale as prime contractor for Puma (90%) and Gazelle (60%); Westland as sub-contractor	1967
2. EH 101	Italy UK	Agusta Westland	(50) (50)	(i) *European Helicopter Industries* (EHI) created as a new international company for joint development of EH 101. Agusta and Westland have equal shares in EHI (ii) UK MoD handling the programme for both countries	June 1980
3. PAH-2 HAP/HAC-3G	France W. Germany	Aerospatiale (50); Turbomeca MBB (50); MTU		(i) New joint company formed – *Eurocopter* based in Paris and controlled by joint board (ii) MBB is programme leader; Aerospatiale is co-contractor (iii) Executive authority for programme is with West German procurement agency	May 1984

4. A 129	Italy UK Netherlands Spain	Agusta (38) Westland (38) Fokker (19) CASA (5)	*Joint European Helicopter* created as new international company for joint development of A 129. Feasibility study stage	May 1985
MISSILES 1. HOT, Milan Roland	France W. Germany	Aerospatiale MBB	*Euromissile* created as new joint company	1972
2. TRIGAT	France UK W. Germany	Aerospatiale British Aerospace MBB	(i) *Euromissile Dynamics Group* created by the 3 companies (ii) Three versions being developed: Aerospatiale team leader on light-weight version; B.Ae leader on long-range land version and MBB leading on long-range helicopter version	January 1980
3. ASRAAM	UK W. Germany	British Aerospace (50) Bordenseewerk Geratetechnik (50)	(i) *BBG* created as new company to act as prime contractor for ASRAAM (ii) ASRAAM and AMRAAM form NATO family of weapons programme	November 1980
4. LRSOM	UK USA W. Germany	British Aerospace; GEC; Hunting Boeing; General Dynamics MBB; Dornier	Two competing international teams have been formed – General Dynamics, Dornier and Hunting form one team; other companies form rival team	July 1984

Note: Date of start based on signing of a joint agreement between partner states or formation of joint company.

(ii) Performance against the original contract specification in the form of cost escalation, delays and 'gold-plating'. Such indicators need to be compared with the typical outcomes on national projects. For example, do collaborative projects involve more ambitious technical advances and hence greater cost escalation?

(iii) Estimated cost savings compared with a national venture. Does collaboration result in inefficiencies; how large are any inefficiencies and have such inefficiencies been falling with experience?

(iv) Wider economic benefits in the form of jobs, technology and balance of payments contributions compared with a national project.

(v) Total development time-scales: do collaborative ventures take longer to develop than a similar national programme?

(vi) Exports and world market shares can be used as indicators of international competitiveness. Has collaboration led to greater export sales and an increased share of world markets? Or, does collaboration create future rivals in world markets?

(vii) Total output. The output of a collaborative venture can be compared with the output of a typical national project and with US scales of output. Has collaboration resulted in Europe's approaching US scales of output and becoming more capable of competing with the USA? Alternatively, the extent to which orders from the partner nations exceed their initial estimates might be used as a further indicator of market performance.

(viii) The creation of larger firms and a European industry which is competitive with the USA and able to obtain the productivity benefits of longer production runs. What have been the effects of collaboration on the size of firms, the structure of European defence industries and on their competitiveness? Furthermore, what is the evidence on the unit prices of collaborative projects compared with European national and US projects?

(ix) Political integration within Europe and within NATO. For example, success might be measured by the number of partners involved in a project and/or where existing partners agree to future projects. Such developments also contribute to military standardisation. This raises the more general question of which types of collaboration have been most successful and why?

The results of collaboration

Various indicators have been outlined for assessing the performance of collaborative projects. Unfortunately, published data are unavailable or at least are not readily available on each of the suggested indicators. In particular, it is not always possible to obtain reliable data on planned or expected results. An official UK study concluded that 'it proved difficult to establish the extent to which the potential benefits of collaboration – which in principle are very significant – were fully secured in practice' (*HCP 626, 1984*, p. 1). Nonetheless, some limited evidence is readily available and is indicative and illustrative of the potential for empirical work in this field.

Table 9.4 presents selected performance indicators for a sample of collaborative aircraft and helicopter projects. Data are presented on output, schedule dates and development time-scales. Evidence on the number of prototypes and airframes for static testing can be used as an indication of the scale of development effort on joint projects and this is likely to be reflected in development times. Obviously, by themselves, the data in *Table 9.4* are not very useful for any evaluations. They need to be compared with typical national ventures (*eg* pairwise comparisons of, say, Alpha Jet and Hawk aircraft) and with the original planned or expected outcomes. Consideration also needs to be given to other performance indicators such as changes in the structure of the European aerospace industry, the creation of larger firms and, ultimately, the effects of collaboration on costs. Significantly, one review of the literature concluded that 'no comprehensive, quantified list of advantages and disadvantages could be found in published papers, yet they must play a significant part in the decision to go ahead with European collaboration, or not' (Farrar and Balthazor, 1981).

Cost savings

In view of the many government references to the cost savings and other benefits of collaboration, there is a surprising absence of publicly-available official evidence on the *expected* and *realised* magnitude of the cost savings and wider benefits. Consider some of the evidence which is available:

(i) There is general agreement that actual collaboration departs from the ideal model (*eg* equal sharing and a doubling of output for two equal partners, *ceteris paribus*), although differences arise about the magnitude of any collaboration premium. On aircraft R & D, estimates range from an extra 15–20 per cent for a bilateral programme to 50 per cent, depending on the number of partners (Farrar and Balthazor, 1981). For the Alpha Jet, collaborative development might have cost an extra 10 per cent compared with a German national programme (Hoffert, 1981). Elsewhere, various rules of thumb have suggested that collaboration increases project costs by 30 per cent for each additional country involved and that

TABLE 9.4. *Performance Indicators*

| Project | Output | | | Date of | | | Total development time | Number of prototypes and test airframes |
	Partner nations	Exports	Total	Start	First Flight	In-Service		
1. Alpha Jet	F = 176 WG = 175	161	512	July 1969	Oct 1973	Summer 1978	9 years	6
2. AMX	It = 187 Br = 79		266	March 1980	May 1984	June 1988	8 years	7
3. Eurofighter	UK = 250 WG = 250 It = 165 Sp = 100		765	December 1983	1991	1996	13 years	8
4. Harrier II	US = 328 UK = 96	12	436	November 1978	November 1981	October 1983	5 years	6
5. Jaguar	F = 200 UK = 203	170	573	May 1965	September 1968	May 1972	7 years	–
6. Tornado	UK = 435 WG = 375 It = 100	80+	990+	July 1968	August 1974	July 1980	12 years	15
7. Gazelle	F = 296 UK = 286	587+	1,295+	January 1967	April 1967	January 1972	5 years	n.a.
8. Puma	F = 175 UK = 48	476	692	Pre-1965	April 1965	May 1969		n.a.
9. Lynx	F = 40 UK = 214+	63+	342+	January 1967	March 1971	July 1976	9.5 years	13
10. EH 101	UK = 75 It = 38	30–50+	143– 163+	June 1981	October 1987	1991+	10+ years	10
11. PAH-2 (Eurocopter)	F = 215 WG = 212		427	May 1984	1991	1997	13 years	5

Notes: (i) Output figures are approximations and include licensed production.
(ii) It is difficult to obtain accurate and standardised data on date of start.
(iii) For projects in the early development stage, the output figures are plans and estimates.
Sources: Taylor (1989); *Flight* (1989); HCP 518 (1986).

collaborative development costs are multiplied by the square root of the number of partner nations – juniors counting as a fraction, say one-half (Pugh, 1986, p. 357; WEU, 1987, p. 7). On aircraft unit production costs, the inefficiency premium on collaboration ranges from an extra 1–2 per cent at the lower bound to an extra 10 per cent at the upper bound, with some experts suggesting that unit production costs are unchanged by collaboration (Pugh, 1986, p. 357; *Figure 9.1*).

(ii) Even with inefficiencies, collaboration should result in cost savings for each partner compared with an identical national project. An estimate for a hypothetical but representative aircraft project suggested that the costs of collaboration might absorb about 50 per cent of its potential benefits; but even so, savings are likely to be substantial and in the region of 10–15 per cent for a two-nation project (depending respectively on whether it used an existing or new engine: (Pugh, 1986, p. 358). A German view estimated the fly-away costs of a three-nation collaborative aircraft project at 92 per cent of a national solution (Farrar and Balthazor, 1981). In one of the few UK government estimates, it was calculated that the collaborative European Fighter Aircraft project would be 20 per cent cheaper than a national venture (saving the UK some £1.2 billion to £1.4 billion, 1987 prices). Interestingly, studies on the Tornado have shown that for production, the extra costs of collaboration (*eg* several assembly lines) were balanced by the economies of a longer production run: hence, the major savings were in development costs. The extra administrative costs of Tornado collaboration were estimated at 1.6 per cent of the annual programme costs (Vredeling, 1986, vol. 2, pp. 119–120). And the Tornado has been presented as 'an excellent example' of a collaborative project (Levene, 1986, p. 9).

(iii) Cost comparisons are usually made between collaborative and national programmes. Further cost savings would be likely if a nation were willing to shop-around, buying its defence equipment from the cheapest suppliers in the world market. For example, it has been estimated that the European governments accepted a 34 per cent cost penalty on the F-16 Co-Production Programme compared with a direct buy from the USA (Rich *et al.*, 1981).

Output

There are a number of criteria which can be applied to the output of joint ventures. It is argued that collaboration leads to a greater output compared with a national requirement; an output approaching US scales of production; and greater export sales (*ie* increased competitiveness reflected in exports and shares of the world market).

Table 9.4 shows the obvious point that all the collaborative aircraft and helicopter projects resulted in a total output greater than the requirements of one of the partners. However, this does not tell us anything about the relative unit costs or competitiveness of a joint programme compared with a similar European or US project. In this context, comparisons might be made between the total output (including exports) of a collaborative and typical national project (but what is typical?).

Some joint aircraft and helicopter ventures have approached closely to US scales of output, depending on the number of partners and/or export sales of the project. Typically, US orders for its national armed forces are in the region of 1,000–2,800 units for a combat aircraft produced at rates of 12.5–15 units per month; and 500–1500 units for a helicopter at production rates of 10–12 per month. In contrast, Britain, France and West Germany might *each* require 200–400 units of a combat aircraft for their armed forces, produced at rates of two to five per month. A UK national order for military helicopters might be in the region of 40–200 units of each type. On the UK–US Harrier II, American production rates exceed twice those for Britain. Thus, compared with US output levels, (1000+ aircraft; 500+ helicopters) by 1989, the Tornado and some of the Anglo-French helicopter package were in the region of American scales of production (Tornado production was 9+ per month).

Export sales are an indicator of international competitiveness. On this basis, the 1967 Anglo-French helicopter package seems to have been sucessful, with exports accounting for some 50 per cent of the total sales of all three types (Crowley, 1981). Indeed, the Anglo-French helicopter agreement has also been successful in relation to its original forecasts. In 1967, the initial sales forecasts were:

	Puma	*Gazelle*	*Lynx*
France	130	170	55
UK	40	250	190
Exports	85	210	120
Total	255	630	365

In 1967, it was expected that France and the UK would require a total of 835 units, with a possible 415 units for export, giving a total forecast of 1,250 units. By end-1985, total sales including the Super Puma were 2,582 units (Hartley, 1983, p. 175; *HCP 518, 1986*, p. xxvi; Sieffer, 1981). Questions arise as to whether the success of the Anglo-French helicopter agreement reflected the choice of projects, collaboration, the package deal or the use of the prime contractor – sub-contractor form of organisation.

Mention should also be made of the F-16 European Co-Production Programme. The initial programme was based on 998 aircraft with 650 for the USA and 348 for the Europeans; and export sales were estimated originally at a further 500 aircraft. By 1989, total orders for the F-16 were some 4,000 units, with the USA ordering 2,700 aircraft and exports accounting for a further 1,253 units (about 32 per cent of the total). Also, the European consortium had increased its order from 348 to 515 aircraft.

Of the remaining projects in *Table 9.4*, the Alpha Jet and Jaguar have achieved substantial overseas sales, with exports accounting for 30 per cent of their total output by 1989. On the Tornado, export sales have not been impressive, accounting for under 10 per cent of total output. However, it could be argued that the Tornado is a highly-specialised aircraft and that its closest substitute is the US F-14 aeroplane – in which case by the end of 1989, the Tornado and F-14 had similar records of both total output and exports. Mention also has to be made of the Euromissile which has achieved substantial overseas sales with its HOT and Milan missiles.

While an analysis of the export sales of collaborative projects is suggestive, it must be stressed that national projects are also sold overseas. The export record of some European national aerospace projects such as the Dassault Mirage and British Aerospace Harrier and Hawk has also been impressive. By 1989, exports as a percentage of total sales were 64 per cent for the Mirage F1, 62 per cent for the Harrier and 73 per cent for the Hawk (*cf* F-16). In other words, there are examples of both collaborative and national aerospace projects which are competitive in world markets. A thorough and proper evaluation requires data on the average export performance of national independent projects and, ideally, reliable and accurate information on the unit costs of national and collaborative ventures.

Comparative data on average prices for some European national, collaborative and US military aircraft are shown in *Table 9.5*. Such data can be unreliable, reflecting the complexity of bargaining between governments. For example, governments can exercise discretion in charging for R & D on export sales, and contracts can vary from the delivery of a standard aircraft to a commitment to supply a 'package' of aircraft, missiles, spares, support and training. Nonetheless, *Table 9.5* shows that the UK Hawk trainer is some 10 per cent cheaper than the collaborative Alpha Jet, whilst the Tornado is competitive with the American F-14 and about 5 per cent more expensive than the F-15. A premium of 5–10 per cent on collaborative projects indicates the amount nations are willing to pay for a degree of independence and for wider economic benefits (*eg* jobs, technology).

Collaboration has brought together the major European aerospace companies into new international organisations embracing military and civil

TABLE 9.5. *Average Prices*

Aircraft	Average price Millions, ECUs
European – national	
Hawk	7.5– 9.0
Mirage F1	13.0–14.5
Mirage 2000	24.0–34.0
Saab Gripen	29.0–30.0
European – collaborative	
Alpha Jet	8.5–10.0
Tornado	39.0–48.0
USA	
F-14	38.0–48.0
F-15	37.0–46.0
F-16	23.0–33.0
F-18	35.0–45.0

Note: Average programme unit costs in 1985 including R & D, initial spares and ground support equipment.
Source: EC 1988.

TABLE 9.6. *Major European Companies*

Company	Project	Nations
1. Panavia	Tornado aircraft	UK, WG, Italy
2. Eurofighter and Eurojet	European Fighter Aircraft	UK, WG, Italy Spain
3. E.H. Industries	EH 101 helicopter	UK, Italy
4. Eurocopter	Light attack helicopter	France, WG
5. Joint European Helicopter	A 129 light attack helicopter	Italy, UK, Netherlands, Spain
6. Euromissile	HOT, Milan, Roland	France, WG
7. Euromissile Dynamics Group	TRIGAT	France, UK, WG
8. BBG	ASRAAM	UK, WG
9. Airbus Industrie	Civil aircraft: A300, 310,320	France, WG, UK, Spain
10. European Space Agency (ESA)	Civil space systems	14 European nations

Note: WG = West Germany.

aircraft, helicopters, engines, missiles and space systems (*Table 9.6*). The result has been the creation of larger European firms and the foundations for a European aerospace industry.

Development times

It is often claimed that joint projects take longer to develop than a similar national programme. Delays are supposed to result from excessive government bureaucracy, frequent committee meetings, lengthy negotiations to reach agreements, elaborate reporting procedures and lots of paper-work. A questionnaire study found support for the view that joint projects take longer to develop, with estimates ranging from an extra 20 per cent longer to an additional 3+ years on collaborative programmes (Hartley, 1983, p. 213). Other estimates have suggested that bilateral projects take 40 per cent longer to develop and trilateral projects 70 per cent longer (Taylor, 1982, p. 173).

Pairwise comparisons can be made between the development period for a collaborative programme and for a similar independent national venture. On this basis, there is some evidence that joint European aircraft projects take longer to develop than similar national programmes, with collaboration leading to possible delays of about one year (Hartley, 1983, p. 167; Hartley, 1986, p. 255). Of course, with such an approach, other relevant factors have to be considered. Projects differ in their complexity, in priority and urgency, in the resources which are allocated to development, in their access to previous experience and in their pursuit of wider government policy objectives (*eg* jobs, technology, entry to EEC).

A US statistical analysis has presented an alternative view. It found that 'the evidence that collaborative European programmes tend to take more time than national European programs is far from conclusive' (Rich *et al.*, 1981, pp. 31–32). The statistical analysis was based on six European multi-national aircraft programmes (G91, Atlantic, Transall, Jaguar, Alpha Jet, Tornado) and the results are particularly sensitive to the inclusion or exclusion of Tornado. The average time from design to delivery for the sample of six collaborative aircraft projects was 100 months; excluding Tornado reduced the development time to 94 months, compared with 87 months for a sample of European national aircraft programmes (Rich *et al.*, 1981, pp. 51–52). The same study found that for a sample of European multi-national aircraft, the median time slippage of actual to planned first deliveries was 1.46; the corresponding figure for a sample of US aircraft was 1.03. However, it was not possible to determine whether the time slippages reflected general European procurement policies or the involvement of additional countries in the programme (Rich *et al.*, 1981, p. vii; p. 34). A similar UK econometric study also found no support for the hypothesis that joint projects take longer to develop (Hartley, 1987).

The Tornado project encountered substantial delays. In June 1969, at the Project Definition Stage, it was estimated that the aircraft would enter service in the first quarter of 1976. In fact, the first aircraft was delivered in July 1980, giving a time slippage of 1.63. Apparently, the delays were not unexpected in a programme of such size and complexity: there were, for example, technical problems associated with the development of the engine and the avionics (*HCP 22-II, 1982*, pp. 452–453). However, compared with some other UK projects (*eg* frigates, Sea Wolf missiles), the delays on Tornado were not unique (*see Table 9.7*).

Cost escalation

Some limited evidence indicates that for aircraft projects European collaboration does not necessarily result in higher cost escalation than on national ventures (Hartley, 1983, p. 167). On Tornado, the cost escalation factor on *unit production costs* in real terms was 1.24 (*HCP 22-ii, 1982*, p. 452) which was lower than the escalation on some other UK projects (see *Table 9.7*). Indeed, more recent evidence suggests that combining R & D and production costs for all versions of the Tornado, the estimated costs to completion compared with the original estimates have risen by less than one per cent in real terms (production costs have decreased: Vredeling, 1986, vol. 2, p. 120).

On the US Roland missile programme (a Euromissile product), real cost escalation exceeded 2.0 compared with an average of 1.2 for other US programmes in the 1970s. It has been suggested that the multinational character of the Roland Programme might have been a major reason for this cost growth (Rich *et al.*, 1981, pp. 57–58).

Conclusion

This chapter has raised more questions than answers – questions which form the basis for a lengthy research agenda and questions which need to be answered if we are to identify the conditions required for, and the characteristics of, successful collaborative projects.

The difficulties of analysis and evaluation are considerable. To summarise, compare the collaborative Tornado programme with the national Hawk programme (*Table 9.7*). Hawk was a simple trainer aircraft, using an existing engine; it was the responsibility of one government and single manufacturers were responsible for the airframe and the engine. In contrast, Tornado was an advanced technology aircraft, involving a new engine, financed and controlled by three nations, with the airframe and engine each developed by three firms, with no clear leadership allocated for either unit (*HCP 22-II, 1982*, p. 461).

Ultimately, in assessing collaboration, questions have to be asked about who gains and who loses. Has collaboration benefited national defence producers rather than offering good value for money to taxpayers, as reflected in protection and security? If so, consideration needs to be given

TABLE 9.7. *Escalation*

	Frigates		Sea Wolf Missile		TOW Helicopter borne ATGW	Hawk aircraft	Tornado (collaborative) strike version
	Type 21.01	Type 22.01	GWS 25	Sea Wolf Missile			
Date of start	Jan. 1968	Feb. 1969	Jan. 1964	Jan. 1964	1973	Dec. 1970	June 1969
Planned In-Service date	end 1971	Sept. 1974	1972	1972	Feb. 1980	1976–77	early 1976
Actual In-Service date	July 1974	Feb. 1979	Oct 1981	Feb 1977	Feb. 1981	Nov. 1976	July 1980
Cost Escalation:							
Development Costs	5.2	0.9	n.a.	n.a.	1.1	1.0	1.4
Unit production Costs	1.9	1.01	2.1	1.4	1.05	1.0	1.2
Time delays	1.7	1.8	2.8	1.7	+12 months	+1 month	1.6

Note: Cost escalation and time delays are actual divided by original estimate. Costs are in constant prices. Figure of 1.0 means actual equals estimated costs.
Source: HCP 22-II, 1982, pp. 438–454; Vredeling (1986), vol. 2, p. 120.

to introducing greater competition and efficiency incentives into collaborative programmes. By the late 1980s, there was increasing recognition of the scope for improving the efficiency of collaborative projects, reflected in the Vredeling Report and UK policy.

The Vredeling Report *Towards a Stronger Europe* (1986), made proposals for improving the competitiveness of Europe's defence equipment industry. The Report aimed to create a more open competitive market with the extensive use of competing consortia and fixed price contracts and with industry taking greater responsibility for managing development and production. However, the Report recognised constraints on its proposals in the form of government concern with employment levels, the desire to maintain a national industrial and technological base, a reluctance to transfer technology and a desire for a fair share of defence work (*juste retour*). The worry is that these constraints will prevent the achievements of the ultimate objective, namely, a more open competitive market.

By the late 1980s, the UK government was committed to developing and producing 'most significant new equipments in collaboration with allies unless there are pressing reasons not to do so' (*Cmnd 344-1, 1988*, p. 45). Its commitment to collaboration had two distinctive features: first, the need to promote efficiency and competitive procurement in international projects and second, the desire to encourage different types of co-operation, especially when the traditional approach is not the most efficient. For example, for less costly equipment, reciprocal purchasing may be more efficient, with nations agreeing to buy from one another equipment that each has developed independently (*eg* Anglo-French reciprocal purchasing initiative of 1987). The incentives for reciprocal purchasing and other more efficient forms of collaboration are likely to increase as defence budgets come under increasing public scrutiny. However, the problems of organising collaborative projects between allies are perhaps relatively minor compared with the difficulties of reaching international arms control agreements between potential adversaries.

References

Cmnd 344-I, 1988, *Statement on the Defence Estimates 1988* (HMSO, London).

Cmnd 675-II, 1989, *Statement on the Defence Estimates 1989* (HMSO, London).

Crowley, T. M., 1981, Official experience with the procurement of collaborative ventures, *European Collaborative Projects*, Royal Aeronautical Society, London.

EC 1988, *The European Aerospace Industry: Trading Position and Figures*, February (Commission of the European Communities, Brussels).

Farrar, D. J. and Balthazor, L. R., 1981, 'Analysis of high technology collaboration', *European Collaborative Projects*, Royal Aeronautical Society, London.

Flight, 1989, 'The world's air forces', *Flight International*, London, 29 November, pp. 37–106.

Hartley, K., 1983, *NATO Arms Co-operation* (Allen and Unwin, London).

Hartley, K., 1986, 'Defence, industry and technology: problems and possibilities for European collaboration', in G. Hall (ed.), *European Industrial Policy* (Croom Helm, London).

Hartley, K., 1987, 'The evaluation of efficiency in the arms industry', in Borner, S. and Taylor, A. (eds.) *Structural Change, Economic Interdependence and World Development*, Vol. 2, IEA (Macmillan, London).

Hartley, K., 1988, Collaboration in K. Kaiser and J. Roper (eds.), *British-German Defence Co-operation* (Royal Institute of International Affairs, London).

Hoffert, F., 1981, The Franco-German Alpha Jet Programme, *European Collaborative Projects*, Royal Aeronautical Society, London.

HCP 22-II, 1982, *Ministry of Defence Organisation and Procurement*, Defence Committee (HMSO, London).

HCP 626, 1984, *International Collaborative Projects for Defence Equipment*, National Audit Office (HMSO, London).

HCP 37-II, 1985, *Defence Commitments and Resources*, Defence Committee (HMSO, London).

HCP 518, 1986, *The Defence Implications of the Future of Westland PLC*, Defence Committee, House of Commons, July (HMSO, London).

Levene, P. K., 1986, *Control and Management of the Development of Major Equipment*, Public Accounts Committee, HCP 104 (HMSO, London).

Pugh, P., 1986, *The Cost of Sea Power* (Conway, London).

Rich, M., *et al.*, 1981, *Multinational Coproduction of Military Aerospace Systems*, Rand, USA.

Sieffer, J. C., 1981, 'Industrial experience in the Anglo-French helicopter collaboration', *European Collaborative Projects*, Royal Aeronautical Society, London.

Taylor, J. (ed.), 1985, 1989, *Jane's All The World's Aircraft*. (Jane's, London).

Taylor, T., 1982, *Defence, Technology and International Integration*, (Frances Pinter, London).

Vredeling, 1986, *Towards a Stronger Europe*, IEPG, NATO, Brussels.

WEU 1987, *Armaments Co-operation Between WEU Member Countries*, Western European Union, Brussels.

Yates, I. R., 1987, Keynote Address, *Development Time Scales – Their Estimation and Control*, Royal Aeronautical Society, London.

CHAPTER 10

The Political Economy of Arms Control

Introduction: the issues

By the late 1980s, arms control was one of the dominant themes of international relations. Following the 1987 Intermediate-range Nuclear Forces Treaty (INF), there were prospects of further successful arms control agreements between the USA and USSR and their allies involving both nuclear and conventional forces (*Table 10.1*). Prospects of the withdrawal of American and Russian troops from Central Europe and of substantial cuts in both countries' nuclear and conventional forces has led some commentators to declare the end of the Cold War and to raise question marks over the future of both NATO and the Warsaw Pact military alliances. Nonetheless, arms control remains controversial.

Supporters of arms control claim that it will lead to stability and less risk of war between the superpowers. As a result, NATO and the Warsaw Pact nations will achieve security at lower levels of armaments. Defence budgets can be cut, so releasing resources for valuable and pressing civil needs such as education, health, housing and improving an economy's international competitiveness. This is believed to be particularly appealing to the Warsaw Pact countries, especially the USSR, which are seeking to improve the efficiency of their economies and to raise living standards for their citizens. Indeed, given all the attractions of arms control, some supporters are looking beyond current negotiations and speculating about the next developments. Should we aim at further reductions in conventional and nuclear forces (*eg* CFE II and START II) or should the focus be on cuts in maritime forces or in stocks, supplies and reinforcement capabilities?

There are, though, critics of arms control who question whether the threat from the Soviet Union will be reduced. They stress the problems of verifying arms control agreements and the possibility of cheating. Worries have been expressed that the Soviet Union's real aim is to create public pressure in NATO for reduced defence spending, to divide NATO and to encourage US troop withdrawals from Europe, all of which might

TABLE 10.1. *Arms Control 1986–90*

Initiative	Participating nations	Major features
1. Stockholm Document 1986	35 nations: all Europe (except Albania), plus USA and Canada	Confidence – and security – building measures: advance notification of military exercises; on-site inspection of exercises.
2. Intermediate-range Nuclear Forces Treaty (INF), 1987	USA USSR	Elimination of all intermediate-range ground-launched nuclear missiles by 1991 (*eg* US nuclear cruise and Pershing missiles).
3. Negotiations on Conventional Armed Forces in Europe (CFE)	16 NATO nations 7 Warsaw Pact states	Covers whole of Europe; aims to reduce conventional forces (*eg* troops, tanks, artillery), eliminate disparities and capacity for surprise attack.
4. Negotiations on Confidence – and Security – Building Measures (CSBMs)	35 nations as at Stockholm 1986	Building on Stockholm 1986: proposals to exchange data on conventional forces in Europe and make military activities more open and more predictable.
5. Strategic Arms Reduction Talks (START)	USA USSR	Ceilings on nuclear warheads and delivery vehicles and proposals to cut superpowers strategic arsenals by 50 per cent. START does not include the strategic forces of third parties (*eg* UK).
6. Other nuclear arms control initiatives	USA USSR	Since 1987, proposals have been made not to withdraw from the Anti-Ballistic Missile Treaty (ABMT 1972) until 1994; and to ratify the Threshold Test Ban Treaty (TTBT, 1974) and the Peaceful Nuclear Explosions Treaty (PNET 1974).
7. Chemical Weapons, Paris Conference 1989	149 nations	Reaffirmed 1925 Geneva Protocol prohibiting use of chemical weapons in war (but not their production).

Source: Cmnd 675-I, 1989.

lead to greater instability. Indeed, some critics suggest that the USSR's willingness to accept arms control agreements reflects its need for time to allow it to re-structure and improve the efficiency of its economy, so that it will be better able to pursue its long-run aim of 'destroying capitalism'.

There are other reasons for caution. To some observers, the pace of political and economic change in Eastern Europe and the USSR creates major uncertainties about future international relations (*eg* East and West Germany) to which NATO should adopt a cautious 'wait and see' response. Others counsel caution about the immediate prospect of massive disarmament and turning 'guns into butter'. Worries are expressed about the possibility of massive unemployment associated with disarmament. Moreover, even successful arms control agreements between NATO and the Warsaw Pact will not mean that the UK no longer faces a threat. The Warsaw Pact will retain substantial armed forces and there remain fears about an accidental nuclear war. Also, there are potential threats from Third World nations through international terrorism and the possible proliferation of nuclear and chemical weapons and their associated delivery vehicles (aircraft, missiles). In the future, new military powers are likely to emerge (*eg* China, India, Japan) so ensuring that the world continues to be a dangerous place in which to live!

Clearly, arms control is a policy area dominated by myths, emotion and special pleading, all of which need to be critically evaluated and subjected to empirical testing. Often independent evaluation has been the preserve of political scientists, and experts in strategic studies and international relations. Questions arise as to whether there exists a satisfactory analytical framework for thinking about arms control policy. Here, economists can contribute to policy formulation by applying models of the arms race, bargaining, regulation and public choice.

The arms race, wars and arms control

If arms control aims to reduce the risk of war, economists need to start with a model of the outbreak of war. The Richardson model of the arms race is an obvious starting point (Chapter 4; Hartley and Hooper, 1990). Using this model it is often assumed that a continuous upward spiral of armaments in two rival nations must inevitably result in a war. Problems arise in operationalising the model so that it can be used to provide guidelines for arms control negotiations. Should policy aim to reduce total defence spending in the rival nations or specific types of forces; and if the latter which forces: nuclear or conventional? And if the focus is on nuclear forces, should it seek reductions in strategic or tactical or all nuclear weapons, and should the cuts be in warheads or delivery systems or both (*eg* ballistic missiles v aircraft)? Some answers are provided by more recent theoretical developments.

Modifications to the Richardson model have resulted in some counter-intuitive predictions. It has been shown that, under certain conditions, an arms race can prevent the outbreak of war while substantial disarmament might actually lead to war! (Intriligator, 1990). For example, a nuclear arms race could lead to peace and stability if it resulted in both sides acquiring sufficient missiles to reach a position of mutual deterrence, where each nation deters the other. This occurs if nation A starting the war would suffer so massive and unacceptable a level of casualties from a retaliatory second strike by nation B, that B has the capability of deterring A from an aggressive first strike (*eg* by the ability to destroy all of A's major cities and vice versa). On this basis, the arms race between the USA and USSR during the 1960s, 1970s and into the 1980s achieved a position of mutual deterrence, so reducing the chances of war. Alternatively, war could result from disarming, if both sides move from a stable position of mutual deterrence to an unstable region in which each can successfully attack the other, or if disarmament gives a military advantage to one side. Here, conflict is likely if one side believes it can start a war and defeat the other side, suffering only a minimal and acceptable level of casualties from a retaliatory second strike. Examples where disarmament was eventually associated with war include Europe in the 1930s and the Falklands in the early 1980s. But uncertainty cannot be ignored: regions of instability are usually identified with hindsight!

The possibility that arms races can lead to war or peace, and that disarmament can result in either peace or war is represented in *Figure 10.1*. This diagram, associated with Intriligator and Brito, represents plans for a war (war scenarios) as they might be viewed by defence analysts in, say, Moscow and Washington (Intriligator and Brito, 1987). In *Figure 10.1*, nation X can deter Y if, after an attack by Y, it has

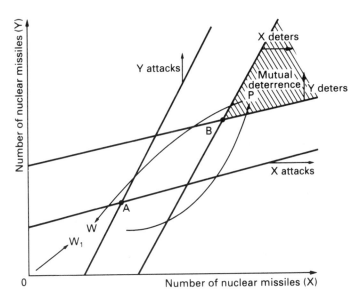

FIG. 10.1. Arms Races, War and Peace. X and Y are two nations. The lines need not be parallel and might be more accurately represented by bands. Position B marks the minimum point of mutual deterrence. Within the inner area between the origin and point A, nation X can attack Y and vice versa, and neither side can deter: hence an arms race leads to war, as shown by path W_1. *Source*: Intriligator and Brito, 1987.

sufficient nuclear missiles to inflict catastrophic damage on Y in a retaliatory strike. Or, for nation X to act as attacker or aggressor through a first strike on Y, it needs to be able to destroy most of Y's missiles to render a retaliatory strike relatively ineffective (*ie* in terms of inflicting damage on X). A similar position is shown for nation Y as an attacker and deterrer. Mutual deterrence or mutual assured destruction is shown by the shaded cone, where each nation deters the other and neither has enough missiles to act as an aggressor and attack the other. An arms race following the path P leads to stability in the region of mutual deterrence. Alternatively, both nations disarming along path W move from a stable to an unstable region in which each side can attack the other!

The Intriligator-Brito model has further implications for arms control. It suggests a selective approach distinguishing between attacking and deterrent weapons. Arms control negotiations should aim to reduce the number of accurate first strike weapons capable of destroying an enemy's nuclear missiles before they can be launched. Similarly, deep cuts in the numbers of deterrent weapons held by the USA and USSR might increase instability. Instead, deterrent weapons might be reduced towards the minimum acceptable number for deterrence, so long as both nations remain in the cone of mutual deterrence: hence the attractiveness of invulnerable systems such as a submarine-based nuclear deterrent. But how many nuclear missiles are required for minimum deterrence? Moreover, a breakthrough in technology such as a more accurate system for detecting submarines or for protecting cities against a ballistic missile attack (*eg* SDI) could render a deterrent system obsolete! To date, defence policy has reflected the fact that the relative costs of destroying populations have been low while the costs of protecting populations (cities) have been high. The possibility also arises that a successful arms control agreement might accentuate the arms race through the search for substitutes!

Arms control and substitution

Economic agents in the military-industrial complex are always seeking alternative ways of making money and protecting their incomes and budgets. Thus, a successful arms control agreement for one set of weapons might encourage the search for new weapons, leading to the continuation of the arms race in new and different forms. For example, controls on nuclear weapons might lead to an expansion of biological and chemical weapons, whilst aircraft might replace cruise missiles, or air and sea-launched cruise missiles could replace ground-launched cruise missiles.

An international agreement on strategic nuclear weapons might not reduce the technological arms race. To the extent that nuclear and conventional weapons substitute for one another, restrictions on nuclear weapons are likely to lead to an expansion of conventional arms. As a result, defence expenditure will increase as nations are required to use costlier methods of obtaining a given level of protection. An example is shown in *Figure 10.2* where an agreement to reduce nuclear weapons leads to greater defence spending, all of which is allocated to conventional forces. Of course, much depends on the perceived threat. If arms control is associated with a reduced threat, then nations might be willing to accept lower levels of protection. However, the armed forces, defence ministries, scientists and contractors have an incentive to exaggerate the threat, to stress the need to maintain 'strong defences' and to point to the possibility of new technological developments which would confer an advantage on a potential enemy.

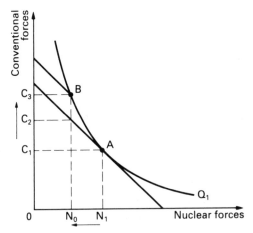

Fig. 10.2. A New Arms Race. Initially, the nation is at position A with N_1 and C_1 of nuclear and conventional forces, respectively, providing Q_1 of protection. If an arms control agreement reduces nuclear forces to N_0, then to maintain Q_1 protection requires increased defence spending, as shown by position B.

Technical progress increases uncertainty and provides an opportunity for one side to obtain a temporary military advantage, as occurred with the US nuclear monopoly after 1945. Uncertainty means that no one can predict accurately the future: a successful SDI might mean that today's nuclear weapons are tomorrow's equivalent of medieval castles and naval dreadnoughts. Who in the 1920s forecast that by 1944 the USA would have developed an atomic bomb and Germany a cruise missile and an embryonic ballistic missile (V1 and V2 rockets)? Does this suggest that arms control should focus on controlling defence R & D? Certainly, technical progress makes life even more difficult for arms control negotiations.

The difficulties of arms control

Arms control involves substantial transaction costs in negotiating and bargaining, and then monitoring and policing the agreement. Each party will have access to unique information about its armed forces and will use skill, bluff and threats to achieve their objectives. An agreement will only be reached if it benefits both parties to the transaction. Possible benefits include a reduced risk of war, the re-allocation of resources from defence to civil uses and the possibility of one side gaining a military advantage over its potential enemy.

The complexity of the subject means that arms control negotiations are inevitably slow and time-consuming. At the outset, agreement is needed on definitions and rules for counting weapons and forces. If, say, a few helicopters of one type are armed and the rest are used for transport roles, should all helicopters in the category be classed as armed helicopters (*ie* if they look alike count them)? What is a weapon in an economy where oil tankers can be converted into aircraft carriers within a few days, and what is a soldier when many societies use heavily-armed policemen? Do strike aircraft capable of carrying nuclear weapons count as nuclear delivery systems or as conventional equipment? Here, though, an emphasis on numbers of aircraft, ships, tanks and troops might divert attention from final outputs in the form of protection and security. After all, a nation's forces will reflect its resources and comparative advantage, so that a labour-intensive economy will use manpower-intensive forces while a capital-intensive economy will use equipment-intensive forces. Each state appears to have an overwhelming superiority in manpower or in equipment and yet both nations might be producing similar levels of defence output (see Chapter 4, *Figure 4.3*).

Cheating is a major problem and fear, which is why nations insist on adequate verification and inspection arrangements. Some agreements are more easily enforced. For example, the 1987 INF Treaty can be enforced simply by observing the destruction of all ground-launched cruise missiles embraced by the agreement – always assuming that both sides have provided accurate data on their total stocks. New technology such as space satellites can also be used to detect non-compliance. The verification problems, however, are much greater with nuclear and chemical weapons where there are large civil industries in these fields (*eg* nuclear power for electricity) and where civil firms will wish to protect their property rights in valuable new ideas resulting from research and development (*ie* commercial secrets). How do nations ensure that each party to an arms control agreement actually abides by the agreement, particularly when there are fears of secret stockpiles of weapons and secret manufacturing facilities? Or what if a nation 'destroys' its tanks by converting them into agricultural tractors with the potential for re-conversion to tanks? In many respects, arms control agreements involve the economics of regulation.

Arms control as regulation

Arms control agreements are about regulating the defence behaviour of nation states. On this view, governments can decide to regulate aggregate defence expenditure, or stocks or flows of specific inputs of manpower and equipment, or the location of forces. Supporters of successful arms control agreements usually stress their benefits, rarely recognising that regulation involves costs. Scarce resources have to be devoted to negotiating, monitoring and policing an agreement. The 1987 INF Treaty involves costs in destroying cruise missiles and in organising on-site inspections to confirm their destruction. The costs of destroying tanks is not trivial and the destruction of nuclear weapons systems and production facilities gives rise to major technical problems and substantial costs in arranging for the safe disposal of radioactive material. Similarly, arms control agreements requiring inspection of production facilities impose costs on the firms which have to be inspected. Further adjustment costs arise as resources are re-allocated from defence to civil activities.

Economic models show that regulators do not necessarily act in the public interest (Chapter 5). Where their employment contract allows some discretion, regulators might pursue policies which benefit themselves. They might, for example, enjoy regular foreign travel and international meetings in attractive locations to review progress and adjudicate on allegations of non-compliance. Or, producers who do not wish to comply with the regulations might capture the regulators by offering inducements in the form of generous hospitality, gifts in cash or kind, or the prospect of future employment.

Regulation also involves the issue of penalties for non-compliance. Here, information asymmetries between regulators on the one hand and a nation's armed forces and its defence producers on the other create difficulties in detecting non-compliance (cheating). Moreover, international agencies cannot impose the same range of penalties as national agencies – (eg the USA could not impose a fine on the USSR!). Nonetheless, possible sanctions include a negotiated agreement to comply; or a nation could impose penalties on its citizens who are found to be cheating; or – the ultimate sanction – the treaty would be cancelled. An alternative view argues that economic factors alone will force nations to disarm.

Economics as the ultimate arms controller

Defence is costly and forecasts suggest that it is likely to become costlier. Increasingly, nations will find that it is too expensive to maintain their traditional defence commitments. Manpower is not cheap, particularly in the 1990s. Conscription involves the loss to the economy of a large proportion of its young adult males, while an all-volunteer force has to be compensated for the non-monetary disadvantages of military service (*eg* danger, discipline, unsociable hours, working away from home). Defence equipment is also extremely expensive, leading to fewer units being bought. For example, since 1945, the real unit production costs of UK combat aircraft have risen at an average rate of 8 per cent per annum. As a result, the reduction in quantity affects both the number of new types of aircraft developed and the number bought of each type (Kirkpatrick and Pugh, 1983). Despite large and rising defence budgets, the general trend in the size of the armed forces has been downwards. Economics is forcing nations to disarm (Callaghan, 1984). On this basis, an economy's limited resources act as the ultimate arms controller.

A nation's defence expenditure results from a combination of both its ability and willingness to pay for defence (Chapter 2). Ability to pay is limited by the efficiency with which an economy uses its resources, the resulting total output and its growth rate. In the end, defence expenditure cannot exceed the economy's maximum output. However, the amount a nation decides to spend on defence will be determined by its willingness to pay, as reflected in society's preferences for military and civil goods and services. Much will depend on perceptions of the threat. A rise in international tension or involvement in a major war is likely to result in society being willing to allocate more resources to defence (as in the Second World War). In contrast, a long period of peace and stability will lead to downward pressure on defence budgets as citizens prefer to reallocate spending towards civil goods and hence signal a willingness to disarm. Rising manpower and equipment costs and small defence budgets combine to result in economic disarmament.

Defence spending might also impose indirect burdens on an economy. Critics claim that defence R & D 'crowds out' valuable civil investment, with adverse effects on economic growth, that there is little technical spin-off from defence to civil activities; and that defence industries are inefficient, relying upon cost-based contracts, guaranteed markets and a cosy relationship with their defence ministry (Chapter 4 and 8). Thus, critics claim that military spending impairs an economy's international competitiveness (Kennedy, 1988). If these views are correct, they reinforce the argument about economic disarmament, with economics as the ultimate arms controller. Defence depends on an economy's performance: a relatively poor performance will contribute to economic disarmament or disarmament by stealth. Pressures on the defence budget will result in smaller forces, reduced buys of new equipment, extending the life of obsolescent equipment and pressure to reduce a nation's defence commitments (Chapter 2). By 1990, such pressures were apparent in both

NATO and the Warsaw Pact. There are, though, major groups in society which depend on defence spending and which will oppose economic disarmament and arms control agreements.

Barriers to arms control

In both NATO and the Warsaw Pact, there is a major interest group comprising the armed forces, ministries, contractors, regions and towns which depend on military spending. Such groups involve large numbers of people and voters who will oppose policies likely to make them worse off. They comprise military personnel in the armed forces and their civilian support staff; scientists, technologists and workers in government defence research laboratories and in defence industries; and their dependents, together with all those whose incomes depend on the spending power of these groups. In the UK, the military-industrial complex employs over one million people, with towns such as Aldershot, Barrow, Catterick, Portsmouth, Rosyth and Yeovil heavily dependent on defence spending. Groups which have invested substantial human and physical capital in the defence sector will find their investments at risk from arms control agreements.

Who gains and who loses from arms control? The potential gainers are society, which might feel safer and which will benefit from resources reallocated from defence to civil uses; the losers will be those bearing the costs of adjustment. On this basis, nations might support arms control so long as the potential gainers are able to more than compensate the potential losers. But the potential losers are unlikely to be passive agents. They will lobby vote-sensitive politicians and governments for new defence or civil contracts (*eg* civil aircrafts), or for generous compensation for job losses. Similarly, civil servants in defence ministries will be conscious of the need to protect their budgets. They will point to new and emerging threats throughout the world (*eg* international terrorism; nuclear proliferation; space weapons) and the need to maintain 'firm and strong' defences. Support might come from the foreign ministry concerned to maintain the nation's power and international prestige, with further support coming from the departments responsible for employment and technology. Elsewhere, other government departments concerned with, for instance, education and health, together with interest groups favouring disarmament, will welcome any release of resources from the defence sector (Chapter 5). Economists can contribute further to this debate by pointing to alternative spending patterns which will provide jobs and promote high technology.

Alternatives to defence spending

Arms control agreements are likely to mean resources released from the armed forces and from industries supplying defence equipment. For example, possible UK troop withdrawals from Central Europe could mean the disbanding of army and air force units and a reduced demand for land and air-equipment. In addition, the economy will respond by signalling that in the future these activities are less attractive. So, arms control has two effects on resources. First, a once-and-for-all release of a stock of resources no longer required in the armed forces and defence industries. Second, an effect on future resource flows, as labour and investors seek more attractive income prospects elsewhere in the economy. Various studies have attempted to estimate the economic impact of disarmament (Chapter 4).

A study of world military spending estimated that, with reductions in defence expenditure, the output of most goods and services would increase, particularly construction, fertilisers, food crops, furniture and textiles. Regions diverting a high proportion of their national output to defence, such as Eastern Europe and the Soviet Union, were likely to experience the greatest percentage increase in GDP and *per capita* consumption. The fact that, by maintaining total employment following reduced military spending, the developed regions could increase their GDP suggests that labour productivity is lower in the military economy than in the civil sector (Leontief and Duchin, 1983).

Another study had estimated the economic consequences of a reduction in the UK defence spending from 5 per cent to 3.5 per cent of GDP (Dunne and Smith, 1984). It considers a scenario where such a cut in military expenditure is associated with a compensating increase in other public spending, particularly on activities such as education, health, housing and roads. Assuming public expenditure remains unchanged after the cut in defence spending, there was estimated to be a net increase in employment of about 100,000 jobs (*ie* after adjusting for job losses in defence). An example is shown in *Figure 10.3*. However, the study emphasises that even with a compensating increase of government civil spending, there will need to be supply-side policies to assist with the conversion of defence activities and the reallocation of resources to civilian use (*eg* retraining and placement policies).

While arms control and disarmament can create major adjustment problems, the scale of the adjustment required needs to be placed into context. First, the UK economy has survived previous examples of large-scale disarmament, especially after 1945 and following the end of the Korean war. Second, a reduction in the UK share of defence in national output needs to be viewed against the background of a long run declining trend in the defence share (Chapter 4). Third, the UK economy has

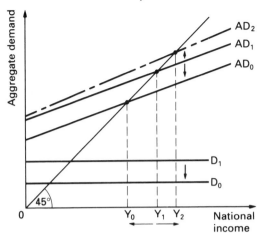

FIG. 10.3. Economics of Disarmament. Initially, defence spending is D_1, aggregate demand is AD_1 and national income is Y_1. Employment is positively related to national income (output). A reduction in defence spending to D_0 reduces aggregate demand to AD_0, income to Y_0 and employment falls. If, however, the cut in defence spending is compensated so that government expenditure remains unchanged, national income and employment might increase to Y_2.

considerable experience of adjusting to the decline of some of its industries. Examples include the decline of the coal, motor-cycle, ship-building, steel and textile industries and, more recently, the tobacco companies have survived and prospered by diversifying into completely new activities (*eg* financial services, engineering, retailing). However, certain features of defence markets are likely to affect the ability of arms firms to convert to civil activities. In defence, the emphasis is on technical performance rather than price, there is a known customer determining market requirements with a considerable willingness to pay and leading contractors are often domestic monopolists (Chapter 8). As a result, arms firms dependent on the sale of high technology and highly specialised defence equipment, with no experience of civil markets, are likely to encounter the greatest problems of conversion and are most likely to disappear (Dussauge, 1987; Hartley and Hooper, 1990). At which point, much depends on how well and how quickly local labour markets work or whether state intervention is required to improve the operation of markets. A similar approach can be applied to prosposals for US troop withdrawals from the UK.

US troop withdrawals

In view of arms control negotiations on US and Soviet troops based in Central Europe, it is useful to speculate on the likely defence and economic implications if American forces were withdrawn from the UK. Are the magnitudes involved so small that, apart from a few local effects, they can be ignored?

In 1986, there were some 32,000 US Service personnel and about 38,500 dependents in the UK. Most of the US presence is in the form of air forces located in East Anglia, Oxfordshire and Gloucestershire. US forces add foreign exchange earnings to the UK's balance of payments account, totalling almost £700 million in 1989–90. Their spending benefits local economies, providing some 30,000 jobs both directly and indirectly.

In predicting the likely effects of US troop withdrawals, it is necessary to make a number of assumptions: an exercise which in itself is illuminating. Assume that an American withdrawal occurs with an unchanged threat, with or without a specific commitment to return in a crisis (the gone-for-good option). Following US withdrawal, the UK could respond by raising or lowering defence expenditure or leaving it unchanged. Even these simple propositions conceal a variety of subsidiary assumptions and complex relationships involving the defence sector, the adjustment period and the operation of the UK economy. Consider the following examples of the types of assumptions which have to be made by the analyst:

(i) *Assumptions about UK defence spending.* At one extreme (unlikely), the UK might increase its defence spending to replace the protection previously provided by US forces. Simple estimates suggest that to replace withdrawn US forces might require the UK to increase its annual defence spending by between £1.8 billion and £3+ billion: an increase of 10–17 per cent on the 1987 defence budget (1987 prices).

(ii) *Assumptions about the transition.* Assumptions have to be made about the time required for US troops to depart, for the UK to respond and the associated adjustment costs.

(iii) *Assumptions about the economy.* US forces inject spending power into the UK economy, so adding to total demand in the UK and contributing foreign exchange to the invisible account of the balance of payments. The withdrawal of US forces will immediately result in lower levels of spending in the UK and the loss of foreign exchange earnings will initially have an adverse impact on the current account of the balance of payments. The effects in subsequent rounds will depend on whether a market or Keynesian view of the UK economy is applied. The regions most at risk are East Anglia and the south of England, areas where local unemployment rates are considerably lower than the national average. Much, then, depends on assumptions made about the operation of local labour markets and how well they are working. Finally, in the case of the exchange rate, some simple estimates suggest that the loss of foreign exchange from US withdrawal would have little noticeable effect on the UK's exchange rate (*eg* a fall of 0.25 per cent or less). Indeed, compared with the adjustments following the end of the Second Word War and the oil price shocks of the 1970s, the *economic* effects of US withdrawal are likely to be relatively small, with some possible local problems. Of course, a complete evaluation would also need to include the defence implications in terms of protection and security in the UK (Hartley and Hooper, 1990a).

Conclusion: future UK defence policy

British defence policy is faced with great uncertainty. Forecasting for 2001 and beyond requires assumptions about the likely threat, about new technology, about who will be our allies, and the UK's ability and willingness to pay for defence. Choices have to be made about the size of the defence budget, its allocation between nuclear and conventional forces, between manpower and equipment and between air, land and sea forces. What are the likely implications of successful arms control agreements between NATO and the Warsaw Pact for future UK defence policy and for UK defence industries? Although the situation is uncertain and changing rapidly, a broad indication of possibilities can be outlined. Readers can cost various options using the data in Chapters 2 and 3 (*Tables 2.1 and 3.2*; and ADC 1983).

During the 1990s, UK defence policy might develop in the following broad directions:

(i) Cuts in real defence spending, probably towards the level of France and West Germany.

(ii) A reduction of army and air forces based in West Germany. In 1990–91, these forces cost over £4.2 billion (Chapter 3).

(iii) A shift towards a smaller army supported by a substantial air force and navy. As a manpower-intensive force, a smaller army is attractive as a response to the demographic problems of the 1990s. A sizeable navy might be required for out-of-area operations, and for protecting the passage of US reinforcements for Europe.

(iv) A reduction in the size of the UK defence industrial base – a reduction already signalled by commitments to cut defence R & D (with implications for future production programmes) and a greater willingness to buy from abroad. Specific sectors at risk in the 1990s and beyond include the warship builders, helicopter manufacture and tank capacity. For example, by 1988 there was over-capacity in UK warship building with too many yards chasing too few orders (*HCP 309 1988*).

(v) The possible development of European solutions involving greater co-operation between European armed forces, more collaborative programmes, the creation of a European defence industry and a common market in defence equipment (Chapter 9).

Finally, in making choices for defence policy in the 1990s, the UK will have to pursue more vigorously the *principle of substitution*. There are alternative ways of achieving protection, such as substitutions between manpower and equipment, between different types of manpower and between different types of equipment. For example, reserves could replace regular forces, helicopters could replace tanks and foreign equipment might replace UK equipment (Chapter 2). These are all difficult choices but ones which will have to be made if the UK is to have an efficient and affordable defence policy. Such difficult choices will embrace air, land and sea forces and the supporting defence industrial base. Something will have to go and the question is what?

References

ADC 1983, *Defence Without the Bomb*, Alternative Defence Commission (Taylor and Francis, London).

Callaghan, T. A. Jr., 1984, 'The structural disarmament of NATO', *NATO Review*, Brussels, pp. 21–26.

Cmnd 675-I 1989, *Statement on the Defence Estimates 1989* (HMSO, London).

Dunne, J. P. and Smith, R., 1984, 'The economic consequences of reduced UK military expenditure', *Cambridge Journal of Economics*, 8, 297–310.

Dussauge, P., 1987, 'The conversion of military activities', in Schmidt, C. and Blackaby, F. (eds.), *Peace, Defence and Economic Analysis*, IEA (Macmillan, London).

Hartley, K. and Hooper, N., 1990a, 'Costs and benefits in the UK' in Sharp, J. (ed.), *Europe After An American Withdrawal*, SIPRI, Oxford UP, Oxford.

Hartley, K. and Hooper, N., 1990, *An Annotated Bibliography of the Economics of Defence, Disarmament and Peace* (Elgar, London).

HCP 309, 1988, *The Future Size and Role of the Royal Navy's Surface Fleet*, Defence Committee, June. (HMSO, London).

Intriligator, M., 1990, 'On the nature and scope of defence economics', *Defence Economics*, 1, 1, pp. 3–11.

Intriligator, M. and Brito, D., 1987, 'Can arms races lead to the outbreak of war?' in Schmidt, C. (ed.) *The Economics of Military Expenditures*, IEA (Macmillan, London).

Kennedy, P., 1988, *The Rise and Fall of the Great Powers* (Fontana Press, London).

Kirkpatrick, D. and Pugh, P., 1983, 'Towards the Starship Enterprise', *Aerospace*, Journal of the Royal Aeronautical Society, London, May, pp. 16–23.

Leontief, W. and Duchin, F., 1983, *Military Spending* (Oxford University Press, Oxford).

Questions

1. 'We regard all military problems as economic problems in the efficient allocation and use of resources' (Hitch and McKean, 1960). Do you agree? What are the implications of this view for future UK defence policy?
2. What are the likely implications of possible arms control agreements between NATO and the Warsaw Pact on the future size of UK defence budgets, on the size and composition of its armed forces and on the UK defence industrial base in the 1990s?
3. Which model best explains the facts of the arms race?
4. Predict and quantify the economic effects on the UK if it required the complete withdrawal of all US Forces located in the UK. Do you regard such a policy as socially desirable?
5. Does the economic theory of alliances explain the facts of NATO defence expenditure? Which NATO nations, if any, are 'free riding'?
6. Is NATO an inefficient organisation for the supply of defence equipment and for the provision of armed forces? If so, how might its efficiency be improved?
7. Predict the effects of abolishing conscription and introducing an all-volunteer force. Does the UK evidence support your predictions?
8. Is defence spending a burden or a benefit? Carefully explain how you would resolve this issue.
9. Why do developing nations spend so much on defence? Illustrate your answer with reference to the facts of military spending in two Third World nations.
10. Predict the effects on the UK economy of complete disarmament. Illustrate your answer with appropriate quantitative evidence.
11. Should the UK buy all its defence equipment from abroad?
12. Critically evaluate the benefits and costs of a competitive procurement policy. Illustrate your answer with reference to the UK.

Index